MW00561667

JULIAN HAWTHORNE

JULIAN HAWTHORNE

The Life of a Prodigal Son

GARY SCHARNHORST

UNIVERSITY OF ILLINOIS PRESS

Urbana, Chicago, and Springfield

© 2014 by Gary Scharnhorst
All rights reserved
Manufactured in the United States of America
C 5 4 3 2 1

♾ This book is printed on acid-free paper.

Library of Congress Cataloging-in-Publication Data
Scharnhorst, Gary.
Julian Hawthorne : the life of a prodigal son / Gary Scharnhorst.
    pages   cm
ISBN 978-0-252-03834-1 (hardback) — ISBN 978-0-252-09621-1 (e-book)
    1. Hawthorne, Julian, 1846–1934. 2. Authors, American—19th century—Biography. 3.
Authors, American—20th century—Biography. 4. Fathers and sons—United States—
History—19th century. 5. Hawthorne, Nathaniel, 1804–1864—Family. I. Title.
    PS1848.S33   2014
    813'.4—dc23   2013040305
    [B]

Again for Sandy

"Wheresoever she was, there was Eden."

Of the romancers of the period the leader for a time unquestion-
ably was Julian Hawthorne, only son of the greatest of American
romancers. In his earlier days he devoted himself to themes
worthy of the Hawthorne name and treated them in what fairly
may be called the Hawthorne manner. His novels . . . were hailed
everywhere as remarkably promising work and there were many
who predicted for him a place second only to his father's. But
the man lacked seriousness, conscience, depth of life, knowledge
of the human heart. After a short period of worthy endeavor he
turned to the sensational and the trivial, and became a yellow
journalist. No literary career so promising has ever failed more
dismally.

    —Fred Lewis Pattee, *A History of American Literature*
      since 1870 (1915)

CONTENTS

INTRODUCTION

Julian Hawthorne would have been a public intellectual had he been an intellectual. Nevertheless, he led, if not a charmed life, a privileged and eventful one. "No other person still alive," he wrote in his *Memoirs*, "could duplicate my story."[1] The only son and second of three children of Nathaniel and Sophia Hawthorne, he outlived his famous father by seventy years. He was born during the Mexican War in the same month Nathaniel published *Mosses from an Old Manse,* and he died eighty-seven years later at the nadir of the Great Depression, soon after Adolf Hitler became chancellor of Germany. While still in short pants, he was acquainted with such Concord, Massachusetts, neighbors as Ralph Waldo Emerson, Henry David Thoreau, Bronson and Louisa May Alcott, as well as Herman Melville, his uncle Horace Mann, his aunt Elizabeth Palmer Peabody, and Franklin Pierce, his father's college classmate and fourteenth president of the United States. "My father was one of the elect," he allowed, "and caused me to become a sort of household intimate of those friends of his."[2]

In 1871, at the age of twenty-four, he began to write for a living. Over the next sixty-three years he was one of the most prolific—or profligate—authors in the history of American letters and a barometer of change in the literary climate. Never a literary lion, he traded on his name, though he sometimes considered it less a blessing than a curse. On the one hand, he banked on its marquee value. "The name has been a great help to me," he admitted. "It proves an open sesame nearly everywhere I go."[3] On the other hand, he complained that his father was his worst enemy. "It would not be so bad if I had chosen a different calling, but whatever I write must always be compared to what he wrote."[4] Still, he published almost nothing during his career without signature. In 1882 the literary historian John Nichol compared him favorably to Wilkie Collins; in 1884 he was ranked twenty-sixth among the "forty immortal" American writers listed by the

New York Critic, along with Henry James, Mark Twain, Walt Whitman, and his father; and the next year the *Critic* pronounced him "the first of living romancers."[5] The cachet of his surname launched magazines much as the face of Helen of Troy launched ships. He was a founding contributor to half a dozen parlor magazines, including *Cosmopolitan* in 1886, *Collier's Once a Week* (later *Collier's Weekly*) in 1888, and the *Smart Set* in 1900. However, his nineteen novels, three dozen poems, and 150 tales and novellas comprise only a small fraction of his oeuvre. In all, he published several million words and more than 3,000 items, on average nearly one a week for nearly six decades, 90 percent of them hitherto unknown to scholarship.[6] As he wrote shortly before his death, "What with fiction, biography, history, journalism, and poetry, I suppose that what I have put on paper during the last sixty-odd years might fill at least one hundred bound volumes."[7] He out-published his father by a ratio of more than twenty to one.

A journeyman of letters, Julian was adept in a variety of genres: he was the author of true crime, mystery, and detective potboilers; of children's stories and bodice rippers; of gothic and fantasy novels; of westerns and science fiction; of textbooks; and of travel, feature, and nature essays. He was also an advice and self-help columnist; a war and foreign correspondent; a sports and political reporter; a literary and theater critic; a poet and playwright; an editor and historian; and a biographer and autobiographer. He was so versatile that in the single October 1900 issue of the *Philadelphia North American* three separate articles appeared under his byline: an interview with William Jennings Bryan, a review of Langdon Mitchell's play *The Adventures of Francois,* and a column of book notices that included a puff of Lafcadio Hearn's *Shadowings.* One of the first celebrity journalists, he interviewed such figures as the scientist Thomas Edison, the novelists Henry James and Jack London, and the jurist Louis Brandeis. A sports aficionado, he covered heavyweight title fights, Ivy League football, and major league baseball, and he even edited the sports pages of the *New York American.* In addition, he was the model for such characters as the child Peony in his father's tale "The Snow-Image" (1851), the villainous George Flack in Henry James's *The Revererator* (1888), and Juliana Bordereau in James's "The Aspern Papers" (1888).

By virtue of his family antecedents, Julian was acquainted with a veritable who's who of Anglo-American authors and other celebrities, both famous and forgotten. "He had among his personal friends probably more of the world's great men and women than any one man of his time," according to his widow.[8] He reminisced about dozens of them, and this biography features cameo appearances by, among others, Theodore Roosevelt; the "millionaire socialist" Gaylord Wilshire; playwrights Bronson Howard and Augustin Daly; actors Charlotte Cushman and Henry Irving; sculptors Hiram Powers and William Wetmore Story; painter James Whistler; the "Gibson girl" Evelyn Nesbit; and writers Hamlin Garland, Harriet Beecher Stowe, W. D. Howells, Coventry Patmore, Robert and Elizabeth Browning, Mark Twain, Walt Whitman, and Oscar Wilde. Gifted with an encyclopedic memory, Julian chronicled a version of American literary and cultural history from the American Renaissance of the 1850s through the modernist revolt. He was no doubt the last living person with intimate knowledge of literary Concord in the 1850s, and as its self-anointed historian he was nothing if not a debunking revisionist. He thought Thoreau a fraud, Ellery Channing mad, and Bronson Alcott a bore and a boor. Virtually the only Concordians immune from his criticism were Emerson and his father. Like an insect preserved in amber, Julian had the genetic coding of a creature long extinct, and at the height of his career he fiercely resisted the realism of Howells and the naturalism of Emile Zola. In his anecdotage he condemned the modernism of James Joyce, Ernest Hemingway, D. H. Lawrence, and Gertrude Stein. A type of turn-of-the-century Zelig, he was also on the scene of some of the most significant events of the period: the 1893 Columbian Exposition in Chicago, Bryan's 1896 and 1900 presidential campaigns, the India famine of 1896–97, the run-up to war in Cuba in 1898 and the subsequent "embalmed beef" scandal, the Pennsylvania coal strike and the Galveston hurricane of 1900, William McKinley's death in 1901, and the trial of Harry Thaw for the murder of the architect Stanford White in 1907.

While not a great man, Julian was an uncommon one. Especially after his felony conviction, he became more circumspect and guarded. His papers at the Bancroft Library at the University of California at Berkeley were sanitized before they were deposited. None of his journals from the period 1900 to 1934 survive save a brief scrap from 1924. Julian certainly expected his surviving diaries to be read by other eyes than his; in his entry for April 12, 1879, for example, he directly addressed his "remote descendants." In a vain attempt to frame his own life story, he edited some of his journals while recopying them. For example, in his original diary he scribbled this entry for January 14, 1879:

> Had a letter this morning from Henry James Junior, who wishes to pump me on his biography of my father, which he is going to do for Macmillan's series. I don't know that I can tell him anything useful; however I shall be glad to see him; he has hitherto kept out of my way, either purposefully or not; but now that he thinks I can serve him, he finds out my address. Well, that is all right and natural; we shall see what sort of an impression we make upon each other.

Here is the redacted entry:

> Letter from Henry James, asking me about his projected biography of my father, for Macmillan's series. I can tell him nothing useful, but shall be glad to see him.[9]

Dozens of pages of his other journals, both in the family's possession and at the Bancroft, have been removed by razor, suggesting that the excisions were made before the documents were divided among the heirs, presumably by Julian himself.

Fortunately, there is still a surfeit of sources detailing the events in Julian's life. As the scion of a famous family, he was always a mote in the public eye, whether in memoirs of his father and sister Rose (aka Mother Alphonsa) or newspaper accounts of his activities. Few nineteenth-century lives are better documented. I have turned up literally thousands of new sources, including many hundreds of his published writings, some two hundred letters, several of his diaries still in the hands of his heirs, the transcript of his trial, his prison file, and a copy of his will. In addition, I have deciphered an elementary code he used in a memorandum book for 1899 preserved among his papers in the Bancroft Library. While some sources have been erased from the record, to be sure, I am confident that this account of Julian Hawthorne's life is complete and reliable, and I hope it will serve to resurrect him from the footnote.

I make no attempt to launder the facts. Instead, this biography develops two overriding themes. First, it portrays a writer of modest talent as he struggled to earn a livelihood, who tailored his tales to the demands of the market in the heyday of sensational fiction, the rise of newspaper syndicates and yellow journalism, and the emergence of "slick" magazines. That is, it is a type of literary history illuminating the plight of professional writers during the late nineteenth and early twentieth centuries. As Herman Melville's narrator observes about Bartleby the scrivener: "I believe that no materials exist for a full and satisfactory biography of this man. It is an irreparable loss to literature." Julian Hawthorne was a type of Bartleby for whom there are abundant biographical sources because he was the son of a literary celebrity and because by a fortunate happenstance (happystance?), he became a semi-famous figure in his own right. He was a writer akin to many others struggling in the maw of the literary market whose lives today are lost in biographical blind spots. In fact, according to Sean McCann, Julian Hawthorne was "perhaps the paradigmatic example of the era's professional writer."[10]

Second, this biography is a cautionary tale about a writer who often exploited and sometimes dishonored his distinguished surname. In his case, the apple fell from the tree and rolled downhill. Like the biblical Esau, he sold his birthright for a mess of pottage. Or as the biographer Jean Strouse has explained, the life stories of semi-obscure figures such as Alice James, sister of Henry and William, and Hawthorne's privileged son "offer new ways of looking at the intersections of public and private experience without the obfuscation of myth." Their lives limn "private drama, personal success and failure, sometimes heroism, sometimes the underside of fame."[11] A pioneer of the "tell all" species of biography, Julian often courted controversy, as when he published his father's private comments about Margaret Fuller in 1884 or his own private conversation with James Russell Lowell in 1886. He abandoned his checkered writing career in 1908 and began to tout stock in worthless Canadian silver-mining companies incorporated in his name. After a controversial four-month trial in 1913, he and two associates were convicted of mail fraud and sentenced to federal prison. To date, however, no one has suspected the reason he so desperately needed money: he had fathered two daughters by a mistress, Minna Desborough, and was responsible for two families, one of them secret—and could no longer support them by his pen. It is a compelling though sometimes dispiriting story.

In relating it I have excerpted parts of articles I have published previously in *Studies in American Naturalism*, *Concord Saunterer*, *Leviathan: A Journal of Melville Studies*, *Henry James Review*, *Nathaniel Hawthorne Review*, *Mark Twain Annual*, *American Periodicals*, *Resources for American Literary Study*, *The Wildean*, and *The Howellsian*. At the risk of seeming overly familiar with the members of the family, I use first names in this book for each of the Hawthornes (Nathaniel, Sophia, Una, Julian, Rose) in order to avoid the redundancy and confusion had I repeatedly used their last name.

*   *   *

Only one book about Julian Hawthorne has hitherto been published: Maurice Bassan's *Hawthorne's Son* (1970), which originated in a 1961 PhD dissertation at the University of California at Berkeley. Bassan's study is a useful overview of Julian's contributions to American letters, and it includes a brief bibliography of his writings, though it is limited in scope and purpose. It largely ignores, for example, his journalism and syndicated or serialized fiction, and it fails even to mention Minna Desborough.[12]

I am pleased to have enlisted the cooperation of the Hawthorne heirs in this project. I am particularly indebted to Imogen Howe, Joan Ensor, Rose Mikkelsen, Tiffany McFarland, Alison Hawthorne Deming, and Rust Deming. I have also depended on the kindness of both friends and strangers, especially David Kessler, Bob Hirst, and Neda Westlake, Bancroft Library,

University of California, Berkeley; Sister Mary Joseph, the Dominican Sisters of Hawthorne, New York; Lisa Long, Redwood Library, Newport, Rhode Island; Roslyn Pachoca, the Library of Congress; Nicholas B. Scheetz, John A. Buchtel, Ted Jackson, Ann Galloway, and Scott Taylor, Lauinger Memorial Library, Georgetown University; Russell Cole and Joe Lane, Zimmerman Library, University of New Mexico; Jane Westenfeld, Pelletier Library, Allegheny College; Karen Schmiege, Bernalillo County Public Library; Catherine Miller and James Newberry, National Archives–Atlanta Region, and Gregory J. Plunges, National Archives–New York City; Caroline Moseley and Leanne Pander, Bowdoin College Library; Mike Takach, Donna J. De-George, and Geoffrey D. Smith, Ohio State University Libraries; Maria Isabel Molestina, Inge Dupont, Sandra Kopperman, and Jill Weinstein, the Pierpont Morgan Library, New York City; Lisa Darms, Fales Library, New York University; Henry Scannell, Boston Public Library; Catherine Rivard; Bill Jobe; Brad Tepper; Garry Boulard; Jeff Haas; Leah Glasser; Joel Myerson; and Nic Witschi. I am also indebted to the staff of the Huntington Library for a fellowship to work on this project.

PROLOGUE

At 9:30 AM on Wednesday, October 15, 1913, two elderly men stepped into the open air through the gate of the Atlanta Federal Penitentiary. Each of them wore a shoddy suit, a vivid scarlet tie, and a pair of paper shoes, and each carried a suitcase as well as a train ticket to New York and a five-dollar bill, their graduation gifts from Uncle Sam.[1] Julian Hawthorne and Will Morton had been college classmates and friends for more than fifty years. They took a streetcar downtown to the Piedmont Hotel, where they rendezvoused with Edith Garrigues, Julian's partner, and Sidney Ormund, a stringer for the *Atlanta Constitution*. For the next forty minutes the four of them cruised around Atlanta in Ormund's car while the ex-cons filled his ear with details about the abuses they had witnessed during their four months behind bars. At 11 AM Julian, Will, and Edith boarded a northbound train. Within twenty-four hours all hell had broken loose.[2]

After the interview, Ormund posted on the wire service a story that dozens of newspapers coast to coast printed the next day: that the warden of the federal penitentiary, William Moyer, was "unfit" to hold his job, corruption in the institution was rampant, and violence against inmates was common. Julian's rant was scathing:

> They are starving men in the name of economy. . . . Prisoners are subjected to treatment which is nothing more than slow murder. There is never enough to eat. The Warden attempts to feed strong men on nine cents a day and boasts when he does it. You hear of clean cells, but you never hear of the "hole." For the slightest fault, sometimes the breaking of a plate, a prisoner is sent to the hole. There the heat is terrific and the stench fearful. Prisoners are chained by their wrists and held with arms outstretched for hours.

Neither he nor Morton had been maltreated—each of them was a high-profile inmate accorded such privileges as congenial work and special diets—but the prison was "a living hell" for most of the convicts.[3] When copies of the *Atlanta Constitution* containing the interview arrived at the Atlanta prison, as one of the convicts later wrote Julian, "there was quite a sensation. You were cheered by the boys in their quarters. . . . The boys are elated but orderly and they are with you."[4]

Julian was interviewed again the next day as he passed through Washington, D.C., where he not only reiterated his allegations but also vowed vengeance. Still sporting the scarlet tie, he told reporters that he would devote the next six months of his life to the cause of prison reform. "I am going to do what I can for the poor devils in that penitentiary," he said. By the time he arrived in New York on the evening of October 16, his charges had become a cause célèbre. A bevy of reporters met him at Grand Central Terminal. "I can't forget that there are eight hundred poor souls down in that hell in Atlanta," he told them, "and I am going to do all in my power to help them in their misery and, if possible, to abolish the tortures practiced upon the prisoners in various forms for the very slightest infractions of the rules." He asserted that the Atlanta jail was "the worst prison in the world."

> There were many prisoners who were [chained in the hole] for three and four days. . . . Some of them were taken out to die. There are eight of these cells, all opening on a corridor like stable stalls. . . . In these cells the stench is almost intolerable, and the heat makes the perspiration pour out. The walls are slimy and covered with crawling things. The floors are covered with filth and are alive with vermin. And into one of these eight hell holes a poor prisoner is thrust for talking out of his turn and fed with one slice of bread a day and one cup of water. Here he must sleep standing up.

One of the reporters asked him if had been permitted to see the dungeon cells. He replied with wry wit, "No, I was not permitted, but I saw them." By the time he arrived in New York, moreover, some thirty hours after his release, Julian was demanding not a pardon but an apology from the federal government for jailing him. To accept a pardon would have been tantamount to admitting he had committed a crime, a concession he was unwilling to make. "There is no disgrace on me or my family, or my name," he insisted. "The disgrace is on those who hounded me."[5] He and his alleged co-conspirators should never have been prosecuted for mail fraud. Their four-month trial had been a monumental waste of taxpayer money. Of the four defendants, only he and Morton had been convicted and imprisoned—and neither of them was the ringleader, much less the mastermind. On his part, Morton continued to insist that he "believed in those mines, and I still believe in them. So does Mr. Hawthorne, but even if they were no good, as the government says, they did not take action against the principal men connected with it."[6]

Julian Hawthorne (right) and Will Morton (left) (*New York Tribune*, October 17, 1913, p. 18).

Julian's charges began to rattle some politicians in Washington. The stern and puritanical U.S. Attorney General James Clark McReynolds conferred with the superintendent of federal prisons, and although he attached "little weight" to Julian's accusations, he agreed to launch an official Justice Department investigation.[7] Congressman William Schley Howard of Georgia, in whose district the prison was located, announced that he, too, would investigate. "I do not know what weight the statements of Mr. Hawthorne and Dr. Morton may have" with the authorities, he told the *Atlanta Constitution*, "but I do know that what these two prisoners just released have said is true in the greater part if not in toto, and I know that the officers actively in charge at the Atlanta federal prison and not the federal government are responsible for the existing conditions."[8] Senator Robert La Follette of Wisconsin expressed his support for "any resolution that might be offered authorizing any inquiry into conditions in the Atlanta prison," and Howard enlisted more than fifty members of Congress to sponsor such a resolution. "I shall not relax in my fight for better conditions in the Atlanta prison," he told the press. He revealed that as the result of Julian's exposé of corruption and abuse, "great quantities of fresh beef, vegetables, eggs, good milk and other foods [are] now daily being bought for the prison commissary." Julian, still in contact with some prisoners, reported that one day "200 chickens were served to the men at dinner. This is the first time in the jail's history that even a single fowl has appeared in the jail dining room, although every fowl raised on the farm [is] the exclusive property of the prisoners."[9]

Of course, there was blowback. Moyer and his defenders asserted that Julian's attacks were "the result of spite."[10] Julian's former cellmate sided with Goliath in the contest; he swore that Julian's "charge about prisoners being chained in a black hole for trivial offenses is as base a lie as the one about the food." In fact, he said, "there was always plenty of good food on the tables."[11] Some critics noted that Julian had gained weight while incarcerated. A volunteer worker at the prison launched an ad hominem attack: "Julian Hawthorne is nothing more than an old grouch. . . . When he says such things as he is reported to have said, he should be made to prove them, or keep his mouth shut."[12] Moyer himself catalogued the reforms he had introduced: the abolition of stripes on the prison uniform, the organization of a Saturday baseball league, and an eight-hour workday. He even permitted inmates to converse during meals and to write letters on plain paper rather than prison stationery.[13] "I do not know what prompted the charges," he averred, "but the fact that Hawthorne and Dr. Morton were once denied parole may throw light on the situation."[14]

Julian made good on his threat to battle the prison system. On October 17 he traveled to Albany, New York, where his daughter Beatrix and her husband lived, and the second day after his release he began to prepare a series of essays titled "Behind Prison Walls." "No one can know what happens to convicts except convicts themselves," he explained, "and no ex-convicts thus far have possessed in combination the knowledge, inclination, and ability" to write about the modern prison experience. He felt "an obligation to take advantage" of the opportunity. "But the series is too long for any one newspaper to handle, and could not get the dissemination which I desire for it, and which is more important to me than money, though of course I need whatever money I can properly get. I felt that a newspaper syndicate was the only effective method of reaching people in all parts of the country, and I arranged with the Wheeler Syndicate of this city to handle my material."[15] He wrote from memory: all of his notes had been confiscated by the guards and, Julian speculated, locked in Moyer's safe.

The twelve essays were serialized between mid-December 1913 and March 1, 1914, in such papers as the *New York Sun*, the *Washington Post*, the *Salt*

Lake Tribune, and the *Kansas City Star*. He contributed an additional piece titled "Our Barbarous Penal System" to *Hearst's* for February 1914, and he collected the baker's dozen articles in a volume titled *The Subterranean Brotherhood* issued even before the serialization was complete. In this philippic he railed against the penitentiary "machine" or "human pound." He proposed alternatives to prisons: some lawbreakers may "belong in hospitals," others in "insane asylums," and still others "should be succored, not punished." The remainder should be placed "under surveillance but not in confinement." He described Moyer as "an oily, comfortable rogue," accused the "wardens of many of our jails" of hypocrisy, and equated prison labor with slave labor. "I had promised my mates in prison" that he would write this book, he announced, "and I was under no less an obligation, though an unspoken one, to give the public an opportunity to learn at first hand what prison life is, and means."[16] Predictably, his "mates" in Atlanta were ecstatic that someone with a voice and a knack for making news had dared to tell the truth. Moyer was so outraged that he barred Julian's writings from the prison,[17] but not before he ordered an inmate thrown in the hole for circulating a paper with Julian's first article in it.[18]

Ironically, Julian obscured a crucial autobiographical detail in his dedication of the book to his wife: "To my beloved Minne from Julian. Oct. 1914. Don't sadden yourself by reading this, dear; let the children read it, if they care to."[19] In fact, Julian and Minne had been estranged for nearly a decade when the book appeared, and their youngest child was thirty. That is, the dedication maintained the polite fiction that they were still happily married and reinforced the public persona of a devoted husband and father—even in a prison autobiography!—that he carefully cultivated his entire adult life.

He was justifiably proud of *The Subterranean Brotherhood*, one of his most critically acclaimed books. He sent a copy to his friend Jack London, who "was especially struck by [the] exposition of 'prison silence'" and gleaned from it some jargon for his novel *The Star Rover* (1915). The *Portland Oregonian* pronounced Julian's book "an extraordinary human document" written "in letters of fire." The reviewer for the *Journal of the American Institute of Criminal Law and Criminology* asked, if Julian's allegations were "not substantially true," why he had not "been called to account in a suit for libel" and concluded that the conditions he described were "worth investigating."[20]

Not only were they true, but Moyer also attempted to cover up the abuse. The Department of Justice investigation, led by Dr. A. J. McKelway, general Southern secretary of the Child Labor Organization, whitewashed conditions at the prison in its official report released in January 1914.[21]

McKelway "was a fraud and the investigation a farce," Julian responded in an op-ed piece in the *Sun*.[22] Howard also had an ace in the hole. Moyer had fired seven prison employees, including six guards, ostensibly for trying to foment food riots among the prisoners in the dining hall after the congressman began his inquiries.[23] In fact, these employees had been critical of Moyer and were dismissed in order to discredit them. The ploy did not succeed. Less than two weeks after the release of McKelway's report, Howard met with Attorney General McReynolds and presented him with a sheaf of evidence including statements from the former guards, other employees, and former inmates that substantiated Julian's allegations and indicated they were, if anything, understated. These documents added a charge against Moyer: graft. The funds the government appropriated for food were largely wasted, the difference pocketed by prison officials. The bread baked in the prison was sold for profit outside its walls.[24] The McKelway report suddenly became inoperative. McReynolds agreed to order a "more careful inquiry" if Howard would not introduce his resolution in the House calling for a congressional investigation.[25]

The second government inquiry savaged Moyer's methods of running the prison and vindicated Julian. Based in large part on the testimony of the fired guards and released on March 22, the report detailed conditions that were worse than Julian had described. The guards avowed that "sick men were left to die without medical care; that convicts, their minds weakened by months and years of imprisonment, were thrown into the 'hole' to become raving maniacs; that other prisoners were chained like beasts among the steam pipes in the superheated tunnel from the power house to the main building; and that discipline was administered by heavy clubs that crushed in the offending prisoners' skulls."[26] By order of the attorney general, Moyer retired from office a week later.

Moyer's successor, Fred Zerbst, the former deputy warden of the federal prison at Leavenworth, Kansas, immediately announced a number of changes in the way inmates were to be treated. He outlawed dungeons and clubs. "The best way to treat these men is to appeal to their manhood and sense of right," he declared. "The whipping post and the 'black hole' are relics of the past."[27] Within a month he had introduced other reforms. Inmates were addressed by name rather than by number. They were allowed two half holidays a week, more tobacco, safety razors, and movies for entertainment.[28]

If only this tale of human frailty and sorrow ended here. Unfortunately, there is a sequel. Eugene V. Debs, a socialist and labor leader, was incarcerated in the same prison five years later. Zerbst was still the warden, and conditions had improved but were still appalling. Debs's prison autobiography, *Walls and Bars*, is so similar in tone and substance to Julian's *The Subterranean Brotherhood* that there can be little doubt that he read it. Debs describes the Atlanta jail as a "dismal cemetery of the living dead," much as Julian's title alludes to the entombed Lazarus. Debs also leveled many of the same complaints. Inmates were still punished with solitary confinement in the hole for offenses such as whistling or waving at a fellow prisoner. The food remained "the one great unending source of complaint," Debs wrote. He could stomach only the bread, which was baked as usual in the prison kitchen but no longer sold illegally to the neighbors.[29] Such is progress.

PART I

THE HEIR

1846–64
"I do not at all despair of seeing him grow up a gentleman"

"A small troglodyte made his appearance here at ten minutes to six o'clock this morning," the proud father announced on June 22, 1846. "He has dark hair and is no great beauty at present, but is said to be a particularly fine little urchin by everybody who has seen him." The "troglodyte" was not christened for nearly a year, because his parents could not agree on a name. They bandied about a few, such as Theodore and Gerald; meanwhile, his father called him the "Black Prince" and "Bumblebreech."[1] For whatever reason, they finally chose Julian, the name of a pagan and apostate.

A well-born child, he was the heir of distinguished New England families. On his mother Sophia's side, he was descended from "Boadicea, queen of the Britons," or so he bragged, and the Revolutionary general Joseph Palmer.[2] His mother's sisters, Mary Mann and Elizabeth Palmer Peabody, were renowned reformers, the first a teacher and wife of progressive educator Horace Mann, the latter an antislavery activist, feminist, and champion of kindergartens. The corpulent Aunt Lizzie—Julian once estimated her weight at "several tons"—"became the honored and loved friend of most of the eminent persons of her time and place," and she "overflowed with unselfish love and good works for everybody, for us children especially."[3]

On his father Nathaniel's side, Julian was descended from the Puritan selectman William Hathorne, who accompanied John Winthrop to the New World aboard the *Arbella* in 1630. His forte was the "adjudication of crime, particularly illegal fornication."[4] William's son John was a presiding magistrate at the Salem witch trials. Julian's great-grandfather "Bold Daniel" Hathorne was a hero of the Revolution, and his grandfather had been a sea captain in the merchant marine and died of yellow fever in Surinam in 1808. Julian's paternal grandmother had been a Manning, a prominent Salem family. Julian's ancestry was not without blemish, however. Philip

Young documents an episode of incest in the Manning family in the late seventeenth century.[5] As Nathaniel remarked in his tale "Main Street," "Let us thank God for having given us such ancestors; and let each successive generation thank him, not less fervently, for being one step further from them in the march of ages."[6]

Sophia bore her second child in the relative safety and comfort of her parents' house in Boston near her mother, her physician father, and her homeopathic doctor. For six months her husband commuted to his job in the Salem Custom House. In August 1846, father, mother, daughter Una, and baby Julian moved to a small house on Chestnut Street in Salem, then two months later to a more spacious, three-story house on Mall Street. Julian's grandmother Elizabeth Clarke Manning Hathorne (aka Madame Hawthorne) and her daughters, Elizabeth (aka Aunt Ebe) and Louisa, were ensconced in rooms on the second floor just below Nathaniel's study. "It will be very pleasant to have Madame Hawthorne in the house," Sophia claimed. "Her suite of rooms is wholly distinct from ours, so that we shall only meet when we choose to do so." The house rented for two hundred dollars a year, a small fraction of Nathaniel's twelve-hundred-dollar annual salary.[7]

Though Julian purported in later life to have been a fragile child, the opposite seems to be true. In November, five months old, he weighed a hearty twenty-three pounds. A month later his mother reported that he was "a Titan in strength & size" and "as large as some children of two years." His father thought he resembled "an alderman in miniature. . . . There never was a gait more expressive of childish force and physical well-being." At twenty months he was a headstrong "little outlaw" fond of mischief. In December 1848, Sophia noted that Julian at age two "rides very far on his hobby-horse,—round the whole earth,—and then dismounts, loaded down with superb presents for us all." Or as Emerson might have said, "Hawthorne rides well his hobby-horse of the night." His father hoped to foster a martial spirit in his son, who possessed "a disposition to make use of weapons—to brandish a stick, and use it against an adversary," what his father considered a normal "masculine attribute." Julian played with a wooden cannon and trumpet at the age of seven, and Nathaniel bought him a toy pistol for his eighth birthday.[8]

In short, the young Julian was indulged by permissive parents. His mother scorned "those who counsel sternness and severity instead of love towards their young children!" She regarded Julian as "the son of a King . . . anointed by Heaven." His father once joked that "if Julian sent for mamma's head, I suppose she would do it up in a bundle" and send it. The biographer Randall Stewart fairly noted that Sophia regarded all of her children as "unfallen angels." Nathaniel, on the other hand, worried that his son was too soft: "Julian has too much tenderness, love, and sensibility in his nature; he needs to be hardened and tempered." As Julian recounted in his biography of his parents, "The mother sees goodness and divinity shining through everywhere; the father's attitude is deductive and moralizing." In contrast to her brother, Una seemed odd-turned, an anomaly who defied the norms, "neither male nor female and yet both."[9] Her father would ascribe some of her eccentricities to the elfin child Pearl in *The Scarlet Letter*.

Nathaniel composed his most celebrated romance soon after he lost his patronage job in the custom house. When he was "decapitated" on June 8, 1849, three months after the inauguration of Zachary Taylor, his dismissal became a national cause célèbre. He did not appeal the decision, however, because he had wearied of the menial labor. According to legend, he began the book the same day he was fired, when Sophia revealed that she had saved about $150 in pin money for just such an exigency. Within weeks, Nathaniel's mother died, which helps explain why the gloomy romance was, he said, "a positively hell-fired story, into which I found it impossible to throw any cheering light." At the age of three, Julian understood nothing about his father's despondency. He only knew that in a chamber on the second floor "lay an old woman of striking aspect, with a brow and eyes resembling our father's own. As the book grew to life, she faded out of existence, and before the fame of it had been sounded she was gone."[10]

Raised on the stories of Hans Christian Andersen, the brothers Grimm, Mother Goose, and Lewis Richter's *The Black Aunt*, Una and Julian "believed in fairies, in magic, in angels, in transformations," and in changelings. Sophia boasted that Julian had "developed a superb creative genius & we think he inherits his father's imagination." In winter, in the backyard of the house on Mall Street, the children "rejoiced in the snow; and my father's story of the Snow Image got most of its local color from our gambols." In the tale a small boy and his sister fashion a girl from snow and it leaps to life. The children are easily recognizable as Julian and Una. With his "broad and round little phiz," the boy runs around "on his short and sturdy legs as substantial as an elephant." In his journal Nathaniel also remarked on Julian's "rozy little phiz," "round little face," and "stout, sturdy, energetic little legs." A year or so later he modeled some of the characters and events in *The Wonder Book* and *Tanglewood Tales* on the adventures of his children. Nathaniel, Una, and Julian were thinly disguised as Eustace Bright, Primrose, and Sweet Fern. As their father finished each of the tales, he read it aloud to the family, and before the manuscript was printed, "the children could repeat the greater part of it by heart."[11]

Una and Julian, ca. 1850. (Courtesy of the Boston Athenæum.)

The sales success of *The Scarlet Letter* enabled Nathaniel to earn a modest livelihood by his pen. No longer tied to Salem, he looked for another place where he could write without distraction. He had hoped to settle near the sea, but when Sophia's friend Caroline Tappan offered a small red cottage on her estate in the Berkshires near Lenox in western Massachusetts, he accepted reluctantly. The family settled there in late May 1850 and remained for eighteen months. Nathaniel wrote *The House of the Seven Gables* in the "Red House," where the Hawthornes' third and last child, Rose, was born on May 20, 1851.

Among their near neighbors was the actress Fanny Kemble, grandmother of the novelist Owen Wister. Infatuated with Kemble, Julian once listened as she read an entire Shakespeare play, and on another occasion she rode her horse to the Red House and asked Julian if "he would like to have a ride; and, on his answering emphatically in the affirmative, she swung him up astride the pommel of her saddle, and galloped off with him." When they returned, Kemble "held him out at arm's length, exclaiming, 'Take your boy!—Julian the Apostate!'"[12]

But by far the most important friend Nathaniel made during these months was Herman Melville, who lived on a farm six miles away. The thirty-one-year old author of *Typee* and *Omoo* "was the strangest being that ever came into our circle," Julian later remarked, although he remembered him mostly as having "a black beard, with a pair of dark, glowing eyes above it, and a white forehead contrasting with darker cheeks." Melville "would tramp over once in a while" to charm the children with his stories, especially during the winter,[13] and he dedicated to Nathaniel the romance he was writing at the time—*Moby-Dick*.

When Sophia and Una left Lenox on July 28, 1851, for three weeks in Boston, Julian remained behind in the care of his father. Nathaniel kept a detailed diary of these weeks titled "Twenty Days with Julian & Little Bunny" to share with his wife when she returned. Julian recalled this period as "one uninterrupted succession of halcyon days," although one of Nathaniel's biographers has detected a different subtext, writing: "Hawthorne spared the rod and made his own life miserable. Julian made nasty comments about visitors, bellowed for more bread at the table, and hit his father when it was refused." As for the pet bunny, Nathaniel found it "stark and stiff" in its box on August 16. "Julian seemed to be interested and excited by the event, rather than afflicted," his father noted. He "laughed a good deal about Bunny's exit." Little did he know that Julian had poisoned it— "my first murder, which I did not confess for twenty years."[14] This sadistic streak sometimes emerged in his adulthood, especially in his relationships with women.

The highlights of these weeks were a pair of encounters with Melville. On August 1 they crossed paths by chance. Melville alighted from his horse, lifted Julian into the saddle, and "the little man" had "a ride of at least a mile homeward." Melville stayed for supper, and after Nathaniel put Julian to bed, the two men "had a talk about time and eternity, things of this world and of the next, and books, and publishers, and all possible and impossible matters, that lasted pretty deep into the night." Five-year-old Julian dozed in the next room while his father and Melville enjoyed one of the most famous conversations in the history of American letters. A week later, Melville, the Hawthornes, and George and Evart Duyckinck visited a nearby Shaker village. Nathaniel was horrified. For all their claims of physical purity, "the Shakers are and must needs be a filthy set" and "the sooner the sect is extinct the better." Much to his father's delight, Julian "desired to confer with himself"—that is, he evacuated on the grass—and "neither was I unwilling that he should bestow such a mark." The next day, Evart Duyckinck wrote his wife that Julian, with "his ringlets and quick electric ways," was "overflowing with life." That day, too, Julian announced that he "loved Mr. Melville as well as [his father], and as mamma, and as Una." Weeks later, Melville replied to a letter from Julian that he was "very happy that I have a place in the heart of so fine a little fellow as you."[15]

By November 1851, the same month *Moby-Dick* appeared, Nathaniel was ready to relocate. He had wearied of the Red House, "the most inconvenient and wretched little hovel that I ever put my head in," and he had the offer of the Manns' home in West Newton for the winter. There the family moved, and there he wrote *The Blithedale Romance*. But the arrangement was only temporary, given the acrimony between the in-laws. Horace Mann disapproved of Nathaniel's smoking and drinking, and Nathaniel disapproved of Mann's radical politics, especially his abolitionism. Even as a child Julian was frightened by his uncle's stern moral strictures. Julian recalled a visit to the village by the Hungarian revolutionary Louis Kossuth that winter. Kossuth was in the United States to raise money for the struggle in his homeland, one of the European revolutions of 1848, and while on his travels he stopped for an hour at the depot in West Newton. Julian had printed the message "God bless you, Kossuth!" on a card and presented it to "the slender, dark, bearded gentleman," who read it, "looked me in the eyes with a quick smile of comprehension, and, stepping towards me, laid his hand upon my head."[16]

In February 1852 Nathaniel began to search for a dwelling where he could settle more permanently. "He is very anxious to get into a home of his own, where his mind will be free to follow the calling on which his bread depends," Sophia's mother wrote. The couple had lived in the Old Manse in Concord early in their marriage, and Bronson Alcott was selling a house a mile east of the village. "My father's first look at 'The Wayside' had been while snow was still on the ground," Julian remembered, "and he had reported to his wife that it resembled a cattle-pen."[17] Still, it was located on several acres of meadow and woodlands along Lexington Road. Ephraim Wales Bull, the developer of the Concord grape, lived next door. Nathaniel paid fifteen hundred dollars for it, the only house he ever owned.

The site of the first battle of the American Revolution, Concord was also the mecca of transcendentalism and home to Alcott, Ellery Channing, Henry

David Thoreau, and Ralph Waldo Emerson. Julian disdained Alcott, "whose unselfish devotion to the welfare of the human race," he once mused, "made it incumbent upon his friends to supply him with the means of earthly subsistence." The joke went around that his daughter Louisa May was his greatest contribution to literature. Julian also belittled the poet Channing, whom he considered "not altogether sane." As for Thoreau, Julian remembered best the day in 1852 when the "hermit of Concord" surveyed the grounds of the Wayside: "Wherever he went I followed; neither of us spoke a word from first to last." When he had finished, Nathaniel "paid him ten dollars, and Thoreau strode away, after remarking, with a glance at me, 'That boy has more eyes than tongue.'"[18]

Whatever he thought of the local cranks, Julian revered Emerson. "If we regard Alcott as the cow that jumped over the moon, Emerson's was the hand that let down the bars of the pasture," in his view. Nicknamed the Concord Sage, Emerson was the greatest American poet, indeed "the only original poet" of his generation. Julian befriended Emerson's children Edward and Edith, and their father reciprocated the affection. "There is no child so fine as Julian," Emerson remarked when Hawthorne *père* and *fils* visited him on July 4, 1852. If George Washington was "the Great Repose," he declared, then "Julian is the Little Repose—hereafter to become the Great Repose!" Emerson once invited Julian to walk with him and his children "to Fairy Land," meaning the Walden woods, and he went "in a state of ecstatic bliss."[19]

Meanwhile, Julian and his sisters were homeschooled. Unfortunately, he was a desultory student. Their mother taught reading, geography, and drawing; instructed them in the Bible; and read to them from Homer's epics, John Bunyan's *Pilgrim's Progress*, and Longfellow's poetry. As an adolescent, Julian knew "the story of all the mythological personages" in the *Iliad* and the *Odyssey*; and he was obsessed with the character of Giant Despair in Bunyan's allegory, who seemed to stalk him. His father taught him elementary French, and Aunt Lizzie tried to instruct him in history, but to little avail. "As a pupil I was always most inept and grievous in dates and in matters mathematical especially," he admitted.[20] Thomas Wentworth Higginson visited the Wayside around this time and recalled that Nathaniel "twirl[ed] his magnificent boy" in the air. Not all the visitors to the Wayside were similarly charmed with Julian, however. Channing complained that the Hawthorne children were "brought up in the worst way" and had learned "nothing but bad manners. They break in when not required, & are not in fact either handsome or attractive." On another occasion the poet Richard Henry Stoddard chatted with Nathaniel in his study while Julian played with the inkstand. "He was ordered to desist, but of course he did not" and soon overturned it.[21]

The Hawthornes' first residence at the Wayside lasted only from February 1852 until July 1853. When Franklin Pierce was nominated for president at the Democratic convention in June 1852, he asked Nathaniel, his friend and Bowdoin College classmate, to pen his campaign biography, and Nathaniel agreed, to the despair of antislavery activists everywhere. Pierce did not favor slavery, but neither did he actively oppose it; he merely hoped it would "vanish like a dream." For his role in boosting Pierce's candidacy, Nathaniel was accused of prostituting his talents. Julian loved Pierce: "None other of my father's friends affected me as he did; his voice was winning; his smile touched my heart; I liked to walk with my hand in his, and to contemplate his face as he talked with my father."[22] After he was elected in November, Pierce appointed Nathaniel to the U.S. consulship in Liverpool, one of the most lucrative diplomatic postings in the world. He was confirmed by the Senate on March 26, 1853, and the family sailed for Liverpool on July 6. They lived in Europe for the next seven years.

* * *

They embarked on the steamer *Niagara*, a wooden paddle wheeler under the command of Captain John Leitch, "a genial, debonair, entertaining little gentleman." They were among a privileged few passengers. Only about twenty thousand Americans sailed for Europe annually in the 1850s, many of them the scions of old money on their *Wanderjahr*. The company aboard the *Niagara* was so small, Julian remembered, that a single cow "sufficed for their needs in the way of milk," and at the end of the ten-day voyage several fowl "were still left alive and pecking." Sophia noted in her journal that "Julian eats nobly" meals of chicken and lobster. The *Niagara* docked in Liverpool on July 16 and the family registered at the best hotel in the city. According to Julian, however, "it was intensely discomfortable" and "the solemn meals were administered with a ceremonious gravity that suggested their being preliminaries to funerals."[23] Ten days after their arrival the family escaped to Mary Blodget's boardinghouse on Duke Street, where they remained for the next month.

Julian was initially homesick for the Wayside. At the boardinghouse he was "very much like an eagle crowded into a canary-bird's cage!" The family soon moved to Rock Ferry, "a pretty, green, quiet be-villa'd little suburb" a half hour by water taxi across the River Mersey. For 160 pounds a year for the next two years Nathaniel rented a furnished two-story villa, "one of the typical abodes of the English respectable middle-class," in a fenced neighborhood. Best of all, the house had a yard and each of the children was assigned a garden plot. Julian cultivated his "so assiduously that it became quite a deep hole."[24]

As in the custom house, Nathaniel's duties as consul were largely me-nial: certifying invoices and collecting tariffs on exports, assisting distressed American sailors, and mediating disputes between American shipmasters and their crew members. The consular office was "a grimy little room barely five paces from end to end" on an upper floor of a brick warehouse in the harbor area. However monotonous the work, at least it paid better than writing books. "We are in good spirits—my wife and I—about official emoluments," Nathaniel acknowledged to Horatio Bridge, his former college classmate. He expected to earn enough money "to educate Julian and portion off the girls in a moderate way." Julian often accompanied his father to the consulate, and after hours they sometimes went "to the museum, or the Zoölogical Gardens, or to some other place of amusement" or took the ferry "to New Brighton and stroll[ed] about on the beach."[25]

The family was joined in Rock Ferry in spring 1854 by twenty-five-year old Fanny Wrigley, who remained with them for the next three years. "We had all liked her at first sight," Julian remembered, and Sophia "called her 'Golden Fancy.'" Her precise job "was never determined; she came as [Rose's] 'nurse,' but she remained as everything and nothing." Once, under the spell of *Don Quixote* and Edmund Spenser's *The Faerie Queene*, Julian "conceived a vehement infatuation for medieval chivalry and knight errantry." Fanny "fit me out with a suit of armor and a helmet," and his father bought him "a real steel sword with a brass hilt." If Una was named for the heroine of *The Faerie Queene*, Julian became her champion, the Red Cross Knight. At the age of eight, he signed his letters "the mighty Knight Sir Julian Hawthorne Esq." or "Sir Julian K[night] of the dragon." Like the hero of his novel *Garth* (1877), he "saw giants and enchanted castles in rocks and trees, and followed the steps of nymphs and satyrs through the woods."[26]

The children continued to be homeschooled. Sophia taught them arith-metic, geography, and drawing; instructed Julian in the fundamentals of Greek; and every evening declaimed two cantos of Spenser. Nathaniel taught him some Latin and read aloud many of the classics of British literature, including Milton and Shakespeare, De Quincey and Coleridge, Byron and Tennyson. He also read Washington Irving's *Life of Washington* and the *Ingoldsby Legends* to the family, and in 1855 he recited *Hiawatha* from a copy sent him by Longfellow. "Before my fourteenth year," Julian boasted, "I had become familiar with the best of English literature." He read none of his father's romances, however, until after Nathaniel's death, because "he had always told me that they were not suited to my age and requirements."[27]

He was also instructed in the social manners of a gentleman in Victor Regnier's dancing school in Liverpool, where he met "an American girl and my first love." "Mary Warren has taken him into her good graces,"

Nathaniel wrote Sophia, "and has quite thrown off another boy. . . . I told Julian he must expect to be cast aside in favor of somebody else, by-and-by. 'Then I shall tell her that I am very much ashamed of her,' said he. 'No,' I answered, 'you must bear it with a good grace, and not let her know that you are mortified.' 'But why shouldn't I let her know it, if I *am* mortified?' asked he; and really, on consideration, I thought there was more dignity and self-respect in his view of the case than in mine."

Julian became a bookworm, an avid reader of juvenile novels such as Mayne Reid's *The Boy Hunters* and *The White Chief* and James Fenimore Cooper's Leatherstocking tales. George Borrow's *Lavengro*, "one of the most fascinating and excellent stories ever written," became a favorite. Philip Gosse's *The Aquarium*, illustrated with pictures of sea anemones and other marine creatures, whetted his interest in natural history, especially conchology. Nathaniel and Sophia hired an English governess to assist in teaching the children, but her ignorance, according to Julian, was possibly even "greater than our own." She "had to sit up nights studying the subjects which she was to introduce" the next day. She "was particularly perplexed by geometry" and was eventually dismissed.[28]

In addition, Julian acquired some skills in the so-called manly arts. He was taught the broadsword by a veteran of Waterloo; to fence by a veteran of the Crimean War; to play cricket and ride a horse; and he practiced gymnastics twice a week at Louis Huguenin's gymnasium. "In all sorts of athletic exercises, in which a young Titan is required," his mother averred, "Julian is eminent." Yet, while dancing, he moves "in courtly measures and motions, and when he runs, he throws himself on the wind like a bird, and flits like a greyhound." His father was no less proud. He declared in June 1855 that "Julian has grown amazingly, and is stronger than any English boy of his age, or two years above it. He is a sturdy little Yankee, and holds himself always ready to fight for his country's honor." He soon proved his mettle. In April 1856 the pugnacious Julian fought "some English boys, who, he says, abused his country," though his father suspected "the quarrel began with his telling them that it was his highest ambition to kill an Englishman!" Julian recalled the scene a quarter century later: "At the age of nine, J. H. had his first stand-up fight with a boy a year older than himself; and he still remembers the thrill of pleasure which visited his heart when his antagonist fell to earth."[29]

In deference to British custom, Nathaniel read aloud from the Anglican *Book of Common Prayer* to the family and servants every morning. However, Sophia assumed responsibility for the religious education of the children. Una and Julian regularly accompanied her to the Unitarian chapel on Renshaw

Street to hear the Reverend William Henry Channing, nephew of the New England theologian William Ellery Channing. "I sat in the pew and listened, and learned my way through the church service and the hymn book," Julian remembered. Channing thought Julian had a "very marked character" and predicted that he would become "a high-minded and energetic man." All the children were baptized by Channing in January 1857, though their father was unobservant. As he conceded, "I have not yet been to hear Mr. Channing preach; but, to make amends, I send Julian every Sunday."[30]

The monotony of life in Liverpool was occasionally relieved by visitors, especially two Englishmen. Henry Bright had visited the Wayside in May 1852 and remarked at the time on Nathaniel's "beautiful glorious" son. Bright was "a thorough Englishman from the marrow out," Julian recalled, "near-sighted, with a monocle; prejudiced, frank, amiable, sturdy, incorruptible, delightful." Not only did he frequent the house in Rock Ferry, but also "he several times had me out to visit at his father's house, where I had the run of a huge English country seat and plenty to eat and anything else a boy could want." Francis Bennoch, the other frequent guest in Rock Ferry, "was a broad-shouldered, deep-chested man, of middle height, with a great head and forehead, curly black hair and beard, and kindling black eyes, which flashed with ardent feeling, and smiled with royal good humor." He was "one of the handsomest men in England," a poet in the tradition of Robert Burns and Sir Walter Scott, "a wealthy and successful wool merchant in London," and "an enthusiastic admirer" of his father's genius. Bennoch, too, invited the Hawthornes to his mansion for weeks at a time.[31]

Then there were the Americans who passed through Liverpool, including the author Sarah J. Lippincott, who wrote under the nom de plume Grace Greenwood, and the actress Charlotte Cushman. Julian thought Cushman was "the most beautiful woman I had ever known." In fact, "she was my first love." (He seems to have had several.) In spring 1854 John L. O'Sullivan, the new U.S. ambassador to Portugal, passed through Liverpool en route to Lisbon. Founding editor of the *Democratic Review* in 1837, O'Sullivan had "become interested," as Julian put it, "in some copper-mines in Spain" that "could be bought for a song and would pay a thousand per cent from the start." Nathaniel eventually loaned him money to help finance the scheme, although the debt was never repaid. James Buchanan, U.S. minister to the Court of St. James and technically Nathaniel's superior, came to Liverpool in early January 1855 to interview the consul—more specifically, Julian realized later, "to sound him out as to his political views" in light of Buchanan's political ambitions. The future president struck Julian as "a curiosity on the way to being a bore." Melville, en route to the Holy Land in November 1856, unexpectedly visited the Hawthornes and noted that Julian had "grown into a fine lad."[32]

While living in Liverpool, Nathaniel often tramped to Eastham, Chester, and other Cheshire villages in company with his son. These walks were Julian's "chief education during my childhood years, an education all joy, wonder, and sunshine. For [my father] not only found answers to my queries, but told me tales of great men and mighty deeds, of heroic valor and endurance." So long as they lived in England, too, vacations were planned around either Sophia's health or Julian's schooling. In July 1854 the family spent "a glorious fortnight at the Isle of Man" in the Irish Channel and on their return stopped at Stonehenge. When Julian realized that "the circle of stones once marked out a temple," Rose remembered, "he curled his lip" and asked "Is that all?" That fall they decamped for several weeks at Rhyll on the Welsh coast. The following June they toured Warwickshire and the Lake District north of Liverpool. Julian recalled "wandering with my father through a grassy old churchyard in search of Wordsworth's grave." The family celebrated Julian's ninth birthday by taking a day trip to Stratford, and the next month they returned to the Lake District.[33]

Sophia suffered with such severe bronchial trouble during her first two winters in Merseyside that her doctors advised her that she "*must* leave England" the next winter or risk dying.[34] She accepted O'Sullivan's invitation to bask in the more hospitable Portuguese climate and sailed with her daughters for Lisbon in October 1855. Meanwhile, her husband and son left Rock Ferry and moved into Mrs. Blodget's boardinghouse.

Nathaniel's months of single-parenting his son were an amplified version of twenty days with Julian and little Bunny. Just as he refused to discipline his son at five, he was loath to spank him at nine. Although Julian was "a real little rampant devil," he fretted to Sophia, "unless I give up the attempt betimes, he will soon be the spanker, and his poor father the spankee." As usual, Julian was stubborn in all things, including his homework. "I have not myself the slightest tact or ability in making him study, or in compelling him to do anything that he is not inclined to do of his own accord; and to tell thee the truth, he has pretty much his own way in everything." Despite his sassiness, Julian's intellect was "very remarkable" and his heart "warm and true and simple," even if it "admit[ted] very few persons into it." Nathaniel did "not at all despair of seeing him grow up a gentleman." Sophia exulted in her son during their separation, praising to her sisters his "intellect," his "power of observation," and his "profound insight." She crowed that Julian had "an endless power of work in him" and was very "poetic & contemplative."[35]

After Sophia, Una, and Rose returned from Portugal in June 1856, the family settled for a fortnight at Bennoch's home while Nathaniel searched for a house with salubrious air within commuting distance of the consulate. They settled in Southport, on the coast sixteen miles north of Liverpool. From that base they continued their trips across Britain. In December 1856 they spent several days in Oxford and London, where they visited Westminster Abbey, the Crystal Palace, and the National Gallery. Julian attended the Grand Christmas Pantomime at Drury Lane, his first live theatrical performance. Leaving Una and Rose with Fanny Wrigley, Julian and his parents toured Yorkshire, Manchester, and Lincolnshire. About this time his parents bought Julian his first diary so that he might chronicle his travels. Between late June and mid-July 1857 they traveled to Scotland, where they visited some of the haunts of Robert Burns, including his birth house. Like one of the relic hunters in Mark Twain's *The Innocents Abroad*, Julian bragged in his diary that he "got a little piece of it from one of the walls inside." In late July, as Nathaniel was preparing to resign his consular job, the family moved near Manchester for six weeks so that they could visit the great Art Treasures of Great Britain exhibition.[36]

On the recommendation of Horace Mann, who had become president of Oberlin College, Nathaniel hired an American au pair for his children before the family left for the Continent. Ada Shepard, a recent graduate of the school, joined the Hawthornes in October. She received no salary but had been promised a position on the Oberlin faculty as an instructor of modern languages on the condition she improve her French, German, and Italian. Julian thought she was "the most amiable and philosophic of young ladies" and "a woman of happy disposition and singular intelligence," although to Nathaniel's dismay she had imbibed "all the women's rights fads and other advanced opinions of the day." Still, she "entered upon her duties as governess with energy and good-will" and taught the children some basic Italian to prepare them to live in Rome. Shepard was particularly impressed with Julian, whom she considered a type of "Hercules in miniature," though she soon discovered that study was to him "a painful instead of a pleasant duty." As for Julian, he was smitten and once asked for a lock of her hair as a keepsake.[37]

On November 10 the Hawthorne family left for London, where they took rooms near the British Museum. Their departure for the Continent was delayed by illness, however. The children caught the measles and were treated by a famous homeopathic physician, J. J. Garth Wilkinson, who also gave Nathaniel a letter of introduction to the poet Coventry Patmore. When he had recovered, Julian explored the city with his father—St. Paul's

Cathedral, the Tower of London, and the Strand. Finally, on January 3, 1858, the family took a train to Folkestone, a ferry across the channel, and reached Paris the following day.

*   *   *

"I was always hungry, but hungrier than ever in Paris," Julian remembered. According to Nathaniel, his voracious son could have consumed "a whole sheep." Two days after their arrival, "Julian was woefully hungry" and his father ordered a fillet of stewed beef "principally for [his] benefit" in the hotel restaurant. By Julian's own testimony, he "never flinched from a meal." During their week in Paris the Hawthornes met Maria Mitchell, "a plain, New England old maid from Gloucester," as Julian put it, and "the greatest woman astronomer of her time," who was traveling to Rome—where the Hawthornes planned to winter—and "joined our party." She became "my first lady-love" (yet another one!) and "accepted my devotion—which I made not the slightest effort to conceal." Within a day or two, "she was 'Aunt Maria' for all time to come."[38]

Most of the week was spent in sightseeing. On January 10 Julian and his parents toured the Louvre. The next day, he and his father strolled along the rue de Rivoli to the Place de la Concorde and the Champs-Élysées to the rue de Beaujon; and the following day they walked to Notre Dame. The family left Paris the afternoon of January 12 and caught the *Calabrese*, an Italian steamer "the size of a large tug-boat," in Marseille on the fourteenth. In Civitavecchia they hired a *vettura* for the eight-hour overland trip to the Eternal City, arriving there during a blizzard the night of the seventeenth, and found temporary lodging in Spillman's Hotel. They soon engaged a suite of rooms on the Via Porta Pinciana near the Spanish Steps. Unfortunately, the Italian winter that year was unusually severe. "I was more interested in sliding on the ice round the fountain basins in the piazza of St. Peter's . . . than I was in the famous church," Julian remembered. His father recreated the moment in chapter 41 of *The Marble Faun*. Nathaniel soon called on the American expatriate sculptor William Wetmore Story, whom he had known in Salem several years earlier. In fact, according to Julian, "we went quite often" to Story's studio in the Palazzo Barberini, where he remembered seeing Story's "statue of Cleopatra while yet in the clay."[39] The sculpture reappears in Kenyon's studio in *The Marble Faun*, particularly chapter 14.

During his year and a half in Italy, in fact, Julian became a devotee of classical sculpture. "My delight in the statues was endless," he remembered, including, of course, the Faun of Praxiteles in the Capitoline Museums. Classical statuary provided a kind of sex education for the budding sybarite.

While his father groused that he did not "see the necessity of ever sculpturing another nakedness" and thought Titian was "a nasty old man," Julian literally went to school on human anatomy in the galleries. "I knew personally every statue and group in the Vatican and in the Capitol," he remembered. "If you examine the torsos of ancient Greek statues of women, you will notice a perceptible and beautiful development of the muscles of the abdomen and of the waist and loins." In his novel *A Fool of Nature* (1895), he alluded to the "Junonian bust" of one of his characters, a reference to the statue of Juno Barberini in the Vatican Museum. Even at the age of seventy-four, he compared the "white and flawless skin" of another of his women characters to "the marble of ancient Greek statues." Not that at the age of twelve he was a sophisticated art critic. Once Julian went with his parents to the Vatican gallery and, spying "a vast porphyry vase, forty-four feet in circumference," he wished "he had it full of soup."[40] In any event, he was learning to satisfy the baser appetites.

Before arriving in Rome, Julian read Edward Gibbon's *The Decline and Fall of the Roman Empire* and memorized Thomas Babington Macaulay's "Lays of Ancient Rome," and his father read Torquato Tasso's epic poem *Jerusalem Delivered* aloud to the family. As a result, Julian reveled in the ancient ruins of the empire. He accompanied his parents on dozens of outings—to the Baths of Caracalla, the Palace of the Caesars, the tombs of Cecilia Metella and the Scipios, and the Columbarium of Pomponius Hylas. They toured the tombs along the Appian Way, mentioned in chapter 46 of *The Marble Faun*. He befriended a boy his own age—Eddy Thompson, son of the painter Cephas Giovanni Thompson, whose family also lived near the Spanish Steps—and together they "climbed over the ruins of twenty centuries," particularly the excavations of the Capitol. Julian collected shards of "verd Antique, Rosso Antico, porphyry, giallo antico, serpentine, sometimes fragments of bas-reliefs and mouldings," and bits of mosaic, and according to his father, he might have furnished "a curious and valuable museum, in America," from "the spoil of his boyish rambles."[41]

To escape the stifling Roman summer, the Hawthornes left for Tuscany on May 24, 1858. They paused in Perugia to admire the paintings by Fra Angelico in the church of the Dominican and to receive "the Bronze Pontiff's benediction," much as Miriam and Donatello visit the church and are blessed by the bronze statue of Pope Julius III in chapters 34–35 of *The Marble Faun*. On June 1, the day after their arrival in Florence, they let the thirteen-room first *piano* of the Casa del Bello for two months at about fifty dollars a month. "The house was all light and grace," Julian remembered, and it was a short walk to the Duomo and the Campanile, the Pitti and

Uffizi Galleries, and the Boboli Gardens. Their second day in the city the family went to the Duomo, so ornate that Julian declared it was "turned outside in." The next several months in Florence were, Julian thought, "the happiest period" of his father's life.[42]

While in the city Nathaniel and Sophia renewed their acquaintance with the poets Robert and Elizabeth Barrett Browning, who lived a short walk away in the Casa Guidi. Julian considered Elizabeth "a sort of miniature monstrosity; there was no body to her, only a mass of dark curls and queer, dark eyes, and an enormous mouth with thick lips." Nor did he care for her husband, with his "air of self-sufficiency." He seemed more auctioneer than poet. Julian thought even less of their son, Pennini, whom Elizabeth called "her Young Florentine." Nathaniel had never seen "such a boy as this before; so slender, fragile, and spirit-like." Julian remembered that Pennini was dressed in black medieval velvet and silk stockings, and "I had the contempt for him which a philistine boy feels" for a sissy he knows he "could thrash without trouble." Aunt Lizzie boasted about this time that, since leaving London, Julian had "put off his shyness, become quite gay, gone into society everywhere—& grown quite a dandy, spending more time than papa over his toilet."[43] He cultivated a taste for finery the rest of his life.

Across the street from the Casa del Bello lived the American sculptor Hiram Powers, whose son Preston became another of Julian's boon companions. His most vivid memory of the Powers family, however, was of the eldest daughter, Anne, who modeled for her father. Once "when I happened to be alone in the studio—Powers had just stepped out—the door opened and I had a glimpse of a white pair of shoulders and a bosom such as Venus or Hebe might have been glad to own. Boys of eleven seldom enjoy such a privilege. The privilege was promptly withdrawn: . . . the door closed upon a little squeak of dismay." He had "gazed at her with a frankness of delight which it never occurred to me to disguise," and "that fleeting glimpse . . . remained distinct with me" as long as he lived. Anne Powers's bare breasts were more provocative than all the marble nudes in Rome. "Whenever I see one of Powers' female busts I remember her, and have pleasure in knowing that I beheld the reality of which the marble is, after all, but an incomplete reproduction."[44]

On August 1, when the lease on the Casa del Bello expired, the Hawthornes moved to the Villa Montauto, ancestral estate of Count da Montauto, on the hill of Bellosguardo, less than a mile beyond the Porto Romana. The villa, with some forty rooms and a tower commanding a view of the Arno River valley, rented for about fifty dollars a month. For two months

Julian occupied a suite of rooms all to himself "at the western extremity of the house; they were always cool on the hottest days."[45] The "ancient country house" reappears in *The Marble Faun* as Donatello's ancestral home.

On the first of October, after the heat began to wane, the Hawthornes left to return to Rome. They paused for ten days in Siena, where Julian and his father rambled about the town, wandering through the cathedral, the Piazza Pubblico, and the Piazza del Campo. They spent a day with Story and his family at their summer villa, where Julian was struck by the sight of the Donati comet, "then in its apogee of brilliance." From Siena they traveled by *vettura* the rest of the way to Rome, where they settled in a flat on the Piazza Poli within earshot of the Trevi Fountain. Nathaniel described the piazza, "filled with the stalls of vegetable and fruit-dealers, chestnut-roasters, cigar-venders, and other people," in chapter 16 of *The Marble Faun*.[46]

He had hoped to finish the romance during the winter and sail for the United States in spring 1859, but those plans were dashed when Una fell ill. Despite precautions against Roman fever or malaria—their rule was to be indoors by 6:00 PM—less than two weeks after their return to Rome, she suffered her first attack. As Julian bluntly observed, it "was of the worst kind" and "we thought that she must die." She was nursed by Sophia and a homeopath who prescribed quinine, with consequences that, in the end, "were probably quite as lasting and injurious as those of the fever." Nathaniel wrote nothing for six months. Fortunately, Una survived, and fortunately, too, Franklin Pierce spent part of the winter in Rome. "My father could bear no other company; but Pierce helped him" tolerate the ordeal. When the former president saw Julian for the first time in years, he remarked that he had become "a stout boy."[47]

Even with Pierce on the scene, Nathaniel spent little time outdoors that winter save for his occasional walks with Julian. They traipsed on December 12 "along the Tiber to the Ponte Molle, & home by the Via Flaminia," for example. On other occasions they walked to the Tarpeian Rock, where in *The Marble Faun* Donatello flings Miriam's model to his death, and to the Palazzo Cenci, which Hilda visits in chapter 42. On March 11 Julian, his parents, and Ada Shepard descended into the Catacomb of St. Calixtus, a site that figures in chapters 3 and 4 of the novel. Meanwhile, they received a few visitors, among them Christopher Cranch, who entertained the children with an imitation of a man attacked by bees.[48]

By spring Una was finally well enough to travel. On May 26 the family left Rome for England, where Nathaniel had decided to finish his romance and secure British copyright before returning to the United States. Their pace was unhurried, given the fragility of Una's health, and their route indirect. From

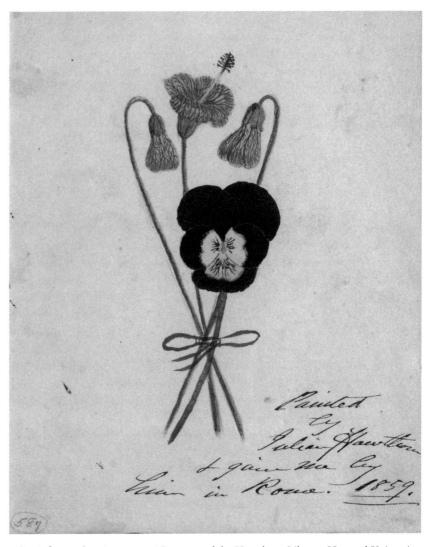

Julian's flower drawing, 1859. (Courtesy of the Houghton Library, Harvard University [bMS 1465 (587)].)

Marseille they traveled to Avignon; in Geneva, Julian learned to swim in the lake; and from Villeneuve he and his father hiked to the Castle of Chillon. Nathaniel noted in his journal that his son sketched "everything he sees, from a wild flower or a carved chair to a castle or a range of mountains."[49] The earliest of Julian's surviving artworks, a floral watercolor, dates from this period. Nearly as erotic as a Georgia O'Keeffe painting, it pictures two veined, purple blooms bordering a flower with a protruding stamen. The family spent five days sightseeing in Paris before departing on June 21 for Le Havre, where they bid adieu to Ada Shepard, who was returning to the United States to marry and assume her teaching duties at Oberlin. "We were sorry to say good-bye to her," Julian recalled. "She had been a faithful and valuable element in our household, and she had become a dear friend and comrade." Little did they know that her marriage would be tempestuous and that fifteen years later she would commit suicide by jumping into the Charles River in Boston.[50]

The Hawthornes also embarked from Le Havre for Southampton and thence to London. Too distracted to write, and with Una's health again failing, Nathaniel moved his family in mid-July to Whitby and a week later to the hamlet of Redcar on the northern coast of Yorkshire. There, Julian remembered, his father "wrote and wrote," and after his daily shift at his desk ended at 3:00 PM, "he walked far along the sands, with his boy dogging his steps and stopping for shells and crabs." Nathaniel wrote over half of the final version of *The Marble Faun* during two months in Redcar, and he took the family to Leamington in early October only when the weather in the north of England turned nasty. On November 8 he finally completed the romance and mailed the last of the manuscript to his British publisher. Meanwhile, Julian was bored. "Papa and I go to walk almost every day," he wrote in his diary, "and we have exhausted all the walks in the vicinity. I am so tired of Leamington that I wish I was a hundred miles away from it."[51]

Upon publication of the book in England on February 28, 1860, Nathaniel took a six-month holiday from work. He moved the family in March to Bath for a vacation. "Bath is a very large town compared to Leamington, and in all other respects its superior," Julian observed. After visiting a local museum with his father and viewing some ancient Roman altars, he noted with more than a hint of intellectual snobbery that they were "very interesting, no doubt, to those who had not seen the Roman Galleries." His father was proud of his teenage son and raved to Sophia that he was "certainly a promising lad."[52]

In finalizing their plans for their return to the United States, the Hawthornes reserved staterooms aboard the steamer *Europa* and departed Liverpool on June 16. James and Annie Fields and Harriet Beecher Stowe, "a little, homely wisp of a woman," booked passage aboard the same ship. Coincidentally, the captain was again "our handsome little Captain Leitch, with his black whiskers." During the voyage Stowe and Sophia "became cronies," according to Julian. "Fresh with the reek of her interview with Lady Byron," in which the poet's widow alleged her late husband had had an incestuous relationship with his sister, Stowe dumped "her whole precious cargo" of scandal onto Sophia. Meanwhile, Nathaniel was eager to reach Concord. When he stepped from the ship in Boston on June 28, a few friends met him at the dock, but he fled with his family on the afternoon train and reached the Wayside before supper.[53]

*   *   *

Julian celebrated his fourteenth birthday aboard the *Europa*, and his father was determined his son would receive an American college education. Nathaniel did not expect his son to become a scholar, "and this was well," conceded Julian. The first order of business was to enroll him in a preparatory school. Julian knew a little Latin and Greek, and he was conversant in the classics and some of the branches of natural history, but of many other subjects, mathematics in particular, he was woefully ignorant. Sophia concluded that Shepard had taught him little or nothing, "but now he understands what he is about." Nathaniel made a few inquiries, and Ellery Channing recommended the Concord Academy under the ferule of Frank B. Sanborn, a Harvard graduate and friend of the executed John Brown. His one-room school on the west side of the village was co-educational, with an enrollment of some forty boys and twenty girls. Among them were Emerson's son Edward; Garth Wilkinson James and Robertson James, younger brothers of William and Henry James; Sam Hoar, son of Judge Ebenezer Rockwood Hoar and nephew of Senator George Frisbie Hoar; Bill Simmons, nephew of George Ripley, Nathaniel's companion at Brook Farm and book editor of the *New York Tribune*; Storrow Higginson, nephew of Thomas Wentworth Higginson; Frank Stearns, son of the abolitionist George Stearns; and Maggie Plumley, Grace Mitchell, Lizzie Simmons, and Lily Nelson, the belles of the school. "The girls were all pretty, except two or three who were beautiful," Julian remembered, and "every week there was a school-dance, and, twice or thrice a year a grand picnic, not to mention other jollifications" As late as 1915, he contended "that the most beautiful girls in the world happened to be gathered together at Concord School" when he was a student there.[54]

Julian began his formal education on September 4, 1860. As Nathaniel apprised Horatio Bridge the day before, "Julian (poor little wretch) begins to go to school tomorrow, for the first time in his life—his education having hitherto been private." Julian faltered from the first, although his father was oblivious to his failures. He wrote Bennoch in December that "Julian goes to school, and takes to his learning pretty well, considering what an idle life he has led hitherto." Ever the overprotective mother, Sophia made excuses for his shortcomings. Her son felt "overwhelmed with his sense of responsibility about his various lessons," she rationalized. "He could not sleep well, and lost appetite, and his hands were almost constantly not damp but *showery* with nervous excitement." She told Sanborn that Julian's problem was not "the result of any study—any effort of intellect." Instead, she blamed Sanborn and his inadequacies as a teacher. She wrote her husband that she "did not like Mr Sanborn. . . . [H]e has a face of Agrippina's type—sharply cut, small features, and the small head of a cruel person."[55]

Still, Julian persevered in the school for three years, and he always considered them among the happiest years of his life. "With the single exception of the studies," he explained, "I came to like the school very much." By his own testimony, he "was one of the dullest and least successful of the scholars. I liked Latin, and that was about all; in arithmetic my failures were preposterous." Instead, he "learned hockey and baseball, and was pretty good at cricket."[56]

His successes at school were not academic but social. He was welcomed to the school by the clique of boys: Sam Hoar had the reputation of an "unruly" lad, though he was merely "overflowing with animal spirits." He was also "perhaps the most brilliant and I think the most lovable of his line." Like Julian, Sam "did not care much for studies. He got through his lessons by the skin of his teeth, when he got through them at all—or else by daring but illicit devices." Rose Hawthorne was infatuated with Sam, whom she thought "a perfectly jolly fellow." Eddie Emerson was "severely moral, with ambitious ideals," Julian remembered, and "as little priggish as the conditions permitted. His bearing was precocious but frank and honest; there was a boy in him, but uniformly repressed." Neither Bob nor Wilkie James was very bright—each of them basked in "sunny ignorance"—but they were "full of the joy of life, and everyone who knew them loved them." Named for the Swedenborgian homeopath who had treated the Hawthorne children for measles in London in 1857, Wilkie was "imperturbably good natured, overflowing with droll humor which never rose to the height of wit."[57] In 1863 he enlisted as an officer in the Fifty-fourth Massachusetts Volunteers, the first regiment of African American soldiers raised in the North, and was wounded on the ramparts of Fort Wagner. His recuperation became the focus of "A Tragedy of Error," his brother Henry's first published story.

By his own account, Julian was a favorite beau of the young women in the school. "I was in love often—all the time perhaps—with one or another of these pretty maids." He remembered a "retreat, made for lovers," at "a point where a small river joined the Concord." There "a high and steep bank was crowned with dark cedars, which cast a deep shadow over the still waters: a commodious rock jutted out" where a couple might "land from their boat, to woo and be wooed." Among the first objects of his affection was Lily Nelson, "a natural princess," whose "face was always of camellia

Una, Rose, and Julian, ca. 1861. Photo by Silsbee, Case & Co., Boston. (Courtesy of the Phillips Library at the Peabody Essex Museum, Salem, Massachusetts.)

paleness, her figure rounded but slender." In March 1862, not surprisingly, Nathaniel admonished his son to resist the lure of the flesh: "I received your letter [which] had a great deal to say about 'sparking' the girls, together with a hint or two about your being destitute of 'tin' [money]. I hope you will not get blown up in this sparking process, for one spark may kindle a great deal of gunpowder; as for tin, your mother may give you any old coffee-pot she can spare."[58] He might as well have offered dating advice to Arthur Dimmesdale.

Sophia was no less worried about her son. She complained to Sanborn that he "literally" threw his students "into each other's arms" by permitting them "to waltz together." She was especially concerned that Julian was "about to plunge into the dissipations of society—all sorts of sport, flirtations, trifling, weary sittings up of nights, reluctant risings in the morning; jaded spirits, plans for fun—everything except a brave and attentive grappling with knowledge." He had been "a sacredly folded bud when we brought him home to America, with a genuine reverence for woman; and now he is forcibly bloomed into a *cavaliere servente* before his wisdom teeth have had time to prick through." Nathaniel had used a similar metaphor with erotic overtones to describe the character Zenobia in *The Blithedale Romance*: "There is no folded petal, no latent dew drop in this perfectly developed rose!" Aunt Ebe dismissed even the suggestion of impropriety, however: Una and Julian "seem to be amusing themselves with all their might. They go to a dance every week and Una dances every dance, to her great delight."[59]

In everything he wrote later about his teenage years in Concord, Julian waxed nostalgic. He remembered especially the parties at the Alcott house, dubbed "Apple Slump" by Louisa May, "with its spacious low-ceilinged living-room, wide fireplace, piano and kitchen. . . . My sisters and I were often invited" there for card parties, private theatricals, or charades. Louisa wrote at the time that Julian was "a worthy boy full of pictures, fishing rods, and fun," and years later she counted these days among "the happiest of my life, for we had charming playmates" in the Hawthorne children. Even Emerson's daughter Ellen thought Julian was "handsome as a picture," was "captivated by his conversation," and "enjoyed him immensely." They sometimes exercised together and Julian would give "my muscles a good pulling." Julian remembered that the "orphic" Bronson Alcott, the paterfamilias, sat apart from the parties, "blinking as though dazzled by the light of his own inspiration." In winter the locals gathered for skating parties on Walden Pond, sometimes by moonlight. Once some eight or nine of the "sons and daughters of persons famous in Concord" and "an elder person or two to represent propriety" camped for ten days on the slopes of Mount Monadnock. Louisa May often joined these gatherings, though Julian kept his distance. "In no other woman that ever I knew was strength of character more manifest than in Louisa Alcott," he observed, and "I was content with an adoring younger brother attitude." Still, he spread the rumor after the publication of *Little Women* in 1868 that he was the original of Laurie, a rumor Louisa was always quick to deny.[60]

One of the young women Julian wooed during his adolescence was Abigail May Alcott, Louisa's younger sister and the model for the comely Amy in *Little Women*. Abby taught art in Sanborn's school and was almost six years older than Julian, but "I was physically well-grown, and the young lady took me at eye-value." As early as August 1862, when he was sixteen and she twenty-two, Julian and Abby were an item. He wrote his mother a year later that he had met another Abby "not looking anything like so divine, enchanting, bewitching &c. &c. &c. as the fair original." Four months later, Julian and Abby escorted Louisa May to the Concord train station for her departure for the military hospitals in Washington. The two of them "formed a private alliance" and cheated "industriously" at cards. Although an anonymous columnist claimed in 1879 that they had once been engaged, Julian passed off their "calf love" as an "interfamily joke" or harmless flirtation. Abby "was endlessly amiable, and good company," he allowed, "and not at the time otherwise occupied. She used to say that she would marry anybody, even me, if he or I would marry her and take her to Europe." By the time Julian was seventeen or eighteen, the age difference seems not to have mattered, if it ever had, though he insisted that their "love-making, such as it was," was "very mild." In any event, he was smitten. Abby once proposed a boy-and-girl swimming party in Walden Pond and Julian was quick to agree. He had read Melville's *Typee,* and he "thought of Fayaway standing up in the bow of their shallop and stripping off her gossamer robe for a sail!" Abby "possessed sex a-plenty." Typee and Walden turned out to be very different venues, however. The Concord women were all attired in "irreproachable blue flannels." But no matter; Julian "glanced at Abby's well-turned figure, her clustered yellow ringlets, her cheerful and inviting expression; she was older than I and must know best; one must follow the customs of the country. I stammered, blushed."[61]

Meanwhile, Nathaniel decided to remodel the Wayside, which had fallen into disrepair during his years abroad. He hired a pair of Concord carpenters, who estimated the price of labor and materials at five hundred dollars. They worked on the project for nearly a year, and the expense eventually reached over two thousand dollars, more than Nathaniel had originally paid for the house. They added a story to its western wing, built two large rooms on the rear, and added a four-hundred-square-foot tower-study inspired by the Villa Montauto. Nathaniel's former study on the ground floor was converted into a library. Not surprisingly, the cost of the renovations strained his resources. As he remarked to his publisher, William Ticknor, "I expect to outlive my means and die in the alms-house." He feared his newest book, *Our Old Home*, based on his English notebooks, would not sell, so "I must try to get my poor blunted pen at work again pretty soon."[62]

Nathaniel's health no less than his finances began to fail after he returned from Europe. He seemed at first to suffer from mere exhaustion and relaxed with Julian at the coast. In July 1861 they vacationed at Pride's Crossing, near Salem on the Massachusetts shore, on the pretext that Julian needed sea air. The next summer they repaired for two weeks to West Gouldsboro, opposite Mount Desert on the Maine shore. "We frequently hear the cry of the Loon, or Great Northern Diver, that Thoreau tells about in 'Walden,'" Julian wrote Una. He and his father attended a chowder party on the beach and a barn dance with some of the locals, but most of the time "we spent on the water" boating and swimming. They lodged at a farmhouse on the bay, where Julian discovered "a very pretty young lady" whom, he joked to his mother, "Papa has already begun to spark," though on his part he had "as yet kept aloof." In a postscript, Nathaniel alluded to "the impertinent jackanapes!—to say that I spark a young lady!!! I have never spoken three words to her. . . . I think Julian is smitten, however, and I fully expect he will be writing poetry to the young lady, unless I bring him away soon." Julian was disappointed by the household library, which included a volume of Zenophon's *Anabasis*, for which he had "as yet found no use," and abounded "with works on Abolitionism and the rights of women." He asked his mother for news of Frank Sanborn: "Is he married, or gone to war? the latter, I hope. I don't feel at all like going to school." Sophia thought Julian's letters were "perfect—the very simplicity and beauty of truth,—nature put into words."[63]

In their correspondence the Hawthornes seldom touched on the burning issue of the hour: the Civil War. In late May 1861, soon after the outbreak of hostilities, Nathaniel conceded to Bridge that one thing "I regret, and one thing I am glad of;—the regrettable thing is, that I am too old to shoulder a musket myself; and the joyful thing is, that Julian is too young." Otherwise, "I shall keep quiet till the enemy gets within a mile of my own house." Julian and some two dozen other fellows from Sanborn's school drilled every evening on Concord Green, but their martial conduct seems to have been mostly (dis)play. Not that their Union sympathies were in doubt. Julian's inclination "was all for war." He faithfully attended Emerson's lectures in the Concord Town Hall, "crammed to the doors with an audience which vibrated like harp strings to any reference to the question." The evening of January 1, 1862, Emerson lectured on the subject of war, and Julian attended the talk with Sophia. In spring 1862 he visited Frank Stearns's family in Medford, Massachusetts, where he met Stearns's father, who, like Sanborn, had helped finance John Brown's antislavery activities.[64]

Unfortunately, Julian had virtually no contact with Thoreau, also an ardent abolitionist, after his return to Concord. But to the end of his life he remembered Thoreau's funeral on May 9, 1862. A crowd filled the Unitarian church on that "sunny pleasant day and all of the mourners filed by the coffin to look at his dead face. I looked with the rest, and I thought it was not Thoreau, but an imitation of him in white wax. It was the first dead face I had seen."[65]

Julian turned his hobby of painting and drawing to advantage during the first months of the war. Sophia had given him an illuminated *Book of Ruth* for Christmas in 1859 that "awoke in me a vehement desire to become an illuminator," and he "zealously pursued" his interest for the next decade. His mother once asked James Fields if the house of Ticknor and Fields would exhibit Julian's drawings in the Old Corner Bookstore in Boston. "Julian wants to buy his wardrobe in part by his own labor," she explained. After one of his portfolios sold for a hundred dollars, he invested the whole sum in watercolors and sheets of parchment and vellum. During the war Julian contributed illuminated poems to Concord benefits to raise money for the Freedman's Bureau and the U.S. Sanitary Commission. "I selected texts from the poets and made them blaze with rainbow hues," as he put it. "There was quite a rush" for his illumination of Browning's "Sordello," according to his aunt Mary Mann, and his illumination of King Arthur's address to Queen Guinevere from Tennyson's *Idyls of the King* was "remarkably fine," according to Annie Fields.[66]

During the winter of 1862–63 Nathaniel began to worry that Julian would fail his entrance exams to Harvard the next summer. Although he wrote Henry Bright that his son was "quite a promising specimen of young America," he was dissatisfied with Frank Sanborn, who thought Julian too young for college. He turned to James Russell Lowell for advice: "I doubt whether Mr. Sanborn, his present instructor, has the faculty of putting a young fellow upon his mettle, and, at all events, Julian does not seem to be thoroughly alive to the emergency of the crisis. Do you think that there would be any advantage in his spending the intervening time under some instructor who would give special attention of filling up the gaps of his knowledge, and giving the precise kind of preparation that he needs?" Lowell soon replied that he thought "it would be very decidedly of advantage to Julian to be put under the training of a tutor." He had discussed the problem with Ephraim Gurney, a Latin instructor in the college, who had "consented to take Julian if you should wish it." Nathaniel soon closed the deal, and Julian was grateful. He thought Gurney was "the greatest Latin scholar of his time in America, and the peer of any in Oxford or Cambridge," as well as "a finished man of the world" with "perfect manners" and "exquisite culture." Best of all, "he was a great smoker" of mild Havana cigars, and he kept a box of them on the table during the tutorials. He seemed to Julian "more like a delightful playfellow than a pedagogue." Gurney coached him in Latin for six months.[67]

Julian was concerned about the exams, too, although less so than his father. He assured Aunt Lizzie in June that he was "studying at Cambridge, to enter College next year. Hitherto I have had to pitch into it pretty hard." Nathaniel similarly advised Bright that "Julian will go to College at the next commencement," even if elsewhere he expressed no such confidence. When his son left for Cambridge to take the exams, Nathaniel shook hands with him "and said, smiling, 'Mind you get in; but I don't expect you will!'" He conceded that if Julian passed, "I shall think less favorably of the wholesome rigor of the examiners than I do now." A day or two later, Julian advised his mother, "If I get in, it will be by the skin of my teeth. . . . I shan't see you again till I have either triumphed or died in the attempt." He sat for the exams in late July along with some seventy other applicants to the class of '67, each "palpitating with ambition, hope, and pride, for to be even a prospective 'collegian' meant something in those far-off days."[68]

He squeezed through with conditions in math, and a week later Nathaniel notified Pierce: "I am happy to tell you that Julian passed a sufficiently creditable examination, and got safely into college, with only a slight rub or two in the mathematical part." As usual, his mother had prepared an excuse in case he failed. She admitted on July 24 that she "was almost destroyed with solicitude about Julian's Examination, not because I feared he did not *know* and was not prepared—but because with Mr. Gurney, I feared he would not recollect what he knew in such a rapid time—rapid and short. But he was triumphant in all but Algebra. . . . He finished his Latin Paper in half the time allowed him. His tastes do not lie in the way of Exact Science—but he is poetic-aesthetic-philosophic." She punned that her son preferred "Ruskin's Immortal Curve to the geometric Curve." Louisa Alcott quipped that Julian "has set up a manly whisker & got into college."[69]

Julian as a Harvard freshman, 1863
(*Memoirs of Julian Hawthorne,* opposite
p. 148).

He matriculated in the fall of 1863 and moved to the second floor of
Hollis Hall, the freshman dormitory. At the time, Harvard College and
Law School boasted a combined enrollment of four hundred men, most
of them the sons of genteel families. He made friends with other students
in his class, among them Eliot Clarke, son of the Unitarian minister James
Freeman Clarke; and Edward Holmes, son of the physician and poet Oliver
Wendell Holmes. He was especially attracted to "a handsome and refined
youth" named William James Morton, son of the physician who discovered
surgical anesthesia. "I knew we would be friends long before I knew who
he was," Julian remembered, "and close friends we came to be, not only
during four years, but till he died fifty years afterward."[70]

As at Sanborn's school, Julian's inclinations at Harvard were more social
and athletic than academic. A hail-fellow-well-met, he took his turn at treating
his classmates, even if he had to sponge off Pierce to do it. "Julian told me
that he borrowed $10 of you," his father wrote the ex-president. "Please to
record it against me, and don't let the little scamp have any more. . . . I want
him never to be a borrower." It was not the last time Julian touched one of his

father's friends for a loan. He also took some liberties during a visit to Maria Mitchell at her home near Swampscott in late September. As Mitchell wrote Sophia, she had enjoyed "a very nice visit from Julian and I think that he more than fulfills his early promise. Outwardly he is amazingly improved—he certainly at his Roman age gave no promise of such manly beauty." She did not mention to his mother an incident Julian later recorded. Alone in her observatory one night, he turned the telescope "on some lighted windows in the town, and sure enough! . . . But Aunt Maria knew boys, and of a sudden there she was." She reprimanded him and "so I blushed and repented."[71]

The Harvard curriculum in the 1860s, before the reforms introduced a decade later, included hefty doses of classical languages, ethics, mathematics, natural science, and history, with virtually no electives. Collegians attended daily recitations and were expected to recite. By any measure, Julian was a failure from the start, especially in math. James Mills Peirce, his math professor, once summoned him to his rooms after class and, while sharing a drink, promised him "that he would never again be asked to recite, but would be given a medium passing mark, say 7 out of a possible 10, at the end of each term."[72]

If, as Stephen Crane once remarked, he majored in baseball at Syracuse, then Julian majored in gymnastics at Harvard. He sported a 48½-inch chest and 16½-inch bicep, and his physical exploits were still legend at Harvard sixty years later. Rather than devote time to his books, he exercised in the gym. Every Saturday he walked sixteen miles from Cambridge to Concord to spend Sunday with his family, returning before dawn on Monday morning. As his doting mother exulted, "He comes home every Saturday and spends Sunday with us, so that we hardly have lost him. He stoutly hates the Mathematics, but is very fond of Latin, and friendly to Greek, and is the greatest gymnast in his class." As his father informed Franklin Pierce, "We think it does him good to keep up a close acquaintanceship with home." Nathaniel's parenting during these months consisted of little more than paying his tuition and urging his son to avoid cheap wine and hard liquor. Julian had been permitted to sample the grape in Italy before he turned fourteen, but once he left for college at seventeen his father fretted he would begin to imbibe. One Saturday in November 1863 Julian and Frank Stearns walked to Concord, where Nathaniel produced a decanter of port and declared, "I want to teach Julian the taste of good wine so that he will learn to avoid those horrible punches." As usual, the admonition fell on deaf ears. The evening he was initiated into Delta Kappa Epsilon in spring 1864, Julian drank from an enormous bowl of claret punch.[73]

During the winter of 1863–64 he also weighed an opportunity to become a professional prizefighter. John Heenan had fought British heavyweight champion Tom Sayers to a draw in a bare-knuckles brawl at Farnborough, Hampshire, in April 1860. Afterward, Heenan and Sayers barnstormed through England, and Julian saw them standing together on a balcony of the Adelphi Hotel in Liverpool holding "two identical prize belts" for "the inspection of the British public crowding the street below." Three years later, Heenan visited Harvard and, impressed with Julian's physique and athleticism, offered to train him for the ring, guaranteeing that he would be "able to lick any man of his weight after three years' preparation." Julian gave serious thought to the idea, even floating it with his father, who, predictably, forbade it.[74]

On May 7, 1864, Julian trekked to Concord to receive Nathaniel's blessing to join a local military regiment that was forming. As he was leaving the room, Julian glanced back at his frail, fifty-nine year old father. "He was standing at the foot of the bed, leaning against it, and looking at me with a smile. He had on his old dark coat; his hair was almost wholly white, and he was very pale."[75] Less than two weeks later, his father died in his sleep, killed by a wasting disease that was never diagnosed.

1864–74
"Julian inherits the princely disposition of his father"

Nathaniel left Concord on May 12, 1864, on a leisurely tour of New Hampshire with Franklin Pierce. He planned to relax in the hamlets along the way and recoup some strength. After retiring to his room in the Pemigewasset House in Plymouth the night of May 18, he seemed to sleep peacefully until, the next morning, Pierce "put his hand on his brow and found it ice," then "laid his hand on the sleeper's heart and found that it had stopped beating."[1] Pierce telegraphed Emerson to ask him to deliver the news in person to Sophia, Una, and Rose at the Wayside, and he notified Fields in Boston. Fields in turn contacted Gurney in Cambridge to inform Julian. Frank Stearns had just returned from his first recitation on the morning of the twentieth when Julian "appeared at my room in the Massachusetts dormitory, and said, like a man gasping for breath, 'My father is dead, and I want you to come with me.'" They hurried to Fields's Beacon Hill house, where Annie Fields shared what she knew. Afterward they "wandered about Boston, silent and aimless."[2] That afternoon Julian met Pierce's train with Nathaniel's body aboard, learned the details of his death, then accompanied Pierce, Fields, and the body to Concord.

He found his mother and sisters "wonderfully sustained and composed," although Sophia reported that Julian seemed "very sad." He had lost his "wise counselor and friend," but her son "tried to comfort me." Aunt Ebe took pity on him, writing Una, "Poor Julian, just entering the world, how much he will miss his father's care. You and Rose will be with your mother, and safe from evil; but a young man's life is full of peril."[3] Still a month shy of his eighteenth birthday, Julian was his father's only male heir and thus titular head of the family. He wrote Fields with news of the arrangements. "As I supposed mamma is willing that the service should take place in the church"—the local Unitarian chapel, where Thoreau's funeral had been held

two years earlier. At Sophia's behest, the officiating minister was James Freeman Clarke, who had married her and Nathaniel in 1842. Julian cautioned
Fields not to tell his mother "nor anyone else, if you can help it," that his
father's body "has been embalmed, for she cannot bear the idea of his being
touched in any way."[4] Emerson, Fields, Longfellow, and Bronson Alcott were
among the pallbearers, and Whittier, Lowell, Pierce, Louis Agassiz, Ellery
Channing, and Abby and Louisa May Alcott were among the attendees at
the funeral and burial in Sleepy Hollow Cemetery on May 23. Julian held
his mother's hand during the funeral, and his "was *ice*," Sophia recalled.
"He feared it would be too much for me."[5]

His plans changed overnight. He did not enlist in the army. "I had become
the Head of the Family," he concluded, "and mustn't leave them unprotected." He literally assumed his father's mantle: Sophia altered Nathaniel's
blue cloak "into an up-to-date Prince Albert coat; for ten years after it was
my best garment." He decided to "give up Harvard and stay at home and
take care of things." He moved into his father's study in the tower of the
Wayside for the summer. His mother believed Nathaniel's death "made a
man of him, for he feels all the care of me and of his sisters." "The children
have taught me rather better than I can teach them," she wrote her sister
Lizzie, "because they are pure mediums of truth and goodness." Perhaps
not. That summer Julian sometimes tomcatted around the neighborhood at
night and ignored the stairs when he returned, climbing the outside of the
house and entering his room "burglariously through a window."[6] So much
for the "Head of the Family."

In early August, Pierce drove to the Wayside behind a pair of black Ham-
bletonian horses and fetched Julian to New Hampshire and Vermont for
a fortnight respite of even more idle pleasure. Upon their arrival at Great
Boar's Head near Rye Beach, Julian remembered, "Pierce and I took a swim
to rid ourselves of the dust of travel. Bathing suits were unknown in that
remoteness. 'You're well set up for a lad of seventeen,' Pierce remarked,
glancing me over." Afterward, they crossed to the Isle of Shoals, fifteen
miles offshore, where the poet Celia Thaxton lived in the Appledore Hotel.
Julian spent the next week trolling for girls. "Celia was there, and so was
a young lady"—one of Lily Nelson's cousins—"for whom I had already
conceived a palpitating interest. The general, seeing with his statesman's eye
how the cat was jumping, suggested that I spend a week at the hotel for the
benefit of my health." Julian "consented with my usual good nature" and
dallied for the next several days with the young woman he later identified
only as "the Appledore Girl," who lived in a ritzy Boston suburb. "Celia
was gracious—at first! But when the fatal propensities of male and female

youth disclosed themselves to her practiced vision, she assumed a sterner demeanor."[7] Ironically, Julian came down with a horrific case of poison ivy during this week. After his return to Concord, he dropped a note to Pierce to thank him for "a most splendid time." Then he again put the touch on the old man: "I am almost ashamed to draw so soon on your generosity, but I received a bill of $22.00 from my tailor for several necessary articles, and as it seems to be the sort of thing you asked me to apply to you for." Pierce sent him the money.[8] He was nearly as blind to Julian's shortcomings as was Sophia.

After deciding to postpone his "grandiose project of being Head of the Family" for a couple of years, Julian returned to Harvard in September, but not, as Sophia doubtless expected, to his studies. He was as dilatory as ever. He confessed to "a constant disinclination to look into a book of any description." The curriculum "was merely an unwelcome and ill-judged addendum of the college career; what I looked forward to was athletics and the companionship of Harvard men." From his perspective, the importance of college was not study but the chance to network. "Before I left Harvard I knew every man of the four classes, besides many law students and scientifics," he bragged, "and I have always thought that this large and varied acquaintanceship was one of the most valuable circumstances of a college career." He rented an apartment near campus where he could board, and he exercised every day in the Harvard gym. As he explained, "Training in the sixties followed the ideas of the great pugilists of the era," his idols Sayers and Heenan. "We lived on red steaks, black bread, and a pint of water a day; we ran distances of ten to twenty miles," walked "from Cambridge to New York at a stretch. Boils broke out on our necks," and "we became all bone and muscle." Una considered him "the flower of ideal chivalry and trust," and Rose addressed him as "dearest Herculian boy."[9]

He did not lack native intelligence, to judge from his ability to cheat. According to Bill Blaikie, class of '66, Julian once dashed off an essay on Tennyson's "Two Voices" for Eliot Clarke in half an hour, "which has since been the wonder of Harvard and surprised the best critics." Or as Will Morton remarked, Julian once composed a paper "for a friend" that "gained the highest mark," even though "it was well known that he never wrote his own forensics." He also penned an unsigned sonnet for a local paper as well as a few anonymous articles on natural history for *Waverley Magazine*. "I never expected to see them in type, and was far too modest to sign my name," he remembered.[10] They were his first publications.

He also became an avid theatergoer. He regularly attended Boston performances of the stars of the Anglo-American stage, including Edwin Booth,

Richard Mansfield, John Drew, and Charlotte Cushman. On opening night of Charles Dickens's last American speaking tour, Julian was in the audience at Tremont Temple with his mother, Rose, the Fieldses, and most of the literary lights of Boston. After the reading, James Fields introduced Julian to the author. The "grip of his hand was impersonal" until Fields "whispered something in his ear, when it tightened for a moment and he looked me in the eye."[11]

Most memorably, Julian attended a performance of Clara Louise Kellogg at the Boston Theater in 1864. After the final curtain, Fields introduced him to the lovely prima donna. Suddenly "she was giving me her hand, and smiling at me, and making some playful remark, and holding my 19-year-old heart captive forever. Then she went to a little table and came back with a carte-de-viste" picturing her in dishabille, "the way they used to photograph stage divinities in the 1860s." Kellogg also remembered her encounter with Julian in her autobiography: "He was a nice lad and I kissed him." He was embarrassed and she told him, "The time will come, my boy, when you'll be glad to remember that I kissed you!"[12]

The distractions from study were soon glaringly apparent to the Harvard faculty. As Julian put it, "In the scholarship lists of the faculty that year I led my class, counting from the bottom." Hardly a month into the fall 1864 term he described his academic "embarrassments" to Pierce and concluded, "I have an amount of work to do which would scare anybody, however smart."[13] Not that he was willing to curtail sports or his membership in Delta Kappa Epsilon, the boat club, the Hasty Pudding, or any other student society. His tone of self-pity in this letter is remarkable. Giant Despair, it seems, was still stalking him.

Though he nominally remained a Harvard undergraduate, Julian devoted most of the next eighteen months to rustication, living and studying mathematics, Latin, and Greek with tutors in rural Massachusetts. Gurney recommended Ferdinand Hoffman in Stockbridge to help him with math. "I know it is the best thing for me," Julian grudgingly admitted to Pierce in October, "though of course I do not look forward with great delight at being separated from everyone I know for a year. However, I shall doubtless get used to it." His regret at the separation was assuaged by the presence in Stockbridge of young Annie Bartlett, with whom he dallied—to Sophia's evident disapproval.[14] The following fall, "the faculty, ever solicitous for the welfare of its infant population," sent him to a Unitarian clergyman in Northborough "who would drill me in my Greek and mathematics and inure me to studious habits." The clergyman had a "beloved daughter" named Elsie, "but my affections at that time happened to be elsewhere engaged [with the Appledore Girl], so she didn't count." "I never was her lover," Julian added, because "she had too much sense to desire it, and quite sense enough to prevent it." Still, the "cure," as Julian termed it, was not efficacious, because, like the hero of his novel *A Fool of Nature*, "the animal was prominent in him." He enjoyed college life only "so long as it was a matter of playing ball, rowing, eating, and genial carousing."[15]

He spent most of the summer of 1865 camping out on the Isle of Shoals. One weekend in August, after a visit to the Wayside, he floated his wherry downstream on the Concord and Merrimack Rivers to Newburyport, a total of over fifty miles. In two days, that is, he retraced the route taken by John and Henry Thoreau in 1839, a boat trip memorialized by the younger brother in *A Week on the Concord and Merrimack Rivers*. On the third day, Julian planned to row across open sea to the isle for a tête-à-tête with the Appledore Girl. He was unexpectedly enveloped in fog, however, and compelled to drift on the ocean swells because he had not packed a compass, "not expecting to be out of sight of land." After the fog lifted the next night, Julian steered by the stars and made landfall on Plum Island the following morning after thirty-six hours at sea.[16]

Sophia was oblivious to all this frivolity. Nathaniel's estate was worth about twenty-six thousand dollars at his death, but his survivors were unable to live on the interest and quickly depleted the principal. "Julian goes to Mr. Hillard"—George S. Hillard, Nathaniel's friend, lawyer, and executor—"for the money he needs," Sophia announced, "and is so childlike that he tells me how he spends the money." Pierce sent Julian a "present" in 1865 that enabled him to pay his "Society fees" and other "college amenities." He thought Julian's career prospects were promising, although he conceded, "I don't know of what particular line." The gift soon went the way of all flesh. "Julian inherits the princely disposition of his father, who said that he would like some day to have money enough to find in his pocket what anyone might ask him for," his mother rationalized. "Julian's ardent friends in college are always entertaining him and inviting him. It is a great pleasure to him to be able to return any favors and Gen P[ierce] said he wished him not to be what the boys call 'scubby.'" When her son was "driven home by an empty purse," his mother blamed not his spendthrift ways but wartime inflation, saying, "Oh for the good old days when charges were moderate."[17]

To make matters worse, Sophia was convinced that James Fields had been cheating her. After Nathaniel's death Fields had in fact reduced his payments to the family from a royalty of 10 percent of gross sales to a flat twelve cents per book. The sums had never been large; Randall Stewart estimates that Fields paid Hawthorne and his heirs on average less than a thousand dollars a year.

Fields's assertion that he actually *overpaid* Sophia failed to mollify her. Gail Hamilton (aka Mary Abigail Dodge), one of the few visitors to the Wayside after Nathaniel's death "whose presence, for my mother, was not irksome but helpful," believed Fields had swindled her, too. As she wrote Sophia, "I am altogether tired of the friendly and familiar style of doing business and should be well content to exchange it for a little hostile and formal accuracy." Julian complained to James R. Osgood, Fields's partner, that "justice was not being done to Mr. Hawthorne's family" and that Fields had taken advantage "of such authors as committed their arrangements" to him. He lamented to his sisters that the Harpers "were not our publishers from the first." "You see how fiercely sharp I am getting," Sophia grumbled—like "a lioness over her cubs" when "their lives are in danger." She permitted Fields to issue her editions of Nathaniel's *French and Italian Notebooks* (1871) and *English Notebooks* (1872) so that all of his books had the same imprint, but, as Stewart remarks, she gave her own *Notes in England and Italy* (1869) to G. P. Putnam and Sons, suggesting "that her relations with Fields continued to be uncordial." The breach would never be repaired. As late as 1924, Julian insisted that Fields had been "a snob in excelsis."[18]

As if Sophia's financial woes weren't bad enough, Julian's plan to return to classes in Cambridge in February 1866 was thwarted by his lack of academic progress. He would "sit all day watching the faces and actions of those about him," according to Will Morton, "and then, late in the afternoon, walk quietly off ten miles or more to call upon a friend." He tried out for the Harvard crew, but for all his strength he was too clumsy to row. "He tipped the crew over in the river one day and gave us all a good ducking," Bill Blaikie remembered. "That was more than we could stand and we put him out. Hawthorne was a stalwart fellow, magnificent build, etc., but human nature couldn't stand everything."[19] Though he considered all women (except his mother and sisters) "beneath contempt," he spent a good deal of his time and money in their company. He took pride "in making a woman forget her reserve & womanly modesty, merely for the pleasure of being able to turn her sacrifice and self-forgetfulness into ridicule afterwards." He would "turn all the blame on her, and say it served her right for being such a fool; how I exulted in whatever power I possessed over weaker hearts and spirits, and how I exercised it without scruple and without conscience."[20]

Meanwhile, Gurney tried to explain Julian's academic failings to his mother. "I do not think he has acted wisely or well at all times in the matter of his college course. I recognize fully the difficulties with which he has had to contend, but I think he would have surmounted them more easily but for his indifference at times to going on with his college life" and his refusal to do "little distasteful things simply because they are to be done." Simply put, Julian was unprepared for the discipline of study. When he went home to Concord on weekends, his mother commiserated, "he wilts and slumbers."[21]

He was finally expelled in the fall of 1866 for his failure to make satisfactory progress toward his degree. He had never worked off his deficiencies in math. In fact, for only about six months of the previous three years had he "been fully connected with the University." He often claimed later to be a member of the Harvard class of '67, omitting the detail that he had not graduated. Sophia was livid. The fault could not lie with her son. She even tried to intervene with the president of the university, without success. As she complained, "My heart has been used for a football by Harvard these nearly three years" and after considerable expense. Julian "bears this upsetting with his usual serene magnanimity—but it is very mortifying after telling all his friends that he was safely back." She blamed in particular Edwin P. Seaver, an assistant math professor, who had "led him astray."[22]

Her "most gifted and noble" son enjoyed a *dolce far niente* for the next several months, loitering in Concord and entertaining pipe dreams. He read books on logic and metaphysics and resolved to study philosophy in Heidelberg. Sophia was amenable: "Everyone says it is cheap to live there if you are once there," she wrote Lizzie. "Maids ask nothing scarcely for service, are very strong, very amiable, eat nothing, and sleep nowhere." The scheme fell through, of course, for want of money.[23]

By the next spring the Hawthornes were in desperate straits. To reduce expenses, Sophia fired her chambermaid and canceled Rose's music lessons. Julian, she wrote, "has been wearing turned and patched clothes and cobbled boots till I am mortified for him." From her perspective, he "bears the grime of poverty like a Socrates or a Plato." Still, to Annie Fields's disgust, Julian resided that summer in the Parker House in Boston, one of the toniest hotels in the country, where in the old days his father and other members of the Saturday Club met for dinner once a month. "In spite of his mother's assertions to the contrary," Annie grumbled, Julian "spends a good deal of money." Ironically, the Fieldses hosted Julian at their summer home in Marblehead, and Annie repressed her disgust long enough to admire "his muscular figure swimming across the rocks with such perfect ease."[24]

Julian was recovering from a romantic disappointment at the time. He had been jilted by a young woman, probably the Appledore Girl, probably the woman named Lulie he mentions in letters of the period. He likely deserved the slight, but his mother and older sister viewed the breakup in an entirely different light. After Julian revealed the sad news, his mother remarked that his letter was "beyond all words in its divine tone of charity, pity, patience, and calmness." From her perspective, he could do no wrong.[25]

By fall 1867 Julian had struck on a course that would enable him to return to Cambridge in good graces. In September he enrolled in the Lawrence Scientific School to study civil engineering. He figured that the profession was "likely to afford plenty of outdoor occupation." He consulted Gurney, who "thought engineering would be a very good thing for me," and Hillard, who concurred. So he announced to his mother that he had settled on a profession and would attend classes in Cambridge. He planned to pay his bills with the remainder of the money he had inherited from his father. "Oh how I wish it could be the Technology School in Dresden—so splendid and free of cost too," Sophia fretted. "But he must burrow down where he is. There never was anything more divine than the way he feels and behaves." When her son had "mastered his profession and made some money," she predicted, "he shall go to Europe with us."[26]

In anticipation of their eventual move to Germany, Sophia advised her son to study the language and recruited James Russell Lowell to tutor him. Two or three evenings a week during the fall and winter of 1867, Julian sauntered to Lowell's mansion a mile west of Harvard Yard to hear him read *Faust*. "I can hardly imagine that my mother really expected me to acquire any practical familiarity with German from those interviews," he conceded. They also played chess and "smoked good tobacco in matured pipes." He had acquired the tobacco habit when he inherited a box of his father's Havana cigars—no cheap cheroots for him—and he soon smoked as many as fifteen a day. Meanwhile, he joined a crew manned by graduate students in the scientific and law schools—at the age of twenty-one, he weighed a rock-hard 170 pounds—and rowed in the Harvard regatta in spring 1868.[27]

But by the end of the academic year Julian was so disillusioned with the Scientific School that he dropped out. He always considered his year there an utter waste of time. The courses focused more on natural science than engineering, and, incredibly, he was surprised to discover that he needed advanced math skills to become an engineer. He returned to "the congenial occupations of fishing, boating, and camping out" in Concord, and he fell in love with Fannie Channing, the daughter of William Henry Channing, whom he had last seen in Liverpool over a decade before. She had been "a beauty" then, but she "became still more beautiful in after years." For six weeks of the summer of 1868 "we were constantly together. I showed her the secret places in the woods," and "after some weeks, when our intimacy had ripened, I used to help her over the fence" to Bull's vineyard next to the

Wayside to pick grapes. "The gap of seven or eight years which seems so impassible when the boy is ten and the girl seventeen shrinks year by year until at twenty one and twenty nine it is easily spanned by a kiss."[28] Fannie later married Sir Edwin Arnold, the author of *The Light of Asia* (1879).

By the first week of September 1868, Julian had decided on his next step: enrolling in the Dresden Polytechnik. Sophia hastily sold the Wayside for four thousand dollars. Julian, his mother, and his sisters lingered for two weeks in Boston and New York, bidding farewell to family and friends. Finally, on October 22 they sailed for their next new home on the *Deutschland*, a steamer "with a very German flavor, an excellent table, and a disturbing tendency to roll in a swell."[29]

*   *   *

It was a rough crossing, with the deck of the ship often tilted at a forty-five-degree angle, but as usual Julian found a silver lining: "I noticed that there were two or three pretty girls" among the first-class passengers. "Once in a while I captured a young lady, and eloped with her to the bows, or behind the Pilot-House." As he observed twenty years later, "women will sometimes captivate men when circumstances are favorable, and a long sea voyage is a very favorable circumstance." At the age of twenty-two he was indiscriminate in his affections. After the ship docked in Bremerhaven, the family railed to Bremen, where Julian quaffed "most excellent Bier, in very large glass tankards, with covers. Everything is absurdly cheap, and much better than in America." By early November they had arrived in Dresden and settled into a fourth-story walkup in the Neustadt. Una and Rose began to study music and art, and Julian, as he put it, studied "music, picture galleries, and beer."[30]

Not surprisingly, the language skills he had acquired while listening to Lowell declaim *Faust* were too slight for him to begin classes in the Polytechnik. Its director referred him to a tutor named Zschoche, "who was in the habit of preparing men for entrance into the Institute" and who smoked "execrable" cigars. Julian eventually named a German character in his novella *Constance* (1880) after him. "I am at present employing myself chiefly in acquiring some idea of the language, especially in connection with mathematics, with a view to entering upon my course at the Polytechnic later in the year," he informed Aunt Lizzie. Meanwhile, he began courses at the local *Realschule*, a type of trade school, though he was unimpressed with the German schoolboys. "The scholars are execrable"—like Zschoche's cigars—and "such unhealthy and hopeless looking creatures I never saw." He eventually acquired basic conversational skills in German, but "it wasn't until I had been in Dresden nearly two years that I awoke one morning and found that I could say what I wanted to and understand what was said to me well enough to get along."[31]

Still, Julian enjoyed an active social life from the moment of his arrival. Though he took an immediate dislike to the Germans—"a stupid, good natured people, with considerable power of acquisition"—on the whole he was content. "I find Europe, as I expected, a far more agreeable and congenial place to live in than America," he wrote Lizzie. "I think we shall find Dresden, as a general thing, the most convenient spot to fix our head-quarters in. It is central in position, and neither too gay for quietness, nor too dull for amusement." He frequented the local museums—like his mother, he admired Raphael's *Sistine Madonna* in the Neues Königliches Museum, but like the hero of his novella *The Professor's Sister* (1888), he also seems to have been driven to distraction by the variety of activities available in the city. The so-called Florence of the North boasted a thriving American colony, and together with a few American friends he "drank beer out of glass schoppen with porcelain covers; we smoked pipes and Laferme cigarettes; we attended open-air concerts in the Grosser Garten, the Bruehlsche Terrace, the Waldschlösschen; we fought schläger duels, and wore high boots, black velveteen jackets, and caps four inches in diameter; we went to masked balls, where neither we nor anybody else behaved quite properly; we went to other dances in queer places; we thought we owned the earth and the fullness thereof; and we talked metaphysics."[32]

In December he escorted a young American woman to a performance of Richard Wagner's *Tannhäuser*, probably the Miss Sherman he mentions in his journal, a "perfectly pretty" expatriate with "alarmingly correct" ideas. Julian harbored Wagnerian designs on her virtue. He thought "that if by any means she could be turned to evil courses, it would be an advantage to her; it might give her a certain form of intellectual development which she can never acquire as it is." She apparently declined to be turned. He received a brush-off letter from her in mid-March in which she broke the news gently: "I *do* care for you as I have done, and I *never* shall try to forget you." If he was wounded he did not show it. His "experimental inquiries into the nature and effects of German beer," he later wrote, were interrupted "by long walks to Saxon Switzerland" twenty-five miles up the Elbe and to such sites as Bad Schandau, Krippen, and Prague.[33]

But in February 1869 Julian met his match in more ways than one. The fair May Albertina Amelung, who went by the nickname Minne, was descended on her father's side from a Bremen émigré who founded a glassworks in Maryland and on her mother's from the Randolphs of Virginia. Minne was living in Dresden with her family for much the same reason Mark Twain would move his brood to Heidelberg eight years later: to save money. She was a type of Daisy Miller—a headstrong young American woman with an unsophisticated mother, Cecelia; an absent father; and a pair of smart-alecky younger brothers, Frederick and Lees. Julian first mentions Minne in his diary entry of February 14, when he danced with her at a "musical soirée." He soon began to transcribe the conversations of "J" and "M." "What a cold, haughty little thing you seemed to me, then," he later wrote her. Finally, in mid-April, he recorded a longish entry.

> Miss A. is a very singular young lady. In appearance she is medium height and well and gracefully formed. She has flaxen hair piled on the top of her head, and flowing down behind. Her complexion is clear and bright, especially when she is excited; at times she is pale, especially about her lips. Her eyes are gray, and shaped differently from each other. . . . Her mouth is small, and her lips gracefully shaped, but thin; her chin curving out prominently. Her cheek bones are high and give her whole expression an air of experience and "hardiness"; but the impression wears off a good deal after a while. She is twenty, but, with the exception of a single occasional expression, she looks two or three years older. She is very handsome altogether. In character she is quite different from what she tries, and tries very successfully, to appear. She wishes to make herself out an ordinary fast American girl. . . . I am pretty sure, if she ever met an individual whom she feared and respected, and for whom she would consequently entertain more or less regard, she would be true as steel.[34]

On Sunday, April 25, the saucy "Miss A." confessed that a man had taught her to smoke "and she had never been able to forget it. I asked her whether it was the smoking or the teaching that she could not forget. She replied, 'No man ever taught me anything that I could not easily forget.'" Julian's journal at this page contains a pressed flower and the initials "M.A.A." He found her pose of haughty detachment alluring. Minne became the model for the heroine of his novella *Ellice Quentin* (1880), a young woman often "silent, repellant, and cold" but possessing "a vein of passion."[35]

Unlike his parents' three-year courtship, theirs was a whirlwind affair. Julian proposed marriage on June 3, less than four months after they met, and Minne accepted. Within a week they quarreled, however. The reason is not difficult to infer from his journal entry for June 11: "I consider it no excuse that the temptation was strong, and the visible evil little or nothing." He had been "fresh" and tested her limits on physical intimacy. They soon reconciled, however, and spent the afternoon of July 19 "sparking" on a park bench, to the dismay of passersby.[36] The next day Minne left with her mother and brothers for Brest and a steamer to America and their home in New Jersey. The young lovers were an ocean apart for the next fifteen months. The separation only stoked his ardor.

Fortunately, the events of this period can be reconstructed from surviving family records. To judge from all available evidence, Julian was genuinely smitten. He expressed contrition for his past misbehavior. "Looking back . . . I am naturally, infinitely displeased with the record I have laid up against myself," he noted in his journal. "When I am with her, I always feel as if I ought to be nobler & better. Well, Love will ennoble me, if anything on earth can." He struck the same note in a sonnet printed in the August 1869 issue of *Putnam's*; it is the first published writing attributable to him: "Shall I, whose life has been a dreary waste / Of misspent years and all unworthiness, / Aspire to love thee, guard thy happiness, / And by thy love and confidence be graced?" (The *Nation* thought his verse "not unpromising.")[37]

Julian wrote to Minne often, at least once a week, sometimes twice a day. At first his letters were merely flirtatious. "Darling, I dreamt of you all last night," he wrote hardly a month after her departure. "I was with you at Orange, & we were having a most delicious time." Soon, however, he began to express his physical longing for her. "Now that I can no longer press your hand, nor kiss your lips, I am forced to turn to your spirit love to feed my own," he declared in July. The longer their separation, the more passionate his expression of desire. Like his parents' letters, they were often written in the familiar form, using "thee," "thou," and "thy." After seven weeks apart, Julian owned that he wished "to take thee in my arms, to have thy sweet self pressed close to my heart, and kiss thee from head to foot from morning till night, and night till morning." He made no secret of his lust: "I shall absorb you, darling, just as a cup of hot tea dissolves the sugar in it." By December he had abandoned metaphor for declarative statement: "I long so to possess thee entirely, body as well as heart, that it seems sometimes as if I could not wait one instant more. . . . Do you remember, love, how I used to kiss you—first all over your face—on your eyes—forehead chin—nose—and at last settle down with content almost too great for this life on your darling mouth—and stay there—Oh!" He recorded sexual fantasies or autoerotic reveries of Minne. "Just at the time when our meeting began" on November 12, "I began to take my bath, which I took care should last half an hour; and I never enjoyed a bath so much. I saw you lying with your back against your pillows, & looking so ineffably sweet, that you almost took my breath away." A few days later, he inserted a similar entry in his journal: "After a sweet meeting with my belovedest, I went to bed."[38]

Meanwhile, he knuckled down to work, or so he claimed. He was eager to finish his studies—not necessarily to complete them—and return to the

United States. He began to attend classes at the Polytechnik on October 5 and wrote in his journal the same day, "I must get through by next fall and go home." For the next several months he tried, as he said, "to familiarize myself with logarithms, theodolites, levels, and descriptive geometry." After all, he expected to have a wife soon, and at the age of twenty-three he had no bankable skills. "I ought to be supporting myself by this time, & you too, you darling," he wrote Minne. "I am punished for my laziness & worse in years past: but it has also given me a good lesson." In November he learned that former president Pierce had died and willed him five hundred dollars, though the news rated only a perfunctory entry in his journal. His mother and sisters largely disappear from the record during these months. Sophia was silent about Julian's fiancé, so far as the surviving record is concerned, although he asserted years later that she had been "very happy" with the match.[39]

Most of the drama in the Hawthornes' lives during this period centers on the son of another expatriate family in Dresden. George Parsons Lathrop had come to Dresden to study music in 1867. He and Julian became friends, and their two families celebrated Christmas together in 1869. Una had ended an engagement to Storrow Higginson the year before, because his family disapproved—they believed she was too good for him. She apparently mistook George's kindness to her for romantic interest and was distraught when she realized he was courting Rose instead. Ironically, Nathaniel had kept company with Lizzie Peabody before falling in love with her sister Sophia, and the pattern was repeated with George Lathrop in the role of Nathaniel and Julian's sisters in the roles of their aunt and mother. The rumors of an assignation were so persistent that as late as 1879 Lathrop was compelled to announce publicly that he had never been engaged to Una, despite his "high regard for her." In any event, Sophia took her older daughter to England in May 1870, a few weeks after George departed for New York, leaving Julian to attend classes in the Polytechnik and Rose to keep house for him. Sophia explained to Rose that she thought the move was necessary to "save Una's life."[40]

Meanwhile, Julian was in the throes of anticipation. "I will kiss you until your mouth is dry; that you will have to spend a whole day in kissing me, so as to get some moisture again," he swore to Minne on March 5, 1870. "I want to take thee on my knee, to press thy soft tender bosom against my great strong one, to suck honey out of thy mouth, to feel thy breath upon my face, & thy arms around my neck: to possess & feel every inch of thy unutterable sweetness, from head to foot." In their home, he imagined, they would have "a most lovely little bathroom, with a big porcelain bath, &

long mirrors & everything that can be imagined of luxurious fittings up. It shall be situated opening from our bedroom, & we will tumble out of bed in the morning, & have a grand time in there for an hour or so." He urged her to meet his aunts Ebe and Lizzie but admonished her to "avoid the Manns. . . . They are not fit company for my darling."[41] He wasted no love on Uncle Horace.

He began to plan their reunion. Minne's mother had agreed to return with her daughter to Dresden in the summer of 1870, a plan that fell through. Julian was disappointed but not distressed. As he explained, "I am afraid the Hotel will be full in summer, & the woods too," so they would have found it "very hard to get into complete solitude." On her part, Aunt Ebe was relieved. "I have not quite so high an opinion of Mrs. Amelung as I might have had," she explained to Una, "if she had not proposed to take her daughter across the Atlantic merely to be with Julian. Being together would not have conduced much to their happiness unless they could be married." In lieu of reuniting with Minne in Germany, Julian fantasized about his own return to the United States.

> I have an idea! that when I come home we can meet in the following way. I will write you word, after disembarking, of the precise day & hour that I shall arrive at your house. You must tell no one, but go off to some secluded place in the woods, which you must previously have described to me so that I shall be able to find it easily, & where we shall be certain not to be disturbed. There I will come & meet you; it shall be in the morning, so that we can be alone four or five hours at least before anyone else knows that I have arrived. Then we can come home to tea together. . . . You must also bring a shawl, to lie upon, & wear (if you have it) that nice hat you had last summer. Of course I shall have on my old straw hat, which seems to be going to last as long as I do. Have on a light dress, with a white waist, over which must be a light jacket that you can throw off. Pink ribbons, & be sure not to have a sign of a corset.[42]

Consciously or not, Julian eerily echoed details of his father's tale "Young Goodman Brown," in which Brown's wife, Faith, festooned with pink ribbons, follows her husband into a forest, where they succumb to temptation and secret sin.

Sophia and Una returned to Dresden from London on June 19 for a reunion with Julian before he departed for the States nine days later. He hoped to resume his studies at the Polytechnik the following winter term, although he elsewhere admitted that he had again left school in "a somewhat unceremonious manner." He sailed from Hamburg to Edinburgh and railed to Glasgow. He embarked on the steamer *Cambria* on July 3. Every morning the captain "would beckon me into his room, and we would drink a little noggin of Scotch together."[43] He arrived in New York the evening of July 15 and hastened to Orange the next day.

Within a week France declared war on Prussia. The war raged until the spring of 1871, preventing Julian's return to his studies, or what passed for them. The Hawthorne women fled a nation at war for sanctuary in London. "Mama, Una, and I rushed for our lives," Rose reported, leaving Dresden "with delight, and plunging headlong into whatever dangers were brewing on our road." Seven months later, on February 26, 1871, Sophia died of typhoid pneumonia. As she was failing she repeatedly called for Julian, thousands of miles distant, who was unaware of the gravity of her illness "until a cablegram told me she was dead." She was buried in Kensal Green Cemetery in London, and Una planted a hawthorn tree on her grave. At Julian's behest, George Lathrop sailed from New York to England, presumably to escort Una and Rose back to the United States. Lathrop improved the occasion by proposing marriage to Rose, however, much to Julian's consternation. As the Head of the Family, he had not been consulted. Later, Lathrop bitterly, if vaguely, alluded to "the false position in which I was placed at the time of my marriage (partly through Julian's agency)."[44]

*　*　*

Julian and Minne were married in Orange, New Jersey, on November 15, 1870, with the Swedenborgian minister Chauncey Giles officiating. George Lathrop's older brother, Frank, attended the ceremony and reported that Julian "looked very grand and noble, and most of the young ladies in the congregation looked as if they would like to be in Minne's place." While in Boston on their wedding journey, they met Aunt Ebe, who halfheartedly approved the match: "Minne is evidently a very nice girl—amiable and artless, I should think." Even better, Julian "seemed quite awake to the necessity of earning money, and his disposition is naturally active, rather than meditative, his habits are good and he is very strong." From all indications, Julian was happy in his marriage. "It grows pleasanter and pleasanter as we go on," he assured Una.[45] By the end of 1870 Minne was pregnant with their first child.

Julian found employment in the New York Dock Department—his first job ever—and moved with Minne into an apartment on East Sixtieth Street. Every morning he walked six miles to his office on Broadway between Canal and Chambers. The department, recently reorganized under Civil War general George B. McClellan, was charged with constructing a granite wall on the Hudson River between the Battery and Thirty-first in order to extend the wharfs and piers. In truth, Julian's job as "hydrographic engineer" required no technical expertise. For eighteen months he surveyed the

Minne Hawthorne's wedding photo, 1870. (Courtesy of Imogen Howe.)

waterfront by taking sounds off the docks and "sometimes sitting for hours at a time in a small boat in the middle of the river, ascertaining with the aid of instruments the exact speed of the current." He put his talent at drawing to good use when he was required "to make mechanical designs." In summer he suffered mosquito bites and in winter freezing cold. In the evenings he often dropped into Wood's gymnasium on East Twenty-eighth to work out. He was able at the time to curl two hundred pounds with either arm and run a mile in four minutes and forty seconds. Once a week, for three cents, he took a Turkish bath at a doctor's house on Lexington Avenue. "I was eating plenty of whatever I wanted, and drank much water, a pint or two of beer, and sometimes a glass of wine. My health was excellent."[46]

But his salary was not. At $66 a month, it was north of adequate but south of satisfactory, especially after the birth of daughter Hildegarde on September 25, 1871. Besides his salary, he received a third of the income from his father's copyrights, about $300 a year. In the fall of 1871, for the first but hardly the last time, he dipped a bucket into the apparently bottomless well of Nathaniel's unpublished manuscripts and memorabilia to score a few extra dollars. In September he received an offer of £1,000 for "absolute copyright of the 'Italian Notes' and 'Septimius [Felton]'" from the firm of James R. Osgood and Company, the successor to Fields, Osgood, and Company. He preferred instead a 10 percent royalty on book sales. When, ten days later, Osgood asked for permission to serialize *Septimius* in the *Atlantic Monthly* prior to book publication, Julian demanded "the largest remuneration per page that is given to any writer in the *Atlantic*"—$15. "In case you should not find it possible to accede to this demand," he warned, "I would request you to forward the MS. of Septimius to me, to be otherwise disposed of for serial publication." The tactic worked. Osgood capitulated, and the "novel" appeared serially in the *Atlantic* between January and September 1872, often as the lead article alongside fiction by Henry James, W. D. Howells, and Bret Harte. Julian received a $140 check in December 1871 for the first installment and two months later a $1,300 check for the balance.[47] Such hard-nosed negotiations eventually alienated him from publishers.

To supplement his city salary, he also began to contribute to magazines, even though his father had advised him years before to avoid a literary career. At the time, Julian had thought the admonition was unnecessary. Still, he "amused myself" one weekend in the winter of 1870 by writing a seven-thousand-word story titled "Love and Counter-Love." He submitted the manuscript to Henry Mills Alden of Harper and Brothers, who passed it along to S. S. Conant, "who, after getting me to cut it down a couple of thousand words, printed it" without signature in *Harper's Weekly* in March 1871. Julian was paid fifty dollars for it, the first money he ever earned by his pen. George Eliot's *Middlemarch* was appearing serially in the magazine at the same time. "If I could make $50 every three or four days by writing such stuff as 'Love and Counter-Love,'" Julian reasoned, "it was plain that literature was a more remunerative business than was engineering."[48]

Over the next two years he published more than a score of light stories, familiar essays, and poems in some of the leading parlor magazines of the day, including *Harper's Monthly*, *Harper's Bazar*, *Independent*, *Scribner's*, and *Appleton's Journal*. His articles routinely appeared in the same issues as works by Stowe, Anthony Trollope, and Wilkie Collins. At the rate of ten dollars per thousand words, Julian received between forty and fifty-five dollars for each of his prose pieces and fifteen dollars or so for his poems. "By the time I had written half a dozen more of the $50 pupil pieces," he and Alden "were pretty well acquainted." The same may be said of his relations with the editor of *Appleton's*, Robert Carter, another of his father's friends and "a man of rare sagacity and wide learning," who persuaded Julian to exploit the cachet of his surname by signing his contributions. Carter's "counsel and conversation did more than anything else to confirm me in my predisposition to make a living by writing." His father's friend Richard Henry Stoddard worked with Julian in the Dock Department, moreover. At a dinner at St. James's Hotel on February 23, 1872, to celebrate Stoddard's accession to the editorship of the *Aldine*, Julian met both Mark Twain, with whom he remained friends for nearly forty years, and Whitelaw Reid, future editor of the *New York Tribune*. Stoddard paid Julian ten dollars a column for his contributions, and so "the virus entered his veins," as he said.[49] His literary career seemed to be off to an auspicious start.

Fortunately so. Under a new city charter, a new Dock Commission and a new chief engineer were appointed in spring 1872, and McClellan and his entire staff were abruptly dismissed. Julian "had the alternative of either taking my family down to Central America to watch me dig a canal, or of attempting to live by my pen." He chose the latter alternative, though "I remember wondering how anybody could write novels." To expand a story "until it should cover two or three hundred pages seemed an enterprise far beyond my capacity," but "Carter urged me to banish fear and go ahead." He bought twelve reams of lined paper and began a novel titled *Bressant*. "I finished it in three weeks; but prudent counselors [Carter in particular] advised me that it was too immoral to publish, except in French, so I recast it" and shopped the revised manuscript around. He hoped Osgood and the Appletons would rise to the bait and compete for it. "I am reluctant, for reasons I have stated to you, that my first book should be issued by your firm," he explained to Osgood. He was unwilling to be identified too closely with his father's publisher. "I should not, however, feel justified in maintaining my objections should you think it worthwhile to offer me a larger percentage than Appleton." Osgood asked to see the manuscript, but it was lost in the mail. Julian, "in my madcap twenties," had no choice but to rewrite the novel from his notes. In the interval Osgood lost interest and Julian eventually sold it to the Appletons.[50]

By a happy coincidence, Julian began his writing career at exactly the moment the market for his wares was burgeoning. Publishing was a growth industry. The number of newspapers almost doubled, to about 7,000, during the 1870s, and by 1890 there were more than 12,000 dailies and weeklies in the United States. By 1899 the number had increased to 18,793. The first important Anglo-American newspaper chains and syndicates— Scripps-Howard, McClure, Bacheller, and Tillotson—were organized in the mid-1880s and drove down the cost of fiction to editors while increasing the profit of producers. The number of magazines also doubled during the 1870s to about 2,400 and ballooned to about 3,300 by 1885; 4,400 in 1890; and 5,500 in 1900; that is, the total number of magazines published in the United States increased by 686 percent between the end of the Civil War and the end of the century. As Daniel H. Borus explains, moreover, "Postbellum publishers concentrated more of their offerings in fiction, which the new consumers preferred over all other types of literature." Before 1880 some 300 to 400 fiction titles were issued annually in the States; by 1881, however, 587 of the 2,991 books published were fiction, and by the end of the decade "nearly 30 percent of the new titles were fiction." Many factors—technological, economic, demographic, and legal—combined to boost sales of the printed word during the era, including the invention of the Linotype machine and the typewriter; the decline in the price of paper, especially newsprint; the passage of the Postal Acts of 1879 and 1885 and international copyright protection in 1891; the growth in population and real income due to immigration and industrialization; increased literacy as the result of compulsory elementary education; and expansion of the public library system. Not least among the changes was the turn to advertising: in 1880 the industry budgeted on average about a hundred dollars to advertise a book, but by 1900 some firms had advertising budgets of seventy-five thousand dollars, and the book trade as a whole spent more than five million dollars on marketing and promotion.[51]

A rising star in the American literary firmament, Julian was perfectly positioned to exploit these trends. If, as William Charvat has observed, "authors' names were brand names," Julian owned the Hawthorne brand and thus a ready-made readership. Edward W. Bok, longtime editor and publisher of the *Saturday Evening Post*, conceded that all middlemen in literary production were "more or less susceptible to the attraction of a famous name," and William Frederic Tillotson, founder of the Tillotson publishing syndicate, once admitted, "I buy the author," not the story.[52] As Julian practiced it, authorship was the world's second-oldest profession. He was a craftsman in the same sense as a carpenter. Not only did he abandon the anonymity of the genteel man of letters, but he also developed no coherent literary credo save a commercial one: A good novel was one that sold well. A great novel sold even better.

Unfortunately, he composed no great novels and few good ones. Moreover, so rapid was the growth of the Anglo-American publishing industry during this era that it was plagued by overproduction. Bret Harte averred in 1867 that even in San Francisco, far from the literary centers of New York and Boston, "We have in fact more writers than readers, more contributors than subscribers." Like many middling men and women of letters, Julian was chronically in debt, the victim of cheap competition. He also retained too many of the ways of his father; that is, he failed to adapt to some of the changes in the market. He never hired an agent, for example, and he never published an original work with a subscription press. As his friend Richard Grant White explained, "A man who undertakes to live by occasional contributions to weekly or daily papers, for which he receives five to fifteen dollars, or to the magazines, for which he gets five dollars a page, unless he secures a steady demand for all that he will furnish, can write by steam, and has no pride or conscience about the quality of his work, will soon find himself a fit subject for the poor-house if he is married." Frank Luther Mott estimates that in order to earn two thousand dollars a year—a comfortable middle-class income—a magazinist needed to write and sell an article per week. Horatio Alger Jr., a Phi Beta Kappa graduate of Harvard, spent several weeks preparing an essay for the prestigious *North American Review* in 1863, for which he was paid a measly dollar per page, so, as he put it, "I leased my pen to the boys" and produced juvenile fiction, a field that paid better, for the rest of his career. Like Alger, Julian might have echoed what Melville wrote to Nathaniel Hawthorne in 1851: "The calm, the coolness, the silent grass-growing mood in which a man *ought* always to compose,—that, I fear, can seldom be mine. Dollars damn me."[53]

*   *   *

Rose and George, both age twenty, were married in an Anglican church in Chelsea on September 11, 1871, without first asking Julian's permission—which he likely would have refused. He "was very bitter against Rose for marrying Mr. Lathrop," or so it was gossiped. Years later, after both Rose and George had died, Julian described their marriage as "an error not to be repaired." George not only failed to defer to Julian's authority as Head of the Family, but he also threatened to supplant him as authority on the writings of Nathaniel. He and Rose returned to the United States in January 1872, leaving Una in London, and George soon became associated with the *Atlantic Monthly*. After the serialization of *Septimius Felton* was completed, Lathrop published a piece titled "History of Hawthorne's Last Romance" in the October 1872 issue. He was Nathaniel's son-in-law, but he had never so much as met the man, and Julian the Prince resented George the Pretender.[54] Not only were they no longer boon companions but they also had become inimical foes.

Unemployed at twenty-five, with a wife and infant daughter to support, Julian rolled the dice. To cut expenses while he again rewrote *Bressant*, he decided to return to the far country. He, Minne, and Hildegarde sailed from New York for Germany on the *Baltic* on June 8, 1872. Julian had contracted with the *New York Times* for a series of eight travel essays for which he was paid twenty dollars each. He mailed the first of them from Liverpool, which he found "as blackish, rainy, and stonebound and stately" as he remembered it. Because they were the first pieces he published in a newspaper, Julian hid his identity behind a pseudonym—"Bellerophon," after an adventurer who travels astride his winged horse, Pegasus, in both Greek mythology and his father's *The Wonder Book*. While in London, he sold British rights to *Bressant* to the publisher Henry S. King in consideration of a one-hundred-pound advance.[55]

Once in Dresden, he leased a five-room flat—drawing room, parlor, dining room, bedroom, and study—on the third floor of a building on Waisenhausstrasse for £150 a year. He lived half a mile from the Sophienkirche, with its "handsome dome of solid stone," and in his study he installed his father's writing desk from the Wayside. Passing through Dresden en route to the South African diamond mines, Will Morton remarked that Julian lived in "one of the finest streets of the new city" and in "one of its best houses."[56]

"Dresden is fast becoming an outpost of American civilization," Julian reported. "It has high prices, bad servants, fashionable bonnets, and a Club, not to speak of horse-railroads and rowing regattas." Though elected vice president of the local American Club, he purported to disdain it: "I find [it] absolutely paralyzing & palsying: it is like a stale burial-vault, haunted by the memory of past gentility, which makes it worse." Instead, he fraternized with a group of young Americans who "were in the habit of assemblying [sic] of an evening in the restaurant known as Stefan's, near the further limit of Prager Strasse." He was in the crowd along the Schloßstrasse that celebrated the golden wedding anniversary of King John of Saxony and his consort, Amalie Auguste of Bavaria, in November 1872. The king died a year later, and Julian remarked ruefully on the occasion of his funeral that had he lingered for just another six months, given the quantity of beer drunk to his health as he was dying, "he would thereby have made the fortune of every saloon-keeper in Dresden."[57]

Julian completed the final draft of *Bressant* on September 17, 1872. He regarded the first version—the one too risqué to publish—as the best. The third he thought was "a good book spoiled," and "were it not for the consideration of lucre" he might have suppressed it, much as his father had suppressed his apprenticeship romance *Fanshawe*. Though "I took with it all the pains I knew how, I know the work must really be a crude, unsatisfactory result, such as in my later years I shall be heartily ashamed of." "It has a morbid taste," he admitted to Carter, "and the plot is not vigorously developed. Boarding-school girls will like it, and luckily there are a great many of them." Carter disagreed, saying the third draft "seemed to me very much improved in every way over the first draught & in my judgment will have a success as a book," although he worried about it as "a serial in the Journal. . . . While there is nothing that can be quoted as positively objectionable there is a tone to which some scrupulous readers might demur."[58]

Julian had hoped to sell the novel to *Appleton's* outright for $5,000, because he needed "ready money." Carter guessed that Julian would "be paid by the Appletons ten dollars a page for its publication in the Journal, and the usual percentage of ten per cent on the retail price for all the copies of the book they may sell." The novel was serialized between February and May 1873, and in the end the firm paid the author only $610 for it on the grounds that the story had damaged the reputation of the magazine "by its immorality"—that is, by Bressant's unholy love for two women. At Julian's direction, his lawyer William Peckham—another of his Harvard classmates—sent an invoice to the Appletons for a total of $900, or $15 per page. Carter replied, correctly, that he had "agreed to pay Hawthorne fifteen dollars a page for *short* articles, but that no rate was fixed for *Bressant*, the understanding about that being that it should be paid for at the usual rate of the Journal which is *ten* dollars a page." Julian was peeved. He wrote the Appletons to complain that the novel in book form had not been sufficiently advertised and to advise them "that I should abstain from business relations with them in [the] future." As he wrote Morton, "I find no redeeming traits whatever" in the Appletons. "O is there no way of wringing from them their ill-gotten gains?" He might have said, with Henry James, "I was born to be victimized by the pitiless race of publishers."[59]

Although he never admitted it, the final version of *Bressant* was a thinly disguised account of the love triangle involving George Lathrop and his sisters. As in all of his long fiction, Julian compensated for his crude technique with sensational effect. The titular character is an "intellectual animal," a type of By(i)ronic hero or amoral, egotistical genius (Lathrop) who trifles with the affections of two beautiful sisters. Moreover, Cornelia (Rose) and Sophie (Una) are portrayed as a dark and a fair lady, much like Zenobia and Priscilla in *The Blithedale Romance* or Miriam and Hilda in *The Marble Faun*; in the sexual shorthand of the period Cornelia is earthy and erotic while Sophie is innocent and ethereal. Though Cornelia is a conniving minx, Bressant is by far the worst sinner, because, a false-hearted lover, he betrays both women. In the end Bressant decides that he "needed more body and less soul: less goodness, and—more Cornelia!" just as Lathrop preferred Rose to Una. In consequence, Sophie will never recover—her "mind and body both have had too great a shock." Similarly, two days after the Lathrops were married, Una had lapsed "into a violent state of insanity."[60]

Despite its imperfections, upon its publication in May 1873, *Bressant* favorably impressed many readers as a harbinger of better things to come. Aunt Lizzie wrote Julian that his debut novel "evinces artistic power of the most decided and unmistakable character," and William James recommended it to his brother Bob, saying it was "a powerful though sinister kind of work, surely of very great promise." In the first published review, Henry Bright, in the *Athenaeum*, praised Julian's "vivid and vigorous" tale. "I hope that number of the *Athenaeum* will have a large circulation, and that its advice will be followed by the entire English Race," Julian boasted to Una, because "I never write so well as with my pockets stuffed full of Bank of England notes." In fact, almost all of the notices in the British press were favorable, and the author was almost always favorably compared to his father. The *Illustrated London News* discerned "the stamp of a true Hawthorne" in the analysis of character, the *London Guardian* concluded it contained "something of the family felicity of description," the London *Graphic* asserted that Julian "has inherited much of the distinctive tone and colour of a genius," and the *London Telegraph* concluded that "the son seems to have more flesh and blood in his composition" and "an even more subtle art" than the father. The *Civil Service Gazette* raved that the book "raises its author at one step into the ranks of recognised American novelists" and "might almost have been written by Nathaniel Hawthorne himself" ("some gushing young lady, I fancy," the author glossed in his scrapbook). Julian concluded that, at least in England, "the critics are uniformly well disposed towards it and me, and one or two are even incoherently laudatory: for nine tenths of which I have my name to thank—not my work. . . . I cannot reach the serene power and purity of [my father's] level, but I shall make a respectable place for myself." He particularly welcomed Richard Henry Hutton's review in the *Spectator*: "*Bressant* is a romance of the same school as *Transformation* [the British title of Nathaniel's *The Marble Faun*] but in some respects superior to it in power." Julian reread this notice until he had memorized it and then wrote Hutton a letter of thanks. In reply Hutton congratulated Julian on his success and expressed the hope he would win "a literary name, if it be possible, equal to your father's."[61]

The reviews of *Bressant* in the United States were decidedly more mixed. On the one hand, the *Boston Globe* hailed it with unwarranted enthusiasm as "the most original novel of the season" and predicted that it "will take high rank among the best American novels ever written." The *New York Times* predicted that Julian "in the majority of his power" would "rank side by side" with his father. Julian's friend and editor Robert Carter, in a sub rosa review of the novel published by his firm, declared it "not palpably inferior to the romances of the elder Hawthorne" ("some maniac in the New York Sun," Julian noted in his scrapbook). The *New York Mail* even ventured to pronounce it superior to the father's stories: "It is as though Nathaniel Hawthorne had reached a second stage of development." On the other hand, Nathaniel's old friend George Ripley censured it in the *New York Tribune* for its lack of restraint. By far the harshest assessment of the novel appeared in the *Christian Union*, an evangelical New York weekly: "It is a novel without hero or heroine, without purpose, without a point," and its author should "cease to glorify mere animal health and a superb body." Julian betrayed his thin skin by carping about this notice to the publisher of the paper, Henry Ward Beecher. According to Julian, the reviewer had misread the novel, and he admonished Beecher to advise him "to use more care in the future." In reply, too, Julian published "a very philosophical poem" titled "A Misanthrope on Calvinism" in the *Spectator,* in which he bitterly denounced "the ghastly dogmas" of Beecher's theology, especially the doctrine of innate depravity. Julian harbored a grudge against Beecher for the rest of his life, once gleefully accompanying the agnostic Robert Ingersoll and his two daughters to Plymouth Church in Brooklyn to hear him preach, on another occasion blasting Beecher's advice book *Royal Truths*: "Such books are of less than no value; they do harm."[62]

Despite its generally favorable critical reception, *Bressant* was at best a modest seller. The Appletons issued a second printing, but the British edition was a commercial disaster. Henry King published it "in two scarlet volumes, with fine open type, and it was, in my opinion, the most beautiful example of the bookmaker's art ever seen. In spite of its beauty, external or internal, I doubt if poor Mr. King sold more than five hundred copies of it, which, at twenty-one and sixpence, with discount to the trade, obviously must have left him on the wrong side of the ledger."[63]

Julian's lucky streak with the magazines also petered out. He submitted a manuscript to the *Atlantic* that editor Howells gently declined: "I am sorry not to have liked your story well enough to take it, but I hope for better fortune another time if you care to send me anything else." At the bottom of the page Julian scribbled, "My first refusal!!" It would not be his last. The cost of living in Germany was higher than he had expected, too, the result of what he called a "brazen system" of theft among Dresden tradesmen. "They can spy a bargain through a stone wall, and a thievish advantage through the lid of a coffin."[64] Meanwhile, his obligations were multiplying, with the birth of sons Jack in December 1872 and Henry eighteen months later. Una left her charity work in London and moved into Julian's flat in late 1873 to nanny his children. Minne's father died, and her mother and younger brothers also joined them. "We find our bullion so much decreased," Julian admitted in January 1873, "that we dare not so much as go to the concert in the Terrasee." The advance from King for the British edition of *Bressant* had long since been spent. What to do? What else could he do? Julian was a writer by profession and refused to undertake "anything else in the world!"[65]

He began a second novel despite the obstacles. "Literature is a path of roses: only the roses grow along the sides, and the thorns are underfoot," he observed dryly. He laid the groundwork for *Idolatry* more carefully. "You would be awfully impressed could you behold the accumulation of my notes and reservoirs for the forthcoming work," he wrote Rose in late February 1873. *Idolatry* "was actually rewritten, in whole or in part, no less than seven times" over thirteen months, or so he claimed. Certainly he considered his second novel "far healthier" than his first, and the part of the manuscript that survives is heavily revised, or "sandpapered," as he termed it. He never worked so hard on a book again, because, he said, "the discipline of *Idolatry*" taught him "how to clothe an idea in words." He considered it "the best thing of the kind I have seen."[66]

Hardly. In truth it is the most fantastic of his romances, the most crudely composed, and perhaps the worst book he ever wrote. By his own admission, Julian never developed a sense of the structure or architecture of the well-made novel. "After reading hundreds [of them] and writing—I don't know how many, I still understand very little about how it is done," he conceded fifteen years later. What Howells said of Bret Harte applies equally to Julian: "the long breath was not his."[67] His talents were better suited to short fiction; he simply could not sustain a narrative that would hold a reader's interest over more than a few dozen pages without resorting to outrageous contrivance.

Idolatry is a perfect case in point. The plot strains credulity and defies brief summary. As one (sympathetic!) critic later explained, it "was full of enchanted rings and Egyptian necromancy and avenging thunderbolts." To the extent it has a coherent story line, it is the quest of Balder Helwyse (Hell-wise) to discover the whereabouts of his family, particularly his eccentric foster uncle and twin sister—but then, as the reader eventually discovers, both are dead before the tale opens. The novel has more plots than a graveyard, more loose ends than a frayed rope, and so many characters, some of them with more than one name, it should include an index. It reads like a parody of one of his father's romances rather than a finished work of serious fiction. The narrative at times resembles *The Marble Faun* narrated from the point of view of an addled Donatello. In a scene reminiscent of the murder of Miriam's model, for example, Helwyse flings a satanic figure overboard, presumably to his death—though he is rescued by a passing vessel. Like Robin in "My Kinsman, Major Molineaux," Helwyse encounters a prostitute; however, her sin is not that she sells her body but that she sells it too cheaply. Deliberately or not, Julian even echoes his father's prose. Much as Dimmesdale "yielded himself with deliberate choice . . . to what he knew was deadly sin" in chapter 20 of *The Scarlet Letter*, Helwyse "yielded himself unreservedly to the influence of the moment" in chapter 13 of *Idolatry*. The second half of the novel is set in a massive faux Egyptian temple on the New Jersey bank of the Hudson River a few miles upstream from Manhattan. The romance also features a mysterious dark lady, in this case a young woman named Gnulemah (H. Amelung spelled backward). Surprisingly, too, given its long gestation and the care with which Julian ostensibly planned it, it contains some glaring grammatical mistakes; for example, sentences that end awkwardly with a preposition ("he had only half an hour to dress for dinner in"), noun-verb disagreements ("what was the odds"), and dangling participles ("although not a stimulating companion, one loves to be where Amos MacGentle is"). Nevertheless, American publishers clamored for the rights to it, and Julian, an incorrigible "house jumper," sold it to Osgood. The Appletons—with whom he refused to deal after the imbroglio over *Bressant*—"feel a good deal disappointed at not getting" *Idolatry*, Carter informed him.[68]

Julian finished the novel on April 8, 1874, and hand-delivered a copy of the manuscript to Henry King, who had contracted to publish the British edition, in London the following week. Julian made the rounds of the editorial offices and met Richard Hutton in his sanctum near the Strand, "a snuffy, dark little place, up two flights of stairs, with a view from the windows of brick walls and a dingy London sky." During their conversation, Hutton invited him to review for the *Spectator* "at the rate of 2 guineas a page—say, $10 to $12—good pay in those days." Over the next few years he assayed dozens of books, often two or three a month, including a volume of Robert Browning's poems, George Meredith's *The Egoist*, Henry James's *Confidence*, and several of Anthony Trollope's novels.[69] Many were the times when the checks from the *Spectator* were all that kept the wolf at bay.

On his twenty-seventh birthday Julian paused to reflect in his journal. His father and mother were dead, and his sister Rose "might be dead for all she is to me." But he was living in Dresden and "supporting myself and my family on no better prop than this pen. I certainly never was so happy as now." His ambition, so long as he lived, would be "to get rich." His most cordial relations were with British publishers. Seduced by the prospect of fame and fortune, he figured that he would more easily "make friends and be supported in his writing" in London than in either Germany or the United States. Like Sophia in Liverpool, moreover, Minne suffered in the Dresden climate. So he decided that as soon as their lease expired, "it will be Ho! for England, or some other place equally as good if there be one."[70]

Julian was also eager to leave the Continent because he had begun another project, a series of comic articles on Saxony. He expected the work to be "more popular than my unfortunate novels." Modern scholars have often compared *Saxon Studies* to Mark Twain's *The Innocents Abroad* or Emerson's *English Traits*, but the more apt comparison is to his father's travelogue *Our Old Home*. Julian was desperate to finish and sell the book. Like the prodigal son of parable, he had spent all the money he had inherited from his father by July 1874. He was "in extreme pecuniary distress . . . rather more so than usual," and his grocer threatened "to sell out our furniture to the amount of his bill."[71]

They settled their debts for pfennigs on the mark, packed their possessions before the grocer could seize them, and left for England in September. They embarked from Hamburg for London on the twentieth and found temporary refuge in the Queen's Hotel on Bond Street while Julian weighed his next move.[72]

PART II

THE HACK

1874–82
"My reputation is much sounder than my bank account"

If the years in bucolic Concord between 1860 and his father's death in 1864 were among the most pleasant of Julian's life, his vagabond years in jolly old England between 1874 and 1882 were among the most difficult. He reminisced most often in his anecdotage not about his childhood or his studies at Harvard and Dresden but about his eight grueling years in and around London. His brood continued to grow, with the births of Gwendolen in 1877, Beatrix in 1879, Fred in 1880, and Gladys in 1881. He published three novels; a travel book; a barrelful of short fiction, familiar essays, and book reviews; and some of his earliest journalism. But he was usually penniless, living hand to mouth or on the charity of others, an increasingly hardscribble existence.

He rented a villa in St. John's Wood, a "pretty and unpretending" neighborhood three miles north of St. Paul's, for six weeks while he scouted for a house he could afford.[1] There he was an ear-witness to a catastrophe a mile away on Regent's Canal early in the morning of October 2, 1874. A barge hauling gunpowder and petroleum exploded near Macclesfield Bridge, killing the crew, demolishing the bridge, and damaging dozens of houses. Ever alert to literary possibilities, Julian sold a short article about the devastation to the *New York Tribune* for fifty dollars.[2]

He reconnected with Francis Bennoch, Nathaniel's friend from Liverpool, who welcomed him to London as a father would greet a son. "For years, I met him almost daily," Julian recalled, "and, outside of my own family circle, no one contributed so much as he did to make those years worth living." Bennoch amassed and lost several fortunes during his life, though at this time he lived in a mansion on Tavistock Square. After reading *Idolatry* in manuscript, he was convinced that Julian was a genius and praised it without stint: "There is stuff enough in it to make a whole library of ordinary Romances—*Bressant* was great. *Idolatry* is ten times greater."[3]

Julian and Minne eventually found a house in Twickenham, "a delightful English suburb of trees, hedges, meadows, and quiet streets" where Alexander Pope and Horace Walpole had resided in the eighteenth century.[4] The village was located on the Thames, six miles from the botanical garden at Kew, twelve miles south of Waterloo Station. The house was situated on a cul-de-sac "so that there is no noise of passing carriages to annoy Julian," Minne reported. It was spacious, with room for the entire family plus servants. The ground floor contained "a good-sized drawing room, dining room and study, kitchen, scullery, larders, &c. Upstairs are four large rooms, for nurseries and bedrooms," and "in the attic are four rooms." Best of all, the house was available for nominal rent—merely the cost of taxes: £55, or $275, per year. On November 12 the family moved into Ways End, as Julian christened it—"partly because it was at the end of the way, and partly because Wayside was the name of our house in Concord"—and lived there for the next four years.[5]

They were initially forced to rent furniture. They had sent their belongings from Dresden, but they had been impounded by the shipping company

Julian Hawthorne at his house in Twickenham. (Courtesy of the Bancroft Library, University of California, Berkeley [72/236 vol. 3, 105].)

until Julian could pay the freight bill. While they may have leased a house in Twickenham, the family lived on "Grub Street." As early as October 1874, Julian tried to pick Bennoch's deep pockets. He solicited "a loan of one thousand dollars for a year or two years" so that he might "put it at interest" and "allow my other investments to accumulate undisturbed." At the end of two years, he would be £250 ahead; in other words, he wanted to claim as his own the dividends on money that belonged to Bennoch. As collateral Julian offered Bennoch a picture by the Italian baroque painter Sassoferrato, claiming it was worth £3000. "You are the only man in England that I know of to whom I can apply," he pleaded.[6] Bennoch declined the opportunity.

Julian's first journal entry for 1875 contains another accounting: "We begin the year in good health," though "in debt nearly £800. To meet this we have assets from various sources of about £665." A month later he was less sanguine, his finances more precarious: "We have spent this month at the rate of over £5000 per annum: and our debts today (Jan 31) amount to over £1000. To meet this we have cash in hand £5.14.8." A week later, "the Gas man made his appearance, and we had to dismiss him unpaid. It is most humiliating." It was a foreshadowing of humiliations to come. Two weeks later Julian received a letter from the shipping company that had impounded his furniture threatening him with prosecution unless he immediately redeemed it. "They say they have paid out the money and must be repaid," so he asked around for "some man of money who could make the loan for a few days."[7] No one volunteered, and the furniture remained in hock for nearly a year.

Certainly Julian had trouble supporting his family by his pen. When *Idolatry* appeared in October 1874, the reviews were almost uniformly hostile. Henry James set the tone with an unsigned notice in the *Atlantic*: "We have not, really, the smallest idea of what *Idolatry* is about." The *London Times* ("a mystic story with no meaning whatever"), *Scribner's* (a "psychological saturnalia in a frog pond," and the *Galaxy* ("astonishing rubbish") followed suit. While *Bressant* had been "full of promise," *Idolatry* "cannot be said to fulfil that promise," complained the *Saturday Review*. Not only did the romance represent a decline from the standard Julian had set in *Bressant*, but also the critics began to contrast him with rather than compare him to his father. The difference between them "is greater than the resemblance," according to the *Athenaeum*. Neither *Bressant* nor *Idolatry* exhibited "a fourth part of the power" of Julian's father, asserted the *Spectator*. Though the younger Hawthorne doubtless had talent, the *Philadelphia Inquirer* asserted, "the transmitted genius has degenerated in the transmission." The

London Academy urged Julian "to disregard the clamour of partisans who have already proclaimed him one of the literary forces of the future."[8]

Only a few critics offered tepid praise. Louise Chandler Moulton, in the *New York Tribune,* opined that it "gives promise of still better things to come," the mantra of virtually all sympathetic reviewers of Julian's early writing. The novel also found favor in the *New York Times.* The reviewer there complained about "the extreme difficulty" in "discovering what is what, which is which, and above all, who is who," but nevertheless recommended it: *Idolatry,* the reviewer wrote, was "one of the most fascinating books of its kind." However "extravagant, audacious, imperfect" it may be, it was also "fascinating." "I thought it was worthwhile having written the book," Julian boasted, "to discover so kind and wise an appreciator." He soon received a letter from Richard Grant White, "the keenest of our literary critics," acknowledging authorship of the review.[9]

Once settled in Twickenham, Julian lost little time in networking with the London literati whose help he needed to scratch out a living. He was nothing if not "clubbable." He joined the historic Savage Club, open only to men who were prominent in the fields of literature, science, or art. In its palmy days the Savage occupied a room on the Strand, and there Julian met such men as Charles Dickens the younger, editor of *All the Year Round*; Joaquin Miller, "a licensed libertine" who was "uncultured as a weed," the so-called poet of the Sierras, and the only other American member of the club; Willie Dixon, son of the historian Hepworth Dixon and club secretary; and Halkett Lord, a staff writer for *Punch* "and a man of singular wit and erudition." After club meetings in the summer, he often strolled "through the transparent exquisite dawn" to Twickenham, sometimes with such friends as Miller or Dixon, crossing the gray stone bridge over the Thames in the ancient town of Richmond at sunrise.[10] Though never a member of the Garrick Club, Julian was a frequent guest and met the novelist Wilkie Collins there. While living at Ways End he also hosted such American visitors as Charles Dudley Warner, Robert Carter, E. W. Gurney, and Will Morton, who was en route back to the United States from South Africa. Leslie Stephen, editor of *Cornhill* and father of Virginia Woolf, invited Julian to join the Sunday Tramps, a coterie of artists and intellectuals who met at the home of George Meredith every week for a hike; and he became a habitué of the salons of George Eliot, T. H. Huxley, and the publisher Nicholas Trübner, where he met Bret Harte, Anthony Trollope, and his father's old friend Richard Monckton Milnes (Lord Houghton). "I was a part of the literary Bohemia of that epoch," Julian later boasted. He reminisced about the feasts he had enjoyed, with decanters of port and Madeira "generally on the table," though "the only man who I saw habitually drink them was Robert Browning!"[11]

Bennoch introduced him to the publisher Alexander Strahan, who "immediately wanted to know what I could let him have" for the *Contemporary Review*. Julian brought him the unfinished manuscript of *Saxon Studies,* and "inside of fifteen minutes" Strahan "jumped up and smote me on the shoulder. 'Just the thing, my boy! Just what we've been looking for! Go on and finish it; give us as much as you like.'" Between November 1874 and November 1875 the series appeared in the *Review* alongside writings by Huxley and Matthew Arnold.[12]

Despite Strahan's enthusiasm, however, Julian repeatedly complained about his stinginess during its serialization, as well as "the constant embarrassments, anxieties and humiliations to which he subjected me." He was forced to apply repeatedly for the money owed him, and Strahan metered out the stipends "in sums of five and ten pounds." While he was paid a total of six hundred pounds by Strahan in 1875, "I never knew, nor could he tell me, whether I were going to starve or not." Henry James complained to Thomas Sergeant Perry about the same time that "it is the deuce to get money out of the London Maga[zine]s. Half the work is done by rich dilletanti [*sic*] gratis." Strahan postponed publication of the essays in cloth covers because he was nearly bankrupt, and Osgood postponed their publication in the United States because he was entirely bankrupt. As a result the book enjoyed virtually no sales or, as Julian noted sardonically, it "was murdered simultaneously on both sides of the Atlantic" and "vanished like a ghost at cock-crow." He expected it to appear in the States and to receive a five-hundred-dollar advance on November 20, 1875, but upon its publication three weeks late he complained that not only had the advance failed to arrive but also that "I have been living on 2/6 for the last nine days, and it was exhausted this morning."[13]

Saxon Studies is a paean to the glories of German beer with sarcastic asides on the German *Mentalität*. Julian derided their love of music (e.g., "the Saxons have a less correct ear for music than any people with which I am acquainted") and ridiculed the porcine women. His father had compared English females to beefsteaks in *Our Old Home*, and Julian compared Saxon women to beasts of burden. The "Gretchens," he declared, "carry on their broad backs, for miles, heavier weights than I should care to lend my shoulders to. Massive are their legs as the banyan-root; their hips are as the bows of a three-decker. Backs have they like derricks; rough hands like piledrivers. They wear knee-short skirts, sleeves at elbows, head-kerchiefs. As a rule they possess animal good-nature and vacant amiability." To the end of his life Julian insisted he had "made fun of the Dresdeners" and "peppered them with sarcasms, though not ill naturedly." But two German-language papers that deigned to notice it were predictably outraged. The *New Yorker Staats-Zeitung* dismissed the author as an *anspruchsvollen Amerikaner,* or "bumptious American," and the *Dresdener Nachrichten* condemned it so forcefully that, according to Julian, "the German emperor was moved to issue an edict forbidding its circulation in his dominions, and I prefixed a translation of the critic's curse to the fly-leaf."[14] The scathing review became one of the most attractive features of the volume.

Though Julian considered *Saxon Studies* "the best book I ever wrote," it was both a critical and commercial flop. The English-language notices were scarcely more favorable than those in German. Richard Henry Hutton opined in the *Spectator* that Julian was "unfair in his judgment on the bovine elements in the Saxon character," and Henry James again panned Julian's work anonymously in the *Nation,* suggesting that *Saxon Studies* not only betrayed "a strange immaturity of thought" but also that it was the type of book "which most young men would very soon afterwards be sorry to have written." It was pervaded by a tone of "snobbishness" (*New York Herald*) and "bitter humor" (the *Athenaeum*), its depiction of Saxony "ungracious and unpleasant" (*Philadelphia North American*). Only *Appleton's Journal* tried to turn Julian's querulousness to his advantage, saying his "contempt becomes a genuine literary inspiration" and *Saxon Studies* "will easily take the first place" among books of hate.[15] No reviewer found evidence in it of Nathaniel Hawthorne's genial humor.

Undaunted, Julian began a third novel. In February 1875 he had mailed a précis of *Garth* to Henry Alden, who replied with undisguised condescension that if Julian would "promise to be a good boy, and do no more silly and extravagant things; but settle down to sober, serious work, and forget about everything except deal boards, dry goods and Mill's logic:—if he will do this . . . I may be persuaded to look indulgently at his proposal." Julian wrote Una that Alden was "rather too demagogic for my taste: but his twelve dollars [per printed page] corrupts me." Still, Alden had a point, and Julian again planned *Garth* with extraordinary care. Much as Sinclair Lewis drew a blueprint of his hero's home before beginning *Babbitt* in 1921, Julian prepared a floor plan of Garth's house, filled notebooks with brief biographies of the characters, and outlined his plot in detail before starting to write.[16] *Garth* would be his longest and most ambitious work of fiction.

Despite his prolixity, Julian was unable from his first weeks in England to support his family in the manner to which he had become accustomed. After a visit to Rose in New York, Una returned to Twickenham in March 1875.

The next autumn, Minne's mother joined them for a year due to reverses in the family produce business in New York. Her support as well as the support of Minne's brothers, Frederick and Lees, "one in Freiberg, the other in King's College London," fell upon Julian. Cecelia was "very miserable" about her dependence on Julian's charity and, as he observed sarcastically, "made it a matter of conscience to be as miserable" as possible.[17]

Yet even as his debts mounted, he failed to curb his extravagances. Minne worked like "a charwoman" around the house while Julian vacationed in France in July. He sailed from Newhaven to Dieppe on the twenty-second, railed to Paris the next morning, and registered at the tony Hotel Brighton on the rue de Rivoli. During the rest of the week he revisited many of the sites he had last toured as a teenager. On the twenty-fourth he sauntered along the Champs-Élysées and went sightseeing at La Madeleine, the morgue, Notre Dame, and the Jardin Mabille, a famous pleasure garden, where he observed "some extraordinary dancing and some very handsome & well-dressed women." He spent a day in the Latin Quarter, another in the Quartier St. Antone. He ascended the Arc de Triomphe and dined at the historic Café Anglais, the Café Riche, and the Café de London. On July 28 he paid his hotel bill—130 francs for five nights—and took a train back to Dieppe before returning to England the next day aboard the *Bordeaux*. No doubt he justified the trip as research. A month later he started a story (never published, if completed) titled "Judgment of Paris."[18]

Julian drove the quill, to be sure, and to help make ends met he collaborated with Minne on a series of housekeeping hints for *Harper's Bazar* published under her name. He covered the Oxbridge boat race for the *New York Herald*, a portent of his later sports writing. Una urged Minne to "tell our blessed boy not to work too hard, and to keep up his heart. He'll set the Thames on fire before long." Instead, he gradually slipped deeper into debt and into the Slough of Despond. He concluded his journal for 1875 by declaring he would "rather die than live to pass through such another Valley of Death as this Hell-born year has been to me!" It had been "the gloomiest, most painful and discouraging of my life. Not a single day in it—not an hour—of unalloyed happiness—of freedom from wearing care and anxiety." He had "heard something of the howling of the wolves in the forest," he wrote Carter. "This may surprise you; for the general impression [is] . . . that I am . . . rolling in gold. The truth is that like many other men of transcendent genius and worth, my reputation is much sounder than my bank account."[19]

The situation did not improve in the new year. In April 1876 Julian got wind of a book in press about his father by George Lathrop. The project stuck in Julian's craw and sparked a very public family quarrel. Nathaniel's literary remains had been in Sophia's baggage when she fled Dresden with her daughters in the summer of 1870. They were in Rose's baggage in December 1871 when she returned to the United States after her mother's death and her marriage to Lathrop. That is, although they belonged in common to Una, Julian, and Rose, the papers were in Rose and George's exclusive possession. Lathrop based his book on them—materials that "do not in any degree belong to him," Julian complained to Osgood. Lathrop had access to them only by a series of unfortunate circumstances—the start of the Franco-Prussian War, Sophia's death, and Lathrop's marriage to Rose. In consequence, Julian and Una were "constrained to withhold our consent" to the publication of Lathrop's book and to denounce the "infringement" upon their parents' privacy. Julian closed his letter to Osgood with an ill-concealed threat: "We should deeply regret being called upon to define our position in any more urgent or public manner." The next month Julian contacted Osgood to express his objections more urgently. Lathrop cited in his book "contraband material" that was "accidentally in his possession," so he had taken "what does not belong to him." If Osgood published Lathrop's book over Julian's objections, "I should feel compelled to discontinue the (to me) pleasant and satisfactory relations which have hitherto subsisted between us." If the book appears, "we must have recourse to the newspapers, and make the best of it."[20]

After Osgood issued Lathrop's *A Study of Hawthorne* in mid-June, Julian made good on his threat. After all, as the self-anointed keeper of the family flame, he had a proprietary interest to protect. In a letter to the editor of the *New York Tribune* for July 8, 1876, he claimed to "speak as the chosen mouthpiece of all [or both] the surviving members of the late Nathaniel Hawthorne's family who yet bear his name; and furthermore I speak in behalf of those whom death has deprived of the power to defend themselves" (i.e., his parents). Lathrop had the temerity not only to reveal details of Nathaniel's private life that were "sacred" to his family but also to do so by citing "papers and letters [that] came into his possession" by accident. Lathrop had never so much as "personally met Mr. Hawthorne." Unable to suppress the publication of Lathrop's book, Julian conceded that "the evil has been done and cannot be recalled." But he warned the reading public that Lathrop had gained access to "many letters of a peculiarly private and delicate nature" that had been "left unprotected" (he echoed here his declaration in 1864 that as Head of the Family he "mustn't leave them unprotected") after Sophia's death and that "no member of Mr. Hawthorne's own family would have ventured" to produce such a book. "It was composed and published in violation of a trust and in the face of repeated warning and opposition."[21]

The letter caused a stir, especially within the family. Rose complained to Aunt Lizzie that her brother's "shocking noise in the papers has been a great grief to me." She particularly regretted his "dishonesty," although she shipped the papers to him as soon as he made a fuss, acknowledging his "equal but *not superior* right" to them. On his part, Lathrop insisted to Lowell that he had tried for "a long time to prevent the breach which has now widened into publicity. Julian was my great admiration, before my marriage, and when he utterly disappointed my conception of his character, it did not rouse hostility in me."[22]

*   *   *

In early 1876, even with *Garth* in progress, Julian sold the Appletons a series of projected essays about England based on his walking tours of the London suburbs and written from the point of view of a cheerful flâneur. The essays "will be mellower and quieter than *Saxon Studies*, but I think quite as good," he declared, and with characteristic bluster he considered them his revenge on "the godly Messrs. Appleton. They would allow me but $10 a page for *Bressant*; so I go off with my $600 and presently return, armed with a little English reputation, and requisition them to the tune of £3.10 [per thousand words] plus 10%. Revenge is sweet. By Jingo, they shall pay £7 sterling [per page] next year, or lose J. H." Fourteen installments of "Out of London" appeared in *Appleton's Journal* between July 1876 and November 1878, but the essays were never collected. Julian calculated that Oliver Bell Bunce, Carter's successor as editor, "underpaid me for the essays at the rate of five shillings sixpence a page" by underestimating the word count.[23] So much for his revenge.

By mid-1876 Julian was chronically short of funds. He was sometimes obliged to cable William Peckham in New York "for money to pay my rent—not an economic proceeding!" Not only was he "under the shadow of the law for debt," but also his servants started a rumor that he was preparing "to bolt" from Twickenham in October 1876, whereupon several of the local merchants filed legal writs against him for sums up to seventy pounds. Though his father had admonished him never to borrow, Julian observed the rule in the breach. He bought on credit without planning to pay. In consequence he became a marked man hounded by creditors. On New Year's Day 1877, he noted in his journal that he had "6d ready money in hand; a pierced sovereign, which we shall try to change at the Bank of England, and a five shilling piece, a rare impression, which we must also try to get changed. Also a thousand pounds & upwards of debts."[24]

Much as he thought he could skate by at Harvard without removing his demerits in math, Julian never fully addressed his financial problems in England. Instead, he daydreamed about ways he might live well despite his debts. By writing an average of only four pages a day, he calculated, "I should make over £1000 a year, which would leave us over £400 balance. Take £200 of this for incidental expenses, and we have £200 to pay debts with. By publishing magazine articles in both England and America, the income would be enlarged to at least £1500, and the percentage on copies of books sold, and on interest on American investments &c. ought to bring at least £500 more, making £2000. If this can be realized, we ought to pay our debts by the end of the year, and have something in hand." Nothing came of this soap-bubble fantasy, of course. Julian confided to his journal the same day that he doubted "whether we shall have enough to eat by day after to-morrow." Only two days later he was resigned to the inevitable: "I can't see that there is much more to do to avert the catastrophe than what I have done." A month later: "After supper, and not till then, did I sit down to write my daily and invariable four pages of ms. . . . and then thought how wrong it was to waste my youth and freshness in this way, and how much better it would be to go to bed. I was in bed before twelve." Moreover, the four pages a day included entries in his journal and his private correspondence. During the month of February he wrote a total of 130 pages, an average of more than 4 per day, but of them "only 36 will 'pay'"—a daily average of slightly more than one publishable page.[25]

In addition, Julian was easily distracted from the regimen of writing. He had an "indolent mental disposition" by nature, he confessed, and Minne was "sweet" and "ravishing" even in the depths of their penury. Julian once half-humorously cracked that he was a "third rate old tomcat," and like a gunslinger he notched his conquests. He often marked an X next to the date in his journal when they had sex. Although Minne suffered a miscarriage in early December 1876 and remained confined to the house for weeks afterward, she continued to offer him "comfort and consolation." On the night of February 22, 1877, she kept Julian awake "by various devices for an hour or so," and two weeks later she discovered that she was pregnant with their daughter Gwendolen, born the following October. Julian worried, however, that the pregnancy would kill her: "Unless we can move to a warmer climate, or live in more decent circumstances, very soon, Minne will not live through it." They planned a two-year voyage around the world after her confinement. "A complete journal of the voyage would be amusing reading," Julian thought. It was an idea whose time would finally come thirty years later, when Jack London struck on it. Julian and Minne considered moving to the South Seas, the Sandwich Islands or New Zealand, or to the West Indies or Central or South America. Or Florida. Or Texas, where

Cecelia owned several thousand acres—"but the accounts we received of this land did not encourage us to persevere in our intention."[26]

Julian's private letters and journal entries in 1877 paint an increasingly grim picture of the family finances. Though he earned more than £100 for his writing in April 1877 and the house expenses totaled a mere £11, at month's end he still owed quarterly rent (£13), income tax (£10), a travel agent (£4), a laundry (£5), his butcher, (£12), "and two or three" other bills, a total of over £100. He had become less a breadwinner than breadloser. He was sometimes so distraught during these months that he contemplated suicide. But for his "glimmering of a doubt as to there being a life hereafter, I would have put an end to myself and family long ago," he admitted to Bennoch. Still, the family vacationed in the summer of 1877 in the seaside resort of Hastings, best known as the site of the battle in 1066 when William the Conqueror defeated the Saxons. An anonymous admirer of his father paid for their lodging, "and I, having regard to Mrs Hawthorne's health, which had long been causing me great anxiety, could not feel myself justified in declining the offer. It may be the means of saving her life, and at any rate her bodily well-being if she survives" her pregnancy. "We are all improving under the sea influences," he added, "& I am about beginning my new novel." Only weeks after returning to Twickenham, however, he warned Bennoch not to "be surprised to hear me talk of bankruptcy or anything else."[27]

Una suffered her own disappointments. While visiting Rose in New York, she had fallen in love with Albert Webster, a young poet whose work coincidentally had appeared in *Appleton's Journal* during the serialization of *Bressant*. After she returned to England, Webster proposed marriage and she accepted. Webster suffered from tuberculosis, however, and in early 1877 he sailed for Hawaii in a vain attempt to recover his health. He died en route and was buried at sea. Una was notified of his death in mid-February by the American consul in Honolulu. As she read his letter in the parlor at Ways End, "her hands holding the paper dropped in her lap and she said, with a sighing breath, 'Ah, yes!'" She "rested her head on the table and sobbed quietly for a few minutes; Minne was crying on the sofa." Julian "sat silent and stared into the fire. It seemed too hard. Has Una had so happy and self-indulgent a life as to need this desolating blow at last?"[28]

She devoted the rest of her life to settlement work, especially to the care of orphaned and destitute children. On September 1, 1877, as Julian and his brood vacationed in Hastings, Una departed for an Anglican convent in Clewer, near Windsor. Ten days later Julian was notified by telegram that his sister was dangerously ill. He boarded the next train to London and arrived in Clewer at midnight—but too late. At the age of thirty-three his sister "had died almost as soon as the telegram was dispatched, and before I had received it." When he saw her "lying on her pallet, in the cold, gray little room in the house of the sisterhood," she looked to him like "a pale and frail nun." Julian had no doubt what had killed her: "Una died of a broken heart. Webster's death affected her, not in any abrupt way, but deeply and slowly. She tried to take an interest in her old occupations, but could not. Life had nothing left for her." She was buried three days later beside her mother in Kensal Green.[29]

*   *   *

During the two years he worked on *Garth*, Julian was sometimes forced to abandon it to pen potboilers to feed his family. He offered "Calbot's Rival," a ghost story thirty manuscript pages long, to George Sala, the editor of *Temple Bar*, in late August 1876 for the bargain price of twenty-five guineas, less than the guinea per page he was accustomed to receiving. He sold "The New Endymion," some thirteen thousand words in length, to George Bentley for twenty-five pounds—a rate of about two pounds, or ten dollars, per thousand words. On still another occasion, he composed a twenty-six-thousand-word tale of illicit love, "The Pearl Shell Necklace," or "The Laughing Mill" (printed in England under both titles), in "twenty-six consecutive hours without pausing or rising from my chair." When he reread the story, "it seemed quite as good as the average of my work." The reviewer for the *Athenaeum* agreed—or not. He declared, with studied ambiguity, "It is hardly possible to give Mr. Julian Hawthorne higher praise." Julian offered U.S. rights to it to Osgood, but Howells discouraged him: the story was "fascinating, but mechanically operated, and coarse as hominy."[30] Osgood declined it.

Julian sold more work than ever before, but often at a discount months in advance. In October 1876, he advised Bennoch that he would be paid five hundred pounds by the Harpers upon the publication of *Garth* in cloth covers eight months later, but he offered to mortgage that sum "for £55 now." As a result his real income declined precipitously.[31]

Garth was serialized in twenty-four issues of *Harper's Monthly* beginning in June 1875. By Julian's own account the convoluted story contains three heroes, two heroines, and a pair of Native American villains. The eponymous character, the least of the heroes, is loved by both heroines, one of them a femme fatale. The plot turns on the discovery of a lost document that ends an ancestral feud like the one in *The House of the Seven Gables*. In fact, Julian often filled his tales with a pastiche of people and a welter of tropes gleaned from his father's fiction. *Garth* also features a character named Lady Eleanor, who seemingly wanders into the novel from Nathaniel's "Lady Eleanor's Mantle."[32] Despite Julian's advance planning, the novel closes with several loose ends dangling from the pages. In January 1877 he listed the problems yet to be resolved: "I cannot see, at this point, how Garth is decently to marry either of the heroines—at least, within the limits of the third volume. . . . Jack must bear his disappointment like a man; poor Cuthbert must die; Nikonis must produce the marriage certificate, and Jack and Golightley must clear up the mysteries. The house shall then be burnt down by Nikonis." But the sprawling story had already tested the patience of Messrs. Harper and Alden, who warned him "that unless I put an end to their misery they would. Accordingly, I promptly gave Garth his quietus." Minne stood beside his desk the evening of March 4, 1877, as he "inscribed the final letters upon the page," and "after they were written she kissed me."[33]

At first blush, Julian believed *Garth* was "not only the novel of the season, but of the age, the century and the Future; in fine, the great American novel which has been prophesied and prayed for ever since the United States became a nation." Within a week, however, he began to curb his enthusiasm. The novel was "a hundred pages too long at least." Nor was he sure after another nine days that he liked "the concluding chapter, with its lovers' silliness and its melodramatic conflagration and its bird-twitterings." By May 1 he was reconciled to critical success and commercial failure. Although "it will have many favourable reviews," he decided, *Garth* was "too dull and too long" to be popular.[34]

The book was not even a critical success. Rarely did reviewers favorably compare Julian any longer to Nathaniel. One critic conceded that the differences between them "are quite as striking as the resemblances." Another judged Julian's fiction "weakest" when he tried to imitate his father. A third complained that the elder Hawthorne's stories featured "a savor and shade" that the son replaced with "metaphysics, morbidness, and moccasins." To be sure, Mayo Hazeltine favorably compared *Garth* in the *New York Sun* to Henry James's *The American*—Julian's canvas "is much broader and more amply peopled than that which Mr. James has chosen to fill," according to Hazeltine—but he was the exception. The *London World* challenged Hazeltine's judgment: "Mr. Hawthorne has inherited from his father a certain bizarre weirdness—which asserts itself in his psychological analyses, as well as in his plots—that Mr. James does not display." Edward Burlingame in the *North American Review* added that Julian lacked the "literary ambition" that "Mr. James possesses very fully." James himself asserted that while *Garth* was "a decided improvement upon *Bressant* and *Idolatry*," it still exhibited an "incurable immaturity and crudity." According to the *Saturday Review*, *Garth* "affords far less hope" than *Bressant* and *Idolatry* that Julian would "ever becom[e] a good novelist." The *New York Times* recommended the book only to readers "whose time is not precious."[35]

After the disappointment of *Garth*, Francis Bennoch and Henry Bright urged Julian to apply for a grant from the Royal Literary Fund, or, as Julian put it, to "go to the Literary Poorhouse and beg the charity of the secretary there." The fund directors awarded needy literary men and women or their descendants a total of some fourteen hundred pounds a year and gave Julian one hundred pounds, five times what he hoped. "It will pay all my tradesmen's debts here, and enable me to turn round and help myself," he crowed to Bennoch. "It is a grand charity." Yet a week later he was back in the doldrums: "I see no escape; and—what is odd—I feel remarkably quiet and composed, as a man who had done what he can, and may leave the rest to Providence with a clear conscience." By January his bankruptcy seemed "inevitable" and local tradesmen had again cut off his credit. His debts soon exceeded sixteen hundred pounds, roughly equivalent to eight years of a normal middle-class income. While he had begun to keep a journal for 1878, he soon destroyed it; to continue it "would have been an ugly business."[36]

Although his father had worked at menial jobs at Brook Farm and the Boston and Salem Custom Houses, Julian was too stubborn or proud to work for a salary. Cecelia suggested such a move to Minne, saying, "It has been proved by experiment that Julian cannot support his family by literature—would it not be better [for him] to try and get a position as assistant on a magazine or paper—if it paid but a small salary it would be certain." But he refused, no matter how broke he became. His only form of alternative employment during his years in England was as an unpaid subeditor of a magazine start-up. In early 1877 Julian and a few other "enterprising spirits" founded a short-lived review called *Tatler* after Joseph Addison and Richard Steele's famous eighteenth-century periodical. "It was to be a weekly journal of literature, society, and of good things in general" along the lines of the *Spectator* and *London World*, and among the contributors were Louise Chandler Moulton; Halkett Lord; Algernon Charles Swinburne, whose epistolary novel *A Year's Letters* appeared serially; and of course Julian, whose "Juno Vetter in Search of a Mission" satirized "all the leading journals in England" as the hapless hero attempts to launch a magazine of his own. *Tatler* first appeared on March 6, 1877, and lasted a year. It "ceased to tattle" because, according to Julian, it was too far "in advance of its epoch" to succeed.[37]

Instead of finding a salaried job, he hustled to put food on the table. "My desire," he advised Bennoch in April 1877, was "to save my wife and children from actual starvation, which now threatens us within the next few days." He literally pawned the silverware. He sold the Sassoferrato painting, supposedly worth three thousand pounds, for a pittance. He worried that if England was drawn into the Russo-Turkish War his career would suffer, because the news from the front lines would be more exciting than "any stories I can write." He begged Bennoch, Strahan, and his banker friend Russell Sturgis to lend him money. "Any sum would be better than none, because, even if I am laid by the heels, I should like to know that my family was not hungry—as they have been more than once lately." Much to Julian's relief, Sturgis canceled a loan of three hundred pounds, although the relief was short-lived.[38]

He had few remaining tangible assets. He owned some railroad stock in the United States, but its value had depreciated until it was virtually worthless. He was desperate to sell a pair of mortgages he owned, one on a house in Brooklyn and another on property on the south side of Chicago. Together they were worth about eighteen hundred pounds, "which would pay my debts with an ample margin, if I could get it." He urged William Peckham in January 1878 to sell the Brooklyn mortgage "at *any* sacrifice, if it were fifty per cent," and to send him the money immediately. For months afterward he expected any day to receive a check for as much as eleven hundred pounds, but it never arrived. The house was owned by Peckham's wife, and Peckham had loaned her Julian's money on advantageous terms. "Without doing anything technically illegal," Peckham "got the use of £800 of my money for ten years" at 7 percent interest, so he had no incentive to sell the mortgage. Too late, Julian put his affairs in the hands of Minne's older brother John Amelung, who found that they had been managed "very recklessly."[39]

The property at Sixty-third Street and Stewart Avenue in Chicago was originally owned by Una and Rose. Julian inherited Una's half "in consideration of my engaging to pay her debts out of it," about £350, including a pledge to the orphanage in Clewer. He traded his and Una's shares of their father's royalties—about £135 annually—to Rose for her half of the Chicago property, because he thought he could flip it immediately or at least borrow £400 or £500 on it. That is, he traded a certain £135, or about $675, per year for several years in return for immediate ownership of a lot he hoped to sell or use as security for a loan. Unfortunately, Julian was unable to obtain clear title to the land. Not only had Una's will not yet been probated, but also there was apparently a lien on the land by a previous owner, so it could not be sold. In effect, he had assumed Una's debts and then traded his and Una's shares of his father's royalties to Rose for nothing. Not surprisingly, Bennoch was warned by his lawyers that Julian was a poor credit risk. If the liquidation of Julian's debt "depends on the sale of [his] mortgages we fear there is a poor prospect of its being paid. Our private opinion is that Mr Hawthorne has no intention of paying it if he can avoid doing so."[40]

Only one alternative remained to bankruptcy: a sale of all his assets in England, mostly furniture. He entertained this prospect as early as January 1878. "If the sale takes place," he warned Bennoch, "everything in the house will have to go, down to the paper on the walls; for all will not amount to the sum needed."[41]

At best, Julian could but postpone the furniture auction in his future. In spring 1878 Julian and Willie Dixon collaborated on a comedy of society life, variously titled "Art" and "The Eastern Question," about "the romance of a prima donna and a great portrait painter, complicated with a subtle young diplomat and a vulgar millionaire and his pretty daughter." A successful play, so long as it remained on the boards, potentially earned more money than a novel—upward of three thousand dollars or six hundred pounds per season. As a result, Twain, Howells, Henry James, and Bret Harte all wrote plays—a total of more than sixty among them. Dixon retreated to Twickenham for six weeks, and after they completed the script he read it aloud to a group of their friends. Later he read it to the actress Ellen Terry, who was interested in producing it, but Dixon died before their negotiations were complete. The next year Julian rewrote it as a prose narrative and published it in *Cornhill* under the title "Pauline" beside work by Robert Louis Stevenson.[42]

To escape their money woes temporarily, the family fled Twickenham in mid-August 1878 for Étretat, a "lively little watering-place" twenty miles from Havre on the Normandy coast. "We have resigned ourselves to losing *everything* at Twickenham," Minne wrote Bennoch in October. She had never fully recovered from her miscarriage and subsequent pregnancy the year before, and Julian hoped she would benefit from the sea air. Étretat was an artists' colony in season, and Swinburne often summered there. Julian later pretended that he and the poet became close friends: "Between 1870 and 1880, Swinburne and I both acquired the Étretat habit in summer, but it was specifically for the enjoyment of each other's company." However, this was not true. Julian vacationed there only once, and elsewhere in his journal he referred to "that unclean idiot Swinburne."[43]

The family saved money by summering on the French coast, according to Julian's peculiar notions of economy. They borrowed a cottage, and the same anonymous benefactor who paid for their lodgings in Hastings the summer before "sent money for our journey hither. Our expenses therefore are less than if we had stayed at home by two pounds a week." He insisted he also "needed seclusion to write." The exasperated Bennoch, who had advanced

Julian hundreds of pounds over the years only to learn that he was vacation-ing at the beach in France, accused him of "bad faith." In reply, Julian was unavoidably contrite: "Do you really think that I have been disingenuous as well as selfish,—that I have come over here to enjoy myself, leaving my friends to mind my affairs,—and that I concealed my departure from them, lest they should question the propriety of my spending for mere pleasure money which was a hundred times over owing to them?" He agreed that his "conduct may be made to bear the construction you put upon it." But he begged Bennoch not to "believe for a moment that I could deceive any one—certainly not *you*!" and assured him that "I have come here for work, and I am working, with such diligence and ability as I have, to lessen the gap that separates me from independence." As soon as he returned to England, however, he touched George Bentley for a loan, because his trip to France "has left my purse almost empty." In addition to working on "Normandy," a novel he eventually abandoned, he knocked out a travel essay, "A New Canterbury Pilgrimage," about his tramp with a Twickenham neighbor along the trail of Chaucer's pilgrims from Tunbridge Wells through Kent to the sea at Dover. He also frequented the casino and swam daily in the English Channel.[44]

By mid-November he realized his family could not winter in Étretat as he had originally planned. He had been "misinformed as to the winter condi-tion of the town. There was no physician, the tradesmen shut up, prices rose instead of declining: and the house we were in let in the wind like a sieve." They returned to Ways End not to live, however, but to sell their furniture, pay some expenses, and move to Hastings. Julian had insured the furniture for £2500, but "if it brought £500," he thought, "that would be enough for present needs." It fetched £133. After paying the auctioneer (£17), half a year's rent (£26), and other debts for pence on the pound (£64), the sale netted a mere £26. "Our double bedstead of solid black walnut, which cost £32, was sold for sixteen *shillings*," he groused. Fortunately, he had asked Bennoch in advance to salvage his father's desk and all of his papers "as being of value only to us."[45]

The Hawthornes lived in Hastings for a year, initially in an "amazingly cheap" boardinghouse. But their rooms still cost £140 a year, or nearly £3 a week, and Julian figured "we can do much better than that on a lease." Their expenses were "about £540 a year" for two adults, five children, and three servants. No matter how desperate his straits, Julian insisted on keep-ing a servant or three. One of the reasons was sheer snobbery disguised as noblesse oblige. The domestic class was different from the genteel poor, he believed: "How intolerant would such a life as theirs be to persons brought up in our rank of life." He was whistling past the proverbial graveyard.[46]

Upon renting a house in Hastings called "the Croft" with a breeze and a view of the English Channel in mid-January 1879, he discovered that the poet Coventry Patmore lived virtually next door. Though Patmore was twenty-three years older, they became fast friends—Julian mentioned in his journal no fewer than twenty-seven visits with the poet between January 13 and July 23. He claimed later that they were together "almost every day." Patmore inscribed to Julian a copy of his latest volume of poems, *Florilegium Amantis*, which Julian then reviewed enthusiastically in the *Examiner*. They borrowed each other's books; they dined in each other's homes; they smoked Patmore's "excellent cigars," drank his century-old Madeira, walked together to Fairlight Glen and Winchelsea, and discussed religion. Patmore was a Catholic convert, and he argued that Roman Catholicism was Julian's Swedenborgianism perfected. They also talked poetry, once "heaping abuse upon the wretched Browning. Patmore questioned whether Mr. Browning were not Mrs. Browning, and compared 'Aurora Leigh' to the shriek of a railway whistle!" Nor was the author of "The Angel in the House" a stodgy moralist, his modern reputation notwithstanding. His demeanor "toward all women was courtly and deferential, but in the privacy of his den he could emit epigrams startlingly profane about them."[47]

*   *   *

Julian wrote no other novel for nearly two years after *Garth* but "produced a couple of novelettes," including *Archibald Malmaison*, perhaps his best story. In it, two star-crossed lovers plan to elope, and the young man locks his betrothed in a secret chamber for safety while he prepares their escape. He then suffers an attack of amnesia and forgets her for seven years. The tale ends as he recovers his memory and discovers her dust-filled dress. With its depiction of premature burial, the story is more akin to Poe's brand of fiction than his father's. Whereas Nathaniel's tales were imbued with a brand of moral speculation, Julian's were fraught with a tone of ghastliness. Julian wrote *Archibald Malmaison* in only two weeks, with time off for illness, in January 1879. It was declined by Kegan Paul in London and "all the leading publishers in New York and Boston" before it was bought by Bentley in March for fifty pounds. After its publication that fall, it "had a circulation larger perhaps than that of all my other stories combined." Wilkie Collins thought the tale was so chilling that he told Julian it should have been a three-volumer. Julian realized it "was the horror of *Archibald Malmaison*, not any literary merit, that gave it vogue," and the reviewers agreed. "The nervous should be warned off," according to the *Nation*. Never the nervous type, Emily Dickinson owned a copy.[48]

Meanwhile, Julian accepted esoteric assignments that paid next to nothing. The theosophists Keningale Cook and his wife, Mabel Collins, editors of the *Dublin University Magazine*, commissioned him to compose an essay on "the mystery of the Fourth Dimension." He admitted he "knew nothing about it"—the riddle "had just emerged into a quasi-publicity"—but "I didn't mind guessing along with the rest." The unsigned essay is a tour de force of meaningless babble, with writing such as this: "If there were a space which is to our space of three dimensions as our space of three dimensions is to a plane surface which is of two dimensions, it would be possible to arrange five points at equal distances from each other." Julian elsewhere joked that the piece might have been titled "Unrecognizable Truths in Their Relation to Non-existent Phenomena." He was not invited to contribute to the magazine again, although he never learned whether it was because "I had settled the matter forever, or for some other reason."[49]

Then there were the stories, like "Judgment of Paris" and "Normandy," that he started but failed to finish or, if finished, to sell. No traces of such projects as these survive among his papers except as titles in his notebooks: "Body and Soul," "Family Conduct," "Profit and Loss," "Cecilia, Queen of Opera," "Notoriety," "A Great Experiment, " "Secrecy, or Mistrust," "Literary Peddler," "Autobiography of a Monster," "Ouida's Mother," "The Haunted Dining Room," "Lucan: A Romance of Wickedness" (a werewolf tale), and a fairy tale titled "Rudolph and Opaline." Even when he completed a project, he was subject to the whimsy and arbitrary practices of editors and publishers. He planned "a quiet domestic story" titled "Two Old Boys" for Strahan as early as February 1878 and submitted an opening installment to him in February 1879, though Strahan rejected it. Julian then sold the yet-unwritten novel to Edmund Yates for serialization in the *London World* for £100 and offered it to Kegan Paul for book publication for £150, though it never appeared in either venue. Julian eventually placed the rewritten fragment under the title "Millicent and Rosalind" with *Lippincott's*. He sold "Cynack Skene," blatant hackwork set in a Western mining camp in pale imitation of Bret Harte, to *Temple Bar* in 1880 for £40, though it was not printed until May 1886.[50]

Julian's problems were simple enough: he wrote more than he could sell, he appraised his writing for more than publishers were willing to pay, and he was usually paid for what he sold only upon publication. From his perspective, he earned six to ten pounds a day by his pen, although he collected only three to six pounds a week, "which does not quite pay my expenses." Henry James wrote his parents at the time that he had heard "poor Julian Hawthorne is (somewhere near London) in great destitution

& distress; & wonder greatly that he doesn't go home." In December 1878
Julian struck on a potential solution to these problems: he would dump all
of his vagrant manuscripts onto Francis Bennoch. "I have at this moment,
floating about the country, or in my desk, nearly £200 worth of unpaid-for
mss.," he notified his friend. He proposed to

> place in your hands all the mss. that I produce, as fast as they are written; you
> to forward them to any publishers you please, and receive for them whatever
> price you can induce the publishers to pay: from these sums you will send me
> as much as you can afford, in a cheque of your own, and retain the remainder
> on account of my debt. You will thus command the whole situation, besides
> enjoying the inestimable privilege of reading my lucubrations in mss. before
> the public see them! And very likely you would have more influence with able
> editors than I have. Damn 'em, they know I want money, and the more they
> know it, the slower they are about opening their cheque-books.[51]

In effect Julian invited Bennoch to become his agent. Bennoch declined.

*   *   *

Of all the authors and artists Julian encountered during his decade in
England, he was most beguiled by three expatriates—James Whistler, Oscar
Wilde, and Henry James—two of them Americans. Like virtually all London
art critics, he was initially unimpressed with Whistler's paintings when he
reviewed the famous exhibition at the Grosvenor Gallery in May 1878 for
the *New York Tribune*: "His pictures have the appearance of being seen
through a medium of unfiltered Thames water." James similarly dismissed
the paintings as "hardly more than beginnings, and fatally deficient in finish."
His "crude first attempts to understand Whistler's paintings were dismal
failures," Julian later admitted. "I could see no beauty in them; the drawing was indeterminate; the colors were not pretty; the pictures all seemed
unfinished." His opinion changed when he befriended Whistler. Though he
did not suffer fools gladly, the painter "admitted me from the first to the
sunniest and most cordial side of his nature." They sometimes crossed paths
at the Arts Club in Hanover Square or at Whistler's studio across the street
from Wilde's home on Tite Street. Julian watched him paint a portrait of
Lady Valerie Susie Meux, "the beautiful wife of [Henry Bruce] Meux, the
rich young brewer." "After she had gone, Whistler asked me what I thought
of it. I had no criticism to offer, but I did say that in my opinion it ought to
have been a nude. Jimmie mused a space, and then gave me an indescrib-
able look, but said nothing." Julian was nonplussed: "Had I been a painter,
I would have been glad to 'do' her for nothing."[52]

Julian met Wilde in 1879, soon after the poet moved from Oxford to London. At first he considered Wilde "a gentleman of an original and audacious turn of mind," and he used him as a model for the hero of "The New Endymion." On his part, Wilde was inclined to rank Julian's romances above his father's. One evening in 1879, they left a reception at Helena Modjeska's home together and Julian offered the younger writer some avuncular advice. "Wilde, you're a clever man, and have brains enough to make your way without humbug," Julian told him. "Why should you waste yourself in these fantastic make-believes? The very tones of your voice are a give-away; you'll be found out sooner or later. . . . Can't you, for a few minutes, at least, be sincere?" Wilde "looked at me," as Julian told the story, and replied, "I am always absolutely sincere!" The two crossed paths occasionally over the months—at a masked ball, a private view at the Grosvenor Gallery, a formal reception at Cromwell House—in the same company as such society favorites as Robert Browning, Arthur Sullivan, and Edwin Booth. But when Wilde toured the United States in 1882 and asked "if he might visit me, I made no answer." Minne, on the other hand, was clearly smitten with Wilde—she once called him "the great one"—and invited him to visit her, though there is no evidence he did so.[53]

In October 1878 Frederick Macmillan invited Henry James to contribute a critical biography of Nathaniel Hawthorne to his company's English Men of Letters series. James equivocated but eventually agreed, and he contacted Julian in Hastings to ask if he might interview him for the book. Julian noted in his journal for January 14, 1879, that James "wishes to pump me on his biography of my father," though "I don't know that I can tell him anything useful. . . . He has hitherto kept out of my way, either purposefully or not; but now that he thinks I can serve him, he finds out my address. Well, that is all right." He replied to James's query by inviting him to stay at his house, but he asked him to delay his arrival until after Minne was confined with their fifth child, Beatrix. James in turn thanked Julian for the offer of hospitality but said he preferred to "betake myself to the inn." While in Hastings he hoped the two of them might "engage in a conversational walk." James arrived in Hastings the afternoon of February 26. Julian met him at the station and introduced him to Minne at Ways End; then they dined at James's hotel and afterward walked the St. Leonard Parade.[54]

The next day they hiked twelve miles to Winchelsea and Rye. During their tramp James protested to Julian that he really did not want to write the book about his father. "I'm not fit to do it," he said, "but I'm afraid if I don't do it, somebody will do it even less fit than I." As they strolled the Hastings

Esplanade, they reminisced about old Concord, and Julian recounted an anecdote he had heard about James and Louisa Alcott. After the publication of *Little Women*, the story went, Louisa was wined and dined by the canaille, much to James's consternation. He was unable to fathom how she had become an object of popular adulation virtually overnight for such a wretched novel, and "his conscience compelled him to let Louisa know that he was unable to join in the vulgar chorus of approval." Finally he blurted out his feelings: "Louisa—m-my dear girl—er—when you hear people—ah—telling you you're a genius you mustn't believe them; er—what I mean is, it isn't true!" On that chill January day, James "couldn't fix the episode." He "made inarticulate murmurs and smiled thoughtfully," Julian remembered, "and looked up at the gray sky and along the populous promenade. . . . 'But—well,' he added, rubbing his chin through his clipped dark beard, conscientious to the last, 'you know, after all, dear Louisa isn't.'" After lunch they hired a fly for the return to Hastings. They dined again that evening at James's hotel, followed by "a long talk in which James told me many things about his pecuniary relations with publishers which amazed me: he has been paid far worse even than I have, owing in large degree, I fancy, to his negligence in looking after his affairs. In America Osgood has paid him even worse than here. But he has received nothing for 'French Poets and Novelists,' and but a few dollars for many of the other books."[55] The next morning Julian accompanied James on the train back to London.

Julian had been careful to offer James no help or advice, though he had a stash of his father's private papers at his house. He was loath to give away what he might publish for profit. Although their conversations were amicable, they were not productive. Like Miss Juliana in James's nouvelle "The Aspern Papers" (1888), Julian impeded the research of the erstwhile biographer. In the story, Miss Juliana declares, "I don't like critics," and she refuses to help any of them "rake up the past." Similarly, Julian gave "little satisfaction or information about his father," as James wrote his brother William. "He has something personally attractive and likeable," he conceded, "though he is by no means cultivated or in any way illuminated." James soon published a short piece about his visit. He concluded that if he "were a quiet old lady of modest income and nice habits—or even a quiet old gentleman of the same pattern—I should certainly go to Hastings" to live. Julian congratulated James upon publication of his *Hawthorne* in January 1880. Though the letter does not survive, James reported to his family that "Julian Hawthorne takes my book about his father kindly."[56]

*   *   *

In late 1878 Charles Dickens the younger commissioned Julian to contribute a serial novel to *All the Year Round* for five to six pounds per weekly installment. *Sebastian Strome* appeared in twenty-six parts between May 3 and November 1, 1879, and it was later issued in three volumes by the Appletons in New York and George Bentley in London. Julian considered it one of his better efforts, liable to be a "much more 'popular' novel than *Garth*." The title character is a hypocrite along the lines of the Reverend Hooper in his father's "The Minister's Black Veil," who is slowly redeemed from his secret sins of lust and pride. George Lathrop "was greatly excited over the first half of the book but," he confided, "it broke in the middle." Still, he thought Julian exhibited "great talent, possibly genius," and he considered *Sebastian Strome* "a remarkable advance" on his earlier efforts. Other readers sharply disagreed. The *Literary World* objected to its "brutality and vulgarity," and the *Examiner* panned it, saying, "a more disagreeable book has scarcely ever been written."[57]

The income from the novel scarcely slowed Julian's spiral into insolvency. He still harbored evergreen hopes of a subsistence from writing. With characteristically false confidence, he noted in his journal in early April 1879 that "I can manage, I think, to support myself on my English sales, and shall certainly not allow anything of mine to appear in America without being well paid for." He never explained, however, how he could prevent the piracy of his work in the United States in the absence of international copyright. Ten days later he noted that his "whole property, both here and in America, at this date, consists of something like seven and sixpence in silver, and two coppers." His lawyer advised him "to change my address, since Hastings would soon be too hot to hold me."[58]

Despite all the warning signals, on May 29, 1879, Julian moved his family into Hastings Lodge, a mansion that had belonged to the late Professor R. W. Jelf of King's College, Oxford. Jelf's heirs wanted "a trustworthy and appreciative person to live in it," and Julian was selected by the rental agent after Patmore vouched for his character. With twenty-plus rooms, stables, and a carriage house, the lodge and its grounds were "the realisation of an ideal." "Never before had I dwelt, nor shall I again dwell, in such dignity." The rent was four hundred pounds a year, but the first six months were complimentary on the condition Julian agree to a three-year lease. "It is now reasonably certain that we shall occupy Hastings Lodge for the next six months anyway," Julian confided to his journal the day before he signed the contract. Minne bought a "new black satin dress, with square cut neck and half sleeves" to celebrate.[59] They planned to take lodgers to help pay expenses, but, as usual, the plan backfired. They never rented a room.

Within a month of occupying Hastings Lodge, Julian feared he would soon be imprisoned for "refusal to pay" his creditors, still a crime in Victorian England. If arrested, "I should not care to survive imprisonment," he exclaimed, and, if necessary, he planned to hide from the sheriff. His income was irregular at best—eighty-seven pounds in January; five pounds in February; fifty-two pounds in March; nothing in April; forty-two pounds in May; and thirty-six pounds in June—but apparently sufficient in the short term to keep the law away. In late September, however, he confessed to Francis Bennoch that he was "nearly insane: and my poor wife is in a state too pitiable to speak of here." He was still willing to cheat local tradesmen; he had "found a butcher who had not heard of me and my difficulties, and who therefore consented to sell me meat on credit for two or three days. I am going today to try to find a similarly ignorant grocer and coal-merchant."[60] The endgame began to play out in late October, when Julian was presented with "a number of writs, amounting in the aggregate to over £90 which are to be paid on or before Nov. 5th. I have three pounds in the house." None of his English friends intervened to save him from public humiliation. He had squandered their goodwill. Bennoch explained to him that his "most ardent admirers" had heard such reports of his residence in a "fine house" as to "cool their ardour." Julian replied bitterly that they must suppose him "either a liar or a fool; a liar to say that I am starving, or a fool to starve." He ended his reply in a tone of self-pity, alluding to "the self-denial I have practiced, the work I have done, and the mental and bodily suffering I have endured during the last six months."[61]

Julian and his family were evicted in late November—at the close of the complimentary half year in the house—and on the last day of 1879 he was forced into bankruptcy. In his journal he makes no mention of these events, merely noting on January 1, 1880, that he had "left Hastings Lodge late last year." Julian found "unhappy and iniquitous lodgings" for his family in a boardinghouse on Tufnell Park Road. In mid-January they moved to a house on Queen's Road in St. John's Wood, where the rent was one pound less per week.[62] The night of April 24, 1880, the nursery in this house caught fire. Minne and two of the children suffered burns to their hands and faces "but not so as to leave permanent scars." They moved to Willie Dixon's empty house in St. James Terrace, north of Regent's Park, where they remained six months, then to 20 Woodstock Road, Bedford Park. Between fall 1878, when they left Ways End, and late 1881, Julian and his family lived in five different places.[63]

In the midst of his financial problems, his family and friends in the United States tried to secure a diplomatic post for him. Aunt Lizzie thought she could arrange a consulship in Germany like the one in Crefeld to which Harte had recently been appointed. Peckham inquired where "in Europe I would like to be a consul." Julian assured Bennoch in July 1879 that President Rutherford Hayes had "promised to attend to the matter," though he doubted he could support his family "on the pittance of £200 or £300 a year which America gives its consuls." In any event, nothing came of the scheme. The next winter Julian sought the job of secretary of legation in London under James Russell Lowell—annual salary four hundred pounds—but nothing came of this overture either. In March 1880 he expected to be appointed to a consulate in Japan. "It is a fortune and a sinecure," he wrote Bennoch. "We would sail immediately after my wife's confinement [with Fred] and probably make our permanent home there." The *Christian Union* even reported that Julian had been appointed to the Japanese consulate, but the story was untrue. Lizzie wrote Lucy Webb Hayes, the wife of President Hayes, in June 1880 to ask her to intervene on Julian's behalf, saying that "*if* he could have some consulship—or secretaryship—which would give him the necessaries of life, he could use his pen exclusively to clear off his debts." She hoped "his father's contributions to American literature . . . constitute some claim perhaps for the son."[64] Again, nothing came of this effort.

*   *   *

Among Julian's most popular works were "Rumpty-Dudget's Tower" (1877) and "Yellow Cap" (1879), both of them first printed in Strahan's *Peepshow*, a magazine for children. Like his father in *The Wonder Book* and *Tanglewood Tales*, he published bedtime stories he originally told his own children. "Rumpty-Dudget's Tower" was a cautionary tale about the consequences of disobeying parents. Julian sold it to Strahan for only fifteen pounds, and it has been praised as recently as 1987 as "a finely-balanced and satisfying story." At Strahan's request, in March 1879 Julian submitted the manuscript of "Yellow Cap," "a parable of the power (and impotence) of wealth—of vanity fair vs. arcadia," as he explained in his cover letter. The first installment appeared in *Peepshow* the next month. After the story concluded, however, Strahan wrote Julian "a very serious letter" in "an indignant tone" informing him he would not pay for it because Julian was in arrears to him for nearly one hundred pounds. Worse yet, Strahan sold reprint rights to Sampson, Low, Marston and Company for forty pounds. Julian was not amused. Strahan's seizure of "my story without my knowledge or consent was so far from giving him any right of possession in it, that I could, had I been so minded, have sued him either for the money, or for unlawful detention of property," he advised Sampson and Low. That is, "Strahan has sold you what does not and never did belong to him." Strahan was not amused. Julian should either have remained silent or told "the truth and nothing but the truth," such as "how you got Mr. Bennoch and myself to become security for you to an Insurance Company for a large amount" and how Julian then threatened to commit suicide unless he could borrow on the policy. Strahan refused to return the forty pounds he had received from Sampson, Low.[65] Julian's oft-strained relations with the publisher ended on this bitter note.

Among the unpublished novels Julian tried to foist upon Bennoch in December 1878 were two unfinished manuscripts, tentatively titled "Happy Jack" and "Perdita." Though Julian began to draft "Happy Jack" in October 1877, it was not yet complete when he sold the story for £450 in November 1880 to Frederick Macmillan. His magazine had serialized James's *The Portrait of a Lady* between October 1880 and November 1881, and Macmillan "wanted to follow it by a story from me." The novel had been on the boards for more than three years, but Julian had not yet worked out all the details. The hero and heroine, though in love, are unknowingly rival claimants for an English estate. Although born in a rustic New England village, the hero is in fact the son of a wealthy English nobleman whose artistic talent he has inherited. As Julian conceded, "This arrangement would need careful handling to render it plausible." He wrote ten of twelve installments by the end of January 1882, and it began to appear in *Macmillan's* under the title "Fortune's Fool"—the title is from *Romeo and Juliet*—in December 1881.[66]

Bentley expressed interest in "Perdita" while it was in embryo. He preferred a novella to "a three-decker," however, so Julian completed an abridged version of the story and submitted it to him in February 1879, remarking in his cover letter that it was "the most powerful novelette I have ever written" and asking fifty pounds for it.[67] Bentley declined. Julian redesigned it to be the full-blown novel he had originally planned, retitled it *Dust*, and sold the outline and opening chapters to the New York weekly *Our Continent*, where it began to appear in May 1882. That is, Julian contracted to write two serial novels in 1880–81—and although both were in serialization by early 1882, neither was finished.

*   *   *

When George and Rose's young son, Francis, died of diphtheria in March 1881, Julian wrote to express his condolences. The "loss of your son is so sacred a matter that I cannot bring myself to speak of it to other persons before I have spoken of it to you," he commiserated. The news of his nephew's death "moved me most deeply." Julian had never lost a child, "but death and sorrow are not strangers to me." He wished that on such an occasion as Francis's passing that "nothing stood between us. I can only think of you two as of my sister and my brother." He and Rose were "all that is left" of the family, "and it is strange that we should stand apart." This letter "healed the breach" between them, as Aunt Lizzie put it. Rose and George visited Julian and his family in England that summer, and Rose remained with them when George left for Spain to research his book *Spanish Vistas*. Rose informed Lizzie that Julian was "lovely to George . . . and is in fact the dearest brother." The Lathrops had bought the Wayside, the family homestead in Concord, and offered it to Julian and Minne when they returned to the United States until they could find a place of their own, and they accepted the offer.[68]

After Minne and the children left England in October 1881, Julian ventured to southern Ireland for the winter to work on *Dust*. The maneuver also enabled him to evade his creditors before departing Britain. He sailed via Bristol and Queenstown to Cork, then railed twenty miles south to the ancient fishing village of Kinsale. "Nobody knows it," he avowed, "but it is one of the loveliest places in the world." A "strange, exotic town" settled by Spanish immigrants in the sixteenth century, Kinsale exhibited a Spanish influence in its local architecture, though many of the buildings had fallen into decay. "Women walk these streets barefoot, with blue eyes, and black Spanish hair and graceful figures," Julian exulted, and "there are no women in the world more beautiful." The winter climate was "mild but exhilarating," so warm that Julian swam in the ocean. He walked the moors and bogs, hiking almost daily to a rocky promontory running into the Irish Channel ten miles south of Kinsale to have lunch with the lighthouse keeper there. The village figures in two of his later tales, "Ken's Mystery" (1883) and "Noble Blood" (1884). He finally left Ireland and crossed to Bristol on February 4, lingered a month in Antwerp at the Carnival of Binche "because I had never seen the city," and embarked from there in early March aboard the *Belgenland* for the United States.[69]

4

1882–87
"My chief annoyance is that I should have
to write in order to live"

When Julian stepped from the steamer in New York on March 13, 1882,
he touched native soil for the first time in nearly a decade. He joined his
family at the Wayside in Concord, where he had last lived in the summer
of 1868. At his home nearby, Ralph Waldo Emerson was dying. In his final
years, Emerson suffered from dementia, or, as Julian put it, his "external
memory seemed to have been wiped clean." W. D. Howells described the
condition as "a sort of Jovian oblivion of this nether world." When Julian
went to Emerson's home to pay his respects, he was met by Ellen Emerson, literally the gatekeeper, who permitted him to visit her father briefly.
The Sage didn't recognize him, but they spoke of Nathaniel, whom he did
remember. "I think of [Emerson] oftenest as I saw him last," Julian wrote
later, "when he had laid aside his shining armor and keen weapons, and in
tranquil patience awaited the summons to depart." He and Minne dined
with the Emersons on April 11 and the Sage died two weeks later. After
his funeral, Julian joined the procession that followed the coffin to Sleepy
Hollow Cemetery, where Emerson was buried on Authors' Ridge a stone's
throw from Nathaniel's grave. Julian reminisced about him in *Harper's* for
July 1882, to Ellen's evident delight: "We didn't know that [Julian] knew
so much about Father or felt so much affection for him."[1]

Pressed for cash as usual upon his return to the States, Julian raised the
price of his fiction from ten dollars to fifteen dollars per thousand words,
and he contracted to contribute all of his short stories to the new Bacheller
syndicate in Brooklyn and the McClure syndicate in New York. Writing
pulp fiction for newspapers was a marked step down for an established
writer like Julian, as if a well-known stage actor could no longer find work
with a respectable company and instead performed in vaudeville. But, as he
admitted, if authors "are not to find an outlet in syndicates, the prospects for

them are dark. The magazines are all overstocked, and no author can live on the royalties of his books." Julian's first order of business, however, was to finish *Dust* for *Our Continent*. Set in London in 1816 during "the 'Vanity Fair' epoch," the historical romance depicts a love triangle among a poet, his seemingly amoral wife, and the beautiful Machiavellian femme fatale Perdita. In this novel, even more than in his earlier ones, Julian stressed the sexuality of his characters, as when Perdita "loosened the front of her dress and exposed a bosom white as milk and curved like the bowl of Ganymede." During the summer of 1882, Julian seems to have suffered occasional writer's block. Because his manuscript had failed to arrive on time, the editor of *Our Continent*, Albion Tourgée, was twice forced to omit installments of *Dust*. The thirty-third and final part of the novel finally appeared in mid-January 1883, and the novel was published in cloth covers the next month. It was surprisingly popular, with a first printing of thirteen hundred copies selling out the first day. Julian earned $525 in royalties for the novel. However, as had become the norm for his books, its critical reception was mixed. While the *Atlantic* praised its "cleverness," "good writing," and "skillful touches," other critics joked it was as "dry" as its title. The *Saturday Review* dismissed it as "silly and tiresome." The *Nation* recognized that it was written in a minor key by a type of small-bore Trollope: Julian not only spurned the principles of "the modern 'analytical' novel," but his latest novel also "has as little analysis in it as any story with which we have met for some time."[2]

Within a month of his return to Concord, Julian again turned the cachet of his surname to account. In mid-April 1882 he proposed to James Osgood to write the definitive biography of his parents. Though he had protested the publication of George Lathrop's *Study* in 1876 on the grounds that his father had forbade his family from cooperating with any biographer, Julian had overcome his scruples six years later. To increase the sales appeal of his biography he planned to append to it his transcription of a fragmentary romance about immortality that his father had started in 1860–61, one of the cache of manuscripts Rose had returned to him in 1876. He had transcribed this fragment, which he titled *Dr. Grimshawe's Secret*, while still in England and then shopped the story around—he offered it to Smith, Elder, and Company in November 1881 for £250. It was "about two-thirds [the length] of an ordinary novel," and he considered it "in many respects equal to any of my father's productions." While Smith, Elder refused to nibble, Julian baited his proposal to Osgood with the fragment. During their negotiations, he explained that he needed fast money "as grist to keep the mill going." They soon struck a deal: according to the contract he signed on May 3, 1882, Julian received an advance of $1,000, or £200 (with $550, or £110, of it immediately and the balance due upon submission of the final manuscript), a 10 percent royalty on sales of the book, plus ownership of the copyright.[3] The advance enabled him to move his family from the Wayside to a house in Nonquitt, Massachusetts, on Buzzards Bay, just south of New Bedford.

In the mythology he later created about *Dr. Grimshawe's Secret*, Julian recounted his miraculous recovery of a virtually complete manuscript in his father's handwriting. When the family left England, their "belongings were packed in about twenty large packing-cases,—deal boxes of an average size of six feet by eight. . . . The packing-cases, upon arrival in New York, were stored temporarily in a loft in a warehouse which happened to be empty; they were piled in a room there not more than large enough to contain them. There they were to stay until we had found a house." Or until he could pay the shipping costs. (The family possessions were still in storage eighteen months after Julian returned to the United States, when he filed suit for five thousand dollars against the shipper for "illegal detention of our furniture.") Given access to these crates in June 1882, a month after signing the contract with Osgood, quite by chance, "I inserted an idle hand, and pulled out a bit of wadding from a crevice between the articles of furniture,—a table-top and a sewing-machine. Before tossing it aside I gave it a glance; after a moment I dropped my hammer and chisel and looked again, incredulously. The bit of wadding was a sort of large envelope, on the back of which was written 'Hawthorne MS.' I opened the envelope: there was no mistake. . . . I held 'Dr. Grimshawe's Secret' in my hands!" What he held was not a complete manuscript, of course, but the opening chapters of another draft of the romance he had tried to sell Smith, Elder the previous November. By the end of June he was trying to decide what to do with the two fragments. "Since coming into possession of my father's papers," he wrote Osgood on June 30, "I have discovered various things which have an important bearing on the story of Dr. Grimshawe: and it will be necessary, before printing any of it, to get all these notes etc. in order, and methodically to develop their significance."[4]

He decided to knit the two parts together and pass the story off as a lost romance by his father rather than merely append the fragments to the biography. As Edward Davidson explains, Julian "realized that he could complete the young American's adventures in England and thereby produce a fairly consistent book." Or as Julian claimed, "My father made two studies of this Romance. . . . I, as editor, pieced on this rewritten first half to the latter half of the original version." Stitched together like two heads on a Frankenstein monster, the story had little motor function but, Julian again insisted, was "in some respects more powerful than anything [Nathaniel] had done." He wondered aloud "why he did not complete it." Throughout the spring and summer of 1882 Julian refused to exhibit the manuscript(s) to Osgood, Ticknor, or others "until it has been transcribed. No one can do this work except Mrs. Hawthorne and myself. It is quite illegible except to us."[5] As a result, Osgood followed the path of least resistance and announced in mid-August 1882 that a posthumous romance by Nathaniel Hawthorne would appear from his press in November.

The Lathrops believed *Grimshawe* was a hoax, and George attested in an interview with the *Boston Traveller* that neither he nor Rose "had the slightest inclination" that such a story existed. Ironically, he had described the manuscript in his *Study* in 1876: "It consists of two sections, in the second of which a lapse of some years is implied." The first fragment was set in England, the second in New England, and Nathaniel had abandoned the romance in this form. Rose insisted in a letter to the *Boston Advertiser* that either *Grimshawe* was fraudulent, or "it cannot be truthfully published as anything but an experimental fragment," because "no such unprinted work" existed. The fragile truce between the families evaporated overnight as Julian and the Lathrops competed to prove their bona fides as Nathaniel's literary heirs. Julian wrote Osgood in a rage that he had read Rose's letter "intimating that the Romance was not written by my father at all, but is a forgery of my own. It is impossible for me to take any notice of such a charge." "Years ago," he wisecracked, his critics asserted "that my novels were written by my sister Una. After she died, it was maintained that my subsequent stories were the work of my wife. But now it appears that I am beyond question the real author of my father's works." George tried unsuccessfully to clear the air in the *New York Sun*. Rose had never doubted that Julian "had in his hands a genuine manuscript sketch by her father, for she sent the said sketch to him [in 1876]. . . . But neither was there any doubt that it was a fragmentary production." She had "neither implied nor intended" to suggest her brother was guilty of forgery. Julian was not appeased. The next day, he addressed Rose privately: "I have looked in vain for any further word from you, retracting the statement made in your first letter." Unless she immediately issued a public statement exonerating him, "you will be always hereafter accused of having brought a charge of forgery against your own brother; a charge calculated to ruin his literary and social prospects, and to disgrace the name he bears." To add insult to injury, Julian proposed to dedicate *Grimshawe* to the Lathrops, an offer they declined. ("Can you imagine why?" he queried Ticknor.) In his preface he took another potshot at George: "So many inspired prophets of Hawthorne have arisen of late, that the present writer, whose relation to the great Romancer is a filial one merely, may be excused for feeling some embarrassment in submitting his own uninstructed judgments to competition with theirs."[6]

He was never able to lay to rest questions about the authenticity of the romance for a good reason: he had in fact doctored the manuscripts. While still in England he had shown the second part to his friend Keningale Cook, who vouched for its legitimacy a year later, but of course Cook could not vouch for the accuracy of Julian's transcription. Julian proposed to Ticknor "to submit the Grimshawe mss. together with my transcription of it to four persons of well-known character, such as [Oliver Wendell] Holmes, Miss [Louisa May] Alcott, James Freeman Clarke, and J[ohn] G[reenleaf] Whittier, and request them to sign a statement to the effect that they have compared them and found them identical, and that the handwriting is that of Hawthorne." Such a plan to prove Julian's trustworthiness was never implemented, probably because it would have had the opposite effect of the one he intended: it would have proved the inaccuracy of his transcriptions. By his own admission, "I ignored so much of the original as is covered by the revise, and omitted the intercalary studies." He deleted entirely some of "that portion of the story which is laid in England," because the American part was "much the richer in colouring and vigorous in treatment." As Davidson has painstakingly demonstrated, "Julian allowed himself every license an editor could arrogate to himself: he ruthlessly excised large sections of the two long drafts and patched together loosely related parts which originally had no connection with each other." What he published bears "scant resemblance to the novel Hawthorne left unfinished." Julian inserted a few facsimile pages of manuscript in the book, but these pages proved nothing except that his father had written them. Over the years Julian sold the manuscript piecemeal to collectors so that it would be impossible (or so he thought) to reassemble it and detect the editorial liberties he had taken.[7]

With rare exceptions, the critics were unimpressed by *Dr. Grimshawe's Secret* when it appeared, and they roundly criticized Julian for publishing it. The story was "often little better than nonsense," a "farrago of absurdities and vulgarities," and nothing "but a fragment." Julian made a grave error by publishing unedited parts of the manuscript in the January 1883 *Century* under the title "A Look into Hawthorne's Workshop." The reviewer of *Grimshawe* for the *Nation* compared the passages there with comparable passages in the book and concluded that Julian was "mistaken" in calling his deletions "few" and "unimportant."[8] Nor did the book sell well. Julian wrote Ticknor in July 1883 that he was "surprised by the small results from 'Grimshawe,' which should at least have paid expenses." He received only thirty-four pounds for its initial sale in England. On second thought, he suspected Osgood was cheating him on the book in order to boost "his chances of getting the Biography" so that Julian could pay back the money the publisher had advanced him on the novel. On third thought, he doubted "the propriety of publishing Dr. Grimshawe" at all.[9]

In March 1881 Julian had written Rose and George upon the death of their son that he had "not yet known" the loss of a child. He was not long spared that sorrow. On Wednesday, September 20, 1882, fourteen-month-old Gladys "seemed strangely sleepy," according to Minne. "Her little head would hang down, and she would sleep in spite of all we could do." Julian was in Boston trying to scare up some money, so she sent for Will Morton. The baby was teething, Morton said, but "as soon as the teeth came through, she would be all right." The misdiagnosis led to a rift between Morton and Julian that lasted for several years. The next day Gladys slipped into a coma. Early on Friday afternoon "she went into convulsions that lasted an hour and a half," and Minne telegraphed Julian to return to Nonquitt. Early on Saturday morning, Minne held Gladys "while she slowly and slowly gasped her little life away, until the last little shudder came." She died of an oral infection. Julian arrived at noon but caught the next train back to Boston to borrow the money to bury his daughter beside his father. Ellen Emerson pitied the parents: Julian and Minne had lost "one of the most exquisite babies the world ever saw." In the throes of grief, they paid their bills— "between three and four hundred dollars"—and moved three weeks later from Nonquitt to Fifth Avenue in Morrisania, now the South Bronx.[10]

*   *   *

Julian's visit to Nathaniel's grave when he buried Gladys coincided with the start of his work on the most ambitious literary project of his life: the biography of his parents. "This biography is the only thing in literature, to which my name is attached, that I have any tender feeling about," he advised Ticknor. "Ever since I began to be a writer, I have looked forward to this work as the culmination of my career." His research was, to his credit, reasonably meticulous. He explained to Horatio Bridge on December 27 that he had been "for some time collecting materials for a biography of my father: for it seems as if, unless I do it, the world will be flooded with bastard biographies of him, founded on hearsay and imagination, and injurious to his name and character." He sought Bridge's cooperation and enlisted the help of Aunt Lizzie. In the end, however, he depended mostly on his parents' notebooks and surviving correspondence. Thomas Sergeant Perry once described this method of life-writing: "The biographer gets a dustcart into which he shovels diaries, reminiscences, old letters, until the cart is full. Then he dumps the load in front of your door. That is Vol. I. Then he goes forth again on the same errand. And there is Vol. II." Julian supported his family while writing the biography with potboilers and advances from Osgood. By the end of September 1883 he owed Osgood more than thirteen hundred dollars.[11]

Nonetheless, Julian was never so intensely devoted to a project in his life. Six months after starting it, he griped about the sheer "physical labor involved in this Biography." The next month, he announced that he had written thirty thousand words "in the last 12 days." He considered the first half of the biography "the loveliest story I ever read; and as my share in it is confined to gumming the various pieces together, I have a right to that opinion." At this point he visited the aging Herman Melville at his East Twenty-sixth Street brownstone in New York. "It was a sad interview," Julian remembered, with a good deal of "incoherent talk." Melville was a "melancholy and pale wraith of what he had been in his prime," and he "merely shook his head" when Julian began to reminisce about "the red-cottage days" in Lenox. Melville hinted that his own literary career had been doomed as the result of a conspiracy against him and expressed his conviction "that there was some secret in my father's life which had never been revealed, and which accounted for the gloomy passages in his books." To the consternation of generations of Melvillians, Julian never wavered in his belief that Melville was mentally ill, or, as he inelegantly put it, that "his mental ship lacked ballast." According to Harrison Hayford, Julian "did perhaps as much as any one person to foster the legend of Melville's insanity."[12]

Part hagiography and part debunking biography of his parents' friends and enemies, *Nathaniel Hawthorne and His Wife* remains an indispensable source for scholars. It contains the reminiscences of several of his parents' contemporaries and a number of documentary sources that have since been lost, including at least one of his mother's letters and four of Melville's letters to his father. It was not a disinterested portrayal of his parents, however. Julian wrote it with an agenda: to build a firewall around their reputations and to denigrate virtually every figure who rivaled them. He idealized his parents and dedicated "these records" of their "happy marriage" to Minne. Julian was at pains to imply that his own marriage, like that of his parents, was blissful. He also designed the biography to settle old scores or exact revenge, as his contemporaries well understood. As John Albee averred after its publication in November 1884, "we remember no biography having so many poorly concealed antagonisms." Aunt Lizzie was alarmed and feared a backlash, saying the biography "speaks of other people in the most careless and reckless manner." Julian had included "some things especially about persons that [Nathaniel] would never have let any mortal eye see."[13] She was right. The various stings and scrapes Julian inflicted in the biography festered for years to come.

Julian's (vivi)section on Margaret Fuller is the most notorious example. He could not have known her personally, as he was a babe in arms when she sailed for Europe in 1846 and only four years old when she drowned off the shore of Fire Island. He had never mentioned her in print before 1884. Yet she was an attractive target because, unlike his mother, Fuller was no "angel in the house" and he was an unrepentant misogynist. Nathaniel's infamous complaint about "the d——d mob of scribbling women" with whom he competed for readers pales beside Julian's declaration in his journal that "no book was ever written by any woman that I should much regret to see burned" or in a letter that it would "be well, at this stage of our literary history, to make it a penal offence for any woman to write a story." Over the course of his long career he complimented only a handful of women writers, among them Georges Sand, Emily Brontë, and Elizabeth Stoddard.[14] Given the chance, he no doubt would have consigned Fuller's *Woman in the Nineteenth Century* to the flames.

In *Nathaniel Hawthorne and His Wife*, Julian published for the first time a passage from his father's journal for April 3, 1858—an entry Sophia had omitted from her edition of the *French and Italian Notebooks*. In it, Nathaniel mused that Fuller "was a great humbug." In Italy she seems to have collapsed "morally and intellectually. . . . On the whole, I do not know but I like her the better for it; because she proved herself a very woman after all and fell as the weakest of her sisters might." As Thomas Mitchell has explained, Julian took unconscionable liberties in editing this entry in order to defame Fuller, omitting the context and failing to explain that his father was recording gossip he had overheard. By distorting the passage, Julian depicted Fuller from Nathaniel's point of view as a feminist shrew and fallen woman.[15]

These two pages in a near thousand-page biography predictably rankled Fuller's friends and family and sparked a war of words, what Aunt Lizzie called in a miracle of understatement "quite a burst of resentment." The furor raged for weeks. As for Julian, he defended his decision to publish the passage and insulted those who questioned his motives. His father had "told the exact truth" about Fuller, and as his biographer he had simply placed his statement on the public record. "I foresaw, of course, that [the passage] would create a fluttering in the dove cotes of Margaret's surviving friends and of the later disciples," he allowed. "The majority of readers will, I think, not be inconsolable that poor Margaret Fuller has at last taken her place with the numberless other dismal frauds who fill the limbo of human pretension and failure." To Christopher Cranch's allegation that he had kindled the uproar in order to promote the sale of his book, Julian replied that he remembered Cranch in Rome during the winter of 1858–59 "as an amiable and inoffensive gentleman with an entertaining talent for ventriloquism." Frederick Fuller, Margaret's nephew, complained that Julian was "not one to spoil a sensation to save a friend," to which Julian responded that such whining reminded him of "the story of the nephew of the Doll Stuffed with Sawdust." He belittled George William Curtis for having been "a gushing and sentimental youth ready to make an idol if he could not find one ready made." While not exactly defending Julian, Aunt Lizzie was ready with rationalizations for his ad hominem attacks. He had been "driving the quill like mad" for years "for daily bread." He "was all worn out nervous with his dozen years of book work, and full of neuralgia," so he had "replied angrily and made bad worse by insulting all the best friends of his father." His mistake "was mainly due to his most unfortunate characteristic, namely, an abnormal impetuosity of temperament."[16]

While the case of Fuller may be the most notorious example of Julian's method of subtle slander by selective editing, others such as Thoreau and Theodore Parker suffered similar fates. Julian nowhere mentioned James T. Fields by name, alluding to him merely as the "publisher" or "the editor," and Fields's friends were mortified. In commissioning Thomas Wentworth Higginson's review of the biography for the *Atlantic*, Thomas Bailey Aldrich expressed the hope "that you will find it in your way, or be willing even to go out of your way, to give Julian a rap on the knuckles for his shabby treatment of Fields." Higginson happily complied. "Of all the pettinesses" in the book, he grumbled, "there is none so petty" as the omission of Fields. Aldrich was delighted. "Your Hawthorne review is cruelly good. Of course I shall make a life-long enemy of Julian Hawthorne [by printing it], but my stock of enemies has recently run so low that I am glad to add to it." Julian could only offer a lame excuse for eliding Fields: "I conceived that he had already sufficiently vindicated, in print and otherwise, his share in the production of the 'Scarlet Letter.'" But he also retaliated, as Aldrich had predicted. He asserted later that Higginson "would have been a better and more useful person . . . had he dwelt among more insignificant people" and that Aldrich's verse was sheer "rubbish."[17]

If Julian designed the biography to spark controversy and sell, he succeeded admirably on both counts. It became a *succès de scandale*. Some 4,350 copies were printed during the final two months of 1884, including

350 copies of a deluxe edition. The following year Chatto and Windus issued it in England, Osgood issued three additional printings, and it was praised as much as panned by critics. On the one hand, of course, Julian was scolded for disregarding his father's wish that no one write his biography and for betraying the confidences of his friends and family. The *Athenaeum* contended that Julian should not have printed the "censures" on Fuller out of respect for his father. The *Saturday Review* thought the passage on Fuller was "probably the most brutal thing ever written by such a man of such a woman in such circumstances." The reviewer for the *London Academy* regretted even reading the biography: "Few hours of a mis-spent life have been more sorrowfully wasted." On the other hand, the *Boston Beacon* pronounced it "the most charming biography of the year"; R. H. Stoddard, in the *Independent,* considered it "the most remarkable [book], all things considered, that I ever read"; the *New York Tribune* declared it "near . . . faultless"; and in his history of American literature, Charles F. Richardson hailed it as a work of genius, "the best biography written in America."[18]

*   *   *

During the year he lived in Morrisania, Julian was a consummate social animal. Between late February and late March 1883, for example, he attended at least eight functions, including meetings of the Harvard Club of New York, the Saturday Night Club, the International Copyright League, and a breakfast at Delmonico's in honor of the German actor Ludwig Barnay. Julian also attended, with Mark Twain, a meeting of the Kinsmen at Laurence Hutton's home and meetings of the Twilight Club, where he made a brief speech about English journalism, and the Nineteenth Century Club at Courtlandt Palmer's home on Gramercy Park, where he spoke on "The Modern Novel." Most importantly, he joined the Authors Club of New York, the literary equivalent of the famed Players Club for actors, founded in November 1882 with membership limited to a total of fifty writers. The club rolls included all the usual suspects, among them Mark Twain, Howells, Lathrop, Charles Warner, and the playwright/impresario Augustin Daly.[19]

The frequent appearance of Julian's name in the society columns of the New York dailies failed to insulate him from serious public embarrassment in March 1883, however. He had ignored too long the unfinished *Fortune's Fool.* The last of the installments Julian had written before leaving Europe in March 1882 was printed in *Macmillan's* the following September. He had "received a friendly reminder" from Frederick Macmillan "in June [1882] or thereabouts" that the remaining installments were overdue, but "by that time I had dismissed the story utterly from my mind, and could not recall it." He requested an extension of time and "it was accorded; but when it had passed, I was still incompetent." Meanwhile, *Macmillan's* subscribers were clamoring for the conclusion, so Macmillan inserted a card in the March 1883 issue to the effect that he had been forced to postpone publication of the final chapters of the novel due to his "inability to obtain" them "from the Author."[20] He publicly charged Julian with breach of contract on the grounds that he had been paid for the entire novel in advance.

To make matters worse, Julian claimed in an interview with the *New York Tribune* that he had completed the entire manuscript before returning to the United States the previous March. "I determined to modify the conclusion of the novel," however, and with Macmillan's consent, "I withdrew the last two monthly installments for the purpose of rewriting them. I had at that time nearly or quite a year in which to make the alterations, for the publication of the serial had scarcely been begun in the magazine." He "brought the debatable chapters" with him to Concord and "rewrote them, with the exception of a few concluding pages," but this manuscript was lost in moving from Concord to Nonquitt to Morrisania, "and my best efforts to find it were unsuccessful. It therefore became necessary to write the final installments a third time." But "the death of my little daughter and other matters totally unfitted me for literary work, and it was impossible to bring my mind to the task of rewriting the concluding chapters." He finally decided "that my only chance of success was to dismiss the whole subject from my thoughts until such time as I could return to it with a certain feeling of freshness and novelty." Macmillan was quick to challenge this version of events. He reiterated that Julian "never supplied the last two installments of *Fortune's Fool*, but did receive pay for them" and that "the novel remains incomplete."[21]

In either case, all the time Julian was gadding about New York in February and March 1883, the novel was hanging fire. Finally, he "took up the work once more," as he put it, and (re?)wrote the final installments. According to his journal, he "finished Fortune's Fool" on May 9, 1883, and its publication resumed in *Macmillan's* in July after a ten-month hiatus. Julian protested that "if the incident has been injurious to anyone, it is to me rather than to the publishers."[22] He was the only victim, the damage was self-inflicted, so no one was entitled to censure him. Macmillan begged to differ. Though he had paid Julian an extra one hundred pounds for British book rights to the novel, he sold them to Chatto and Windus, and he buried each of the final installments, after he finally received them, on the final pages of the issue in which they appeared. He wanted nothing more to do with Julian, who never again placed a serial novel with a major magazine.

In his last public statement on the fiasco, Julian conceded that *Fortune's Fool* had been "a failure." The story "lacked wholeness and continuous vitality" because of the haphazard manner of its composition, "but I did not realize this fact until it was too late, and probably should not have known how to mend matters had it been otherwise." As in *Dust*, he indulged at one point in a kind of narrative voyeurism or erotic gaze, in this case a slow pan of the heroine's body: "Her bust was small, but exquisitely moulded; below her waist, the full arch of her hips swept down with an elastic curve to the knee, and thence tapered to the ankle of her slender foot." In the final chapters, Julian's unpracticed prose was remarkably slipshod, as when the omniscient narrator cannot determine an exact number of characters or identify which of them the protagonist recognized: "There were three or four persons in the room, some of whom he may or may not have known." The novel ends on an outlandish note, with the hero murdered in the stage pit of a burning theater while the heroine commits suicide by asp in her dressing room. "I have no reverence for anything, and would sacrifice anything, truth included, for the sake of a startling or picturesque effect," Julian confessed. He eventually admitted, too, that he had not finished a draft of the novel months in advance and withdrawn the last chapters in order to revise them, as he had claimed. On the contrary, those "two remaining installments were not written and published until 1883, and this delay and its circumstances spoiled the book."[23]

The critics certainly shared his opinion that the novel was a failure, the literary equivalent of processed sugar. According to the *Spectator*, the story in its last chapters "drops swiftly down into a sensation novel of the poorer sort, and winds up as a 'penny dreadful,'" and the *Century* agreed it was redolent of "a blood-and-thunder" juvenile novel. Julian had never learned to chasten his style, the *Critic* carped, and *Fortune's Fool* reads "like the first book of an author who has thrown into it all that he has ever thought, or learned, or experienced. There is material enough for twelve stories or novels." "If the secret of successful Romance writing was the concoction of improbable tales," averred the *Nation*, "then Mr. Hawthorne would be the greatest Romance-writer living."[24]

*   *   *

On May 11, 1883, only two days after finishing *Fortune's Fool*, Julian began *Beatrix Randolph*, a six-part novel for the *Manhattan*, for which he was paid one thousand dollars. He finished it in less than two months. It dealt "with New York society life, of which the author has been of late making a personal study." Julian's club-going turns out to have been research.

In the novel, an impresario sponsors the U.S. tour of a Russian diva, who unexpectedly cancels at the last moment. The heroine of the novel, a young and beautiful American woman, is persuaded to impersonate the diva during the entire operatic season and of course earns accolades and buckets of money. The prima donna hears of her success and sails to New York to confront her—only to hear Beatrix sing and then abruptly to retire from the musical stage. The story earned few kudos. According to *Life*, Julian depicted the musical producer and prima donna "with all the realism of a two-cent journalist," and the *Literary World* reviewer could not "think of a single reason to justify the production of this book."[25]

*   *   *

In July 1883, at the invitation of Bronson Alcott and Frank Sanborn, Julian joined the faculty of the Concord School of Philosophy. Every summer between 1879 and 1887, "battalions of late-Victorian highbrows," as he put it, congregated in the "chapel" behind Orchard House (aka Apple Slump) to hear speakers on such arcane topics as "Dialectic Unity in Emerson's Prose" and "Platonism in Relation to Modern Civilization." The morning of July 31, Julian addressed the largest audience at the school that year on "Agnosticism in American Fiction," a paper subsequently published in the *Princeton Review*.[26]

The lecture was an early skirmish in what came to be known as the war against realism. As editor of the *Atlantic* for most of the previous decade, W. D. Howells had argued that in the evolution of literary forms, such imaginative tales as *The Scarlet Letter* and *The Blithedale Romance* (and *Vanity Fair* and *Oliver Twist*, for that matter) were a more primitive type of fiction than realistic novels such as Henry James's *The Portrait of a Lady*, Leo Tolstoy's *War and Peace*, and Émile Zola's *L'Assommoir*. Julian had known Howells since August 14, 1860, when the young Ohio poet visited the Wayside during his first trip to New England. Though he still professed a "strong personal regard" for Howells a generation later, he disparaged Howells's theories and the school of fiction he championed. Literary realism was, in his view, the narrative equivalent of Kodak photography and a step down the slippery slope to base materialism and nihilism. In the mecca of transcendentalism, he was literally preaching to the choir. The novels of James and Howells, he held, represent "life and humanity not in their loftier, but in their lesser manifestations." Julian spoke at the Concord School the next summer on "Emerson as an American." Ellen Emerson thought this lecture was "very good," too, and it was subsequently published in both the *Manhattan* and a Festschrift in Emerson's honor edited by Frank Sanborn.[27]

In early September 1883 Julian and Minne decided to leave Morrisania, "because we found that the expense of maintaining the house was leaving us no margin." They planned to move to Sag Harbor, a former whaling port at the eastern end of Long Island about three hours from the city. Minne's brother John visited them before they began to pack and promptly collapsed with congestive heart failure. "The whole nursing fell to Minne and me: we neither of us went to bed for ten days," Julian allowed. Still, he found time to complete a children's tale titled "Almion, Auria and Mona" for *St. Nicholas* magazine. "It is a little parable of Regeneration, and I have endeavored to make the ending bright and hopeful," he explained to editor Mary Mapes Dodge, although "it has been written under sad circumstances,—a dear friend and relative of mine is now lying in this house at the point of death." Though John briefly rallied, he suffered a relapse and died in Julian's arms the morning of September 18. The next day, Julian received a check for $112 from *St. Nicholas* for his story.[28] He spent it on John's funeral.

Three weeks later the family left for Sag Harbor and the Mortons' summer cottage there. Will and his wife Bessie "did not wish to leave it unprotected, and they could not live in it" while Will worked in the city, Julian explained. "We offered to occupy it during the winter, and they were glad to accept the arrangement." He expected expenses would "be reduced to a minimum" even while they lived "on an island of a hundred acres, with woods and fields, and a delightful bay, entirely to ourselves." Trouble is, the house had no insulation and its walls were the thickness of a single board. Seven years later he remembered that "very cold winter that I spent in a summer cottage by the sea." Julian built a heated "chalet" on a bluff overlooking the bay about a hundred yards from the house, much like Mark Twain's study at Quarry Farm near Elmira, so it was "perfectly removed from all sound of children or human disturbance of any kind." Once settled in Sag Harbor, Julian curtailed his activities in Manhattan, though he kept a pied-à-terre on the north side of Washington Square.[29]

His "chief annoyance" during the winter of 1883–84 was "that I should have to write in order to live." He wrote and sold U.S. serial rights to a fifty-thousand-word potboiler, *Noble Blood*, to Whitelaw Reid of the *Tribune* for seven hundred dollars, and he had another novel, "Mercy Holland," on the boards, although he never finished it. He sold British serial rights to *Noble Blood* to the magazine *Belgravia*, which published it under the more polite title "Miss Cadogna," and he sold book rights to the Appletons in the United States and Chatto and Windus in England. Not only was it "one of my best yarns," he assured the editors, but it also "ends well," unlike *Fortune's Fool*. The money he earned was "indispensable to providing sustenance" to his family (hence the term "potboiler") while he worked on his "opus magnum," the biography of his parents. (In truth, there is no neat distinction between Julian's potboilers and his "serious" writing.) He also quarreled in February 1884 with the staff of *Youth's Companion*. They had asked him to become a regular contributor and announced in December 1882 that his essay about Kinsale, "Life in an Irish Fishing Village," was forthcoming. The essay never appeared, however, prompting him to describe the editors of the magazine in February 1884, with his bile up, as "a loathsome gang of thieves, murderers, whoremongers, and hypocrites."[30]

Minne was in frail health throughout that winter: mourning her brother and Gladys, homeschooling seven children ages twelve or younger, and pregnant with their eighth child. She could never abide Sag Harbor, though she lived there most of the next decade. At least she could depend initially on help from Rose, who announced her separation from George Lathrop on April 27, 1883, and joined her brother and his family in Morrisania. She had "decided to sever all further connection with her husband, who, it appears, has been treating her abominably—keeping her in fear of her life and so on," Julian confided to Osgood. The marriage had long been troubled, particularly after the death of their son. Rose assisted in the move to Sag Harbor and remained with the family until the spring of 1884 when she and Lathrop reconciled.[31]

With the birth on May 11 of Imogen—the name of a virtuous daughter in Shakespeare's *Cymbeline*—Julian and Minne added another fledgling to the nest. He informed Osgood on May 14 that he was too broke to pay train fare to the city, and the next day he joked halfheartedly with William Ticknor that he would "have to write a new story" to pay for the baby. He was nominated for the Yale professorship of literature about this time, although, as with his nomination for diplomatic posts while he lived in England, nothing came of it. Donald Grant Mitchell, aka "Ik Marvel," the author of *Reveries of a Bachelor* (1850), was appointed to the position instead. Julian finished *Nathaniel Hawthorne and His Wife* in the summer of '84 and wrote a friend a few weeks later that he was "living in this lonely sea-side seclusion, very quietly, and am not just now engaged in anything of importance." Determined not to winter again in a summer cottage, he moved the family a few miles to a two-hundred-acre farm on Peconic Bay. The house stood on a knoll with a view of the water. Hildegarde described the house in her autobiographical novel, *Makeshift Farm* (1925), as a "two-story wooden structure with wide verandas." In the spring, with the help of a hired man, the boys planted a garden, kept cows, and raised pigs and chickens.[32]

With his success on the platform of the Concord School of Philosophy, Julian decided to earn some extra money and escape Sag Harbor occasionally during the winter months by lecturing part-time. With the draw of his name "it cannot pay worse than literature," he reasoned, "and may pay better: at any rate it will be variety." Though never a headliner, he routinely received one hundred dollars plus expenses for each talk during the next three winters. According to contemporary reports, he was "polished and dignified in bearing" on the stump. "His voice is low, but his enunciation is distinct. He gives the broad sound to the vowels, but there is little of the drawl in his speech." Managed by the Redpath Lyceum Bureau in Boston and James B. Pond's bureau in New York, Julian averaged around twenty dates per season, either reading from his father's writings or speaking on "Pieces of London," "London Environs," "Walks in London," or "English and American Society." He was mostly booked into towns in western Massachusetts, upstate New York, Pennsylvania, and Ohio. By the end of the third winter, Julian had wearied of the "beastly business," however, especially the rigors of travel. As he wrote Pond, "I am resolved never to attempt to lecture further away than Philadelphia in future."[33]

His brief career as a professional speaker coincided with the period of his greatest activity on behalf of his college fraternity, Delta Kappa Epsilon (DKE). On November 11, 1884, he addressed the Long Island Historical Society in Brooklyn on "English and American Society"—he long remembered his "cordial reception" there—and then caught an overnight train to Rochester, where he spoke at a conference of DKE alumni the next evening and was elected president of the New York chapter of the organization. He hosted a ten-course dinner and acted as toastmaster for nearly three hundred Delts at the fashionable Delmonico's restaurant in February 1885, where he ran across Hubert Thompson, the brother of his childhood friend Eddy, and Theodore Roosevelt, a former New York state assemblyman. Julian and Roosevelt had first met on Prager Strasse in Dresden in the summer of 1873. Teddy, or TR, was fourteen, anemic, and wore "spectacles on his short nose." Julian "told him that he might make himself athletic if he stuck to the job; but, privately, I didn't think he would." He later conjectured that his advice to the spindly asthmatic that day "may have been more important to him and to the United States than I then suspected." When they crossed paths at Delmonico's eleven years later, TR invited Julian to dine with him the next time he was in the city, and in early April, at a farewell banquet for the actor Henry Irving at Delmonico's, he again rubbed shoulders with TR as well as Sam Hoar, James Whistler, Henry Ward Beecher, Henry Cabot Lodge, and U.S. Attorney Elihu Root. At the DKE convention in Meriden,

Connecticut, in late October, he was introduced by Senator Matthew Butler of South Carolina and read a poem, subsequently published in the *DKE Quarterly*, in which he parodied Alfred Lord Tennyson, Robert Browning, Algernon Charles Swinburne, John Greenleaf Whittier, James Russell Lowell, and Walt Whitman to the delight of the delegates.[34]

For little reason other than his reputation as a public speaker, Julian was invited to address the Conference of Charities and Corrections in Washington, D.C., in June 1885. After registering at Willard's Hotel a day early, he visited some tourist sites, including the White House; the Corcoran Gallery; the Smithsonian; the Capitol, where "inconceivable rascalities have been plotted"; and the recently completed Washington Monument, beside which "Cleopatra's needle would look like a hitching-post." He was impressed with the city: "In its worst aspects, Washington is like the best of New York; in its average, it is like the best of Paris; in its best, it is like nothing but Washington." He saw Charles Warner, with whom he shared a mint julep, and his old master Frank Sanborn, who told him a joke about the recent revelation that the Democratic candidate for president had fathered a child with a woman who was not his wife: "Do you know what mechanical forces Cleveland represents?—Screw and leave her (lever)!" On June 9 Julian read his paper—"essentially a defense of the criminal"—before a large audience. He was even more tolerant than Hollingsworth, the prison reformer in his father's *The Blithedale Romance*, in his attitude toward criminals. Julian began by conceding that he was unqualified to speak on the subject and urged his auditors to "supply what was lacking in his paper, each for himself." What followed was "an abstruse and mystical paper of nearly 5000 words" inspired by Swedenborgianism, in which, like his father in *The Marble Faun*, he defended the Miltonic notion of the "fortunate fall." "Without salvation there can be no heaven," he declared, "and there can be no salvation without sin." As he wrote Minne the next day, "it was taken very cordially by the majority, who did not understand it: and created some consternation among the few who did."[35]

Somehow he found the time to knock out another potboiler, ironically one of his better novels. Titled *Love—or a Name*, the hero Warren Bell (a play on "Warning Bell") is loosely modeled on the young Julian: he has been dismissed from college, attended engineering school, and worked for the New York Dock Department. He foils a conspiracy by a group of corrupt politicians to annex Mexico and destroy American democracy under the guise of patriotism. "The dictatorship must seem to be forced upon us by the popular desire," the villain announces. That is, in this tale of political intrigue—serialized in the camping magazine *Outing* between April and

September 1885 and published between covers by Ticknor later the same year—Julian anticipated by a half century such antifascist, Depression-era novels as Sinclair Lewis's *It Can't Happen Here* and Nathanael West's *A Cool Million*. It was not well received, however. The *Washington Post* dismissed it as a "wretched" melodrama, and the *Literary World* said it was "stupidly dull." According to the *Nation*, "No one could open 'Love—or a Name' a second time, supposing it possible to read the dreadful tale to the end even once."[36]

In the wake of the critical failure of the novel, Julian reassessed his career and wrote his father's friend James Russell Lowell for advice. Lowell assured him that he had "not failed except as all men feel that they have failed when they contrast what they have done with what they dreamed of doing." Julian did not abandon writing, but he tempered his literary ambitions. "I have never had the opportunity to write as I would wish," he wrote the poet Paul Hamilton Hayne. "I used to fancy that time might come: but I know better now. And, were it to come, very likely I should do nothing."[37]

*   *   *

When Rose reconciled with George Lathrop in the spring of 1884, Julian reconciled with him, too. They were both members of the Authors Club and moved in the same social circles. They participated on successive days in late April 1885 in what Mark Twain called "a new and devilish invention," public readings by authors for charity, in this case for the International Copyright League. Twain remembered that the Madison Square Theatre "was packed, and the air would have been very bad only there wasn't any. I can see that mass of people yet, opening and closing their mouths like fishes gasping for breath." Among the other readers were Howells and Warner. Julian read an excerpt from *Dust* and some of his passages about beer-drinking from *Saxon Studies*. Though the event was widely publicized, Julian thought that, "like all such affairs, [it] was a failure."[38]

In late 1885 he and George laid plans to found a new weekly paper titled *Ours*, though they soon abandoned the project. They also began to collaborate on several theatrical scripts, including a drawing-room comedy variously titled "Good Society," "Tactics," and "Love and Passion," based at least in part on the play Julian co-wrote with Willie Dixon in 1878, in which an urbane and snobbish American traveler and a sheltered American ingénue debate the merits of the caste system in England. They approached the producers A. M. Palmer and Augustin Daly with it. "Lathrop and I have two or three plays on the stocks, one of which we think may possibly suit your theatre," Julian advised Daly. "It is modern society comedy, not so light as you have been producing lately, but with emotional passages alternating with amusing ones." Nothing came of these overtures. In 1886 Julian persuaded the Polish-born actress Helena Modjeska to add the play to her repertoire, although she never produced it. "Like most persons who follow literature for a living, I had a persuasion that I might write a play," he later admitted, but his friend Bronson Howard discouraged this ambition. "I arrived at the conviction that the proper end and aim of my existence (if there were any) was not playwriting."[39]

Julian supposedly collaborated on a different project around this time with another writer—a dead one. As a Swedenborgian he had long been interested in spiritualism, particularly such psychic phenomena as telepathy and astral bodies. He sometimes lectured on the philosophy of magic and mysticism; followed the investigations by the London Psychical Research Society; attended at least one séance; had his hand read by the famous palmist Cheiro; and often featured trances, clairvoyance, and hypnotism in his fiction. In his story "Ken's Mystery" (1883) he expressed sympathy for the victims of vampires. One reviewer compared it to a "wild dream" that "might have been evolved from the fumes of a good hot whiskey punch." At Sag Harbor in the summer of 1885, he played with a planchette, a type of Ouija board. Experimenting with the device (so Julian claimed) with one of his daughters, a farmer from beyond the pale recounted over a period of twenty days "a sensational and tragic tale" of disappointed love. In an attempt to prove its authenticity, Julian insisted that "the spelling of the planchette-writing" was "much better than in [his daughter's] own letters and journals." He transcribed the story and sent it to the *Independent*, which not only published it under the title "A Planchette Tragedy" and under Julian's name but also paid him a hundred dollars for it.[40]

In December 1885 Julian, Lathrop, Mark Twain, and others were allied in a fight over membership rules in the Authors Club. Its rolls over time had swelled to include archeology students at one extreme and the multimillionaire Andrew Carnegie at the other. The popular newspaper poet Will Carleton, author of *Farm Ballads* (1874), stood for election and was blackballed by the Richard Watson Gilder faction of the club on the ground that his verse was lousy. Julian came to Carleton's defense by lobbying other members, including Lathrop and Twain. Carleton had received the requisite four-fifths of the vote, but the Gilder group challenged the results, whereupon the club's executive council "went into session and determined that the election must be held over again" at the next meeting. Julian was so troubled by the ploy that he decided "to do all I can now to get Carleton elected over again." He had never politicked before. "This is the first electioneering document I ever penned, and the first election in which I ever voted," he quipped to Twain. He didn't like Carleton's poetry either, "but I voted for him, because he is *par excellence* an American author, a man who had done honest work," and "such transactions as those of last night will ruin the Club if they are allowed to stand."[41]

Twain replied from Hartford a week later. He was troubled, too. He agreed with Hawthorne "in all your points—except one. You think certain conduct *will* ruin the club; whereas I think that that sort of procedure has already ruined it. It isn't an Author's club at all. It is no more an Author's club than it is a horse-doctor's club. Its name is a sarcasm." Whether or not Twain assigned his proxy vote to Julian on "the Carleton question" or voted in person, Carleton was reelected to membership and Julian elected to the executive council of the club at its next meeting. Twain and Julian occasionally socialized during these years, too. They were among a retinue of writers who sometimes met at the Hoffman House near Madison Square after club events to swap stories over drinks. They rendezvoused in other ways: both of them contributed to the September 1893 issue of *Cosmopolitan* and the September 1895 issue of *Harper's Monthly*. Although Julian's critical judgments were notoriously harebrained, he was right at least on this point: Mark Twain "is probably our best writer now living."[42]

*   *   *

Julian was not a particularly astute critic of his father's writings. He considered the character of Pearl, for example, "the true creation" of *The Scarlet Letter*: "Every touch upon her portrait is a touch of genius, and her very conception is an inspiration." Nor did he appreciate the portrayals of Zenobia ("too hard") and Priscilla ("too diaphanous") in *The Blithedale Romance*. His blinders did not prevent him from writing dozens of articles about his father's fiction over the years, however, especially in the mid-1880s. He contributed a series of four essays between May 1884 and May 1886 to *Century* and the *Atlantic* based partly on his visits to the sites where the stories were set (e.g., Salem and Brook Farm). He hoped eventually to collect these and other pieces in "a book of 500 pages homogeneous with the Biography; and fitted to be a supplement to that work."[43] The volume never materialized.

All the while his own stories were becoming more sensational and less mannered. Henry Cabot Lodge, the owner of the *Boston Evening Record* and future U.S. senator from Massachusetts, invited him early in 1886 to contribute a novella to the newspaper. Julian submitted a sensational success story titled *John Parmelee's Curse*, for which he was paid $616. "It is written in the paragraphic style and in a popular vein," he informed Ticknor, "and will have a wider circulation, I think, than anything I have done." Set partly in a New England village and partly in a New York opium den, the tale piles coincidence upon coincidence as the hero is promoted from office boy to clerk to cashier of the bank. One of the characters, Newsboy Bob, is first cousin to Horatio Alger's Ragged Dick. As the *San Francisco Bulletin* sniffed, "There is not a page of it which could not have been written by a lively miss of fourteen."[44]

* * *

Though he had initially been welcomed to Sag Harbor, Julian's honeymoon there ended abruptly in July 1885 when he thrashed the teenaged son of a neighbor for throwing rocks at his barn. His parents charged Julian with assault and the local magistrate fined him forty dollars. Unfortunately, the incident did not end there. For months afterward he was harassed—his wire fences cut, his livestock poisoned, and strange cattle herded into his gardens. As usual, he was also in desperate financial straits, working "at syndicate stories or anything that offered itself." In early June 1886, he begged William Ticknor for an advance of three hundred dollars. When Joseph Pulitzer offered him the literary editorship of the *New York World* a couple of weeks later, he jumped at the job and decided to move. He leased a large house he named Hawthornden in Scotch Plains, New Jersey, less than an hour's commute from the city.[45]

The job with the *World* seemed to be a godsend. Pulitzer started him at a salary of sixty dollars a month and soon raised it to one hundred dollars, though the rumor got around that Julian was paid over four hundred dollars a month, or five thousand dollars a year. The first book he reviewed for the paper was Tolstoy's *Anna Karenina*, and soon his department was attracting attention for "its masterful and discursive style." He "read all I could get hold of [Ivan] Turgenieff" and the other Russians, and noticed new translations of Gustav Flaubert, Nikolai Gogol, and Honoré de Balzac as well as more typical fare—stories by H. Rider Haggard, Elizabeth Stuart Phelps, and Charlotte Yonge. He solicited contributions from Gail Hamilton, and he covered the dedication of the Statue of Liberty in New York Harbor ("she seems but a moment ago to have assumed the attitude which she will retain through centuries to come").[46] And then he overreached.

In fall 1885, a few months after the publication of Julian's biography of his parents, James Russell Lowell had agreed to contribute the volume on Nathaniel to the American Men of Letters series issued by Houghton Mifflin. No doubt the report alarmed Julian. Lowell, who made only cameo appearances in *Nathaniel Hawthorne and His Wife*, had known his father before Julian was born, and was a respected man of letters who was well connected with all the leading writers, editors, and publishers in the Anglo-American literary establishment.

As literary editor of the *World*, with a circulation of about three hundred thousand, Julian hit upon a surefire method of warding Lowell off the project: by embarrassing him before the world. He visited his former tutor at his home, Deerfoot Farm, in Southborough, Massachusetts, for four hours one day in mid-October 1886. A few days later, on Sunday, October 22, Julian published a version of their conversation titled "Lowell in a Chatty Mood." During their talk, as Julian reported it, the former U.S. ambassador to England spoke indiscreetly on many subjects, including the British royal family. He remarked that the Prince of Wales was "very fat" and predicted that Queen Victoria would outlive her consort because "she is very tough." The late Prince Leopold, the duke of Albany, had been "the greatest cad I ever knew in my life." Prime Minister William E. Gladstone he found "rather unmanageable." He didn't like Thomas Hardy's fiction. If he could afford the expense, he would immigrate to England permanently, because "I have more personal friends" there "than I have here."[47] Lowell said more than enough to offend readers on both sides of the Atlantic.

When the interview appeared, Lowell was thrown on the defensive. He insisted in a card to the *Boston Advertiser* that he had not been told that he was speaking on the record and that he did not expect Julian to breach his confidence: "It never entered my head that the son of my old and honored friend was 'interviewing' me. If it had he would have found me dumb." Privately, Lowell protested Julian's "scurvy trick" and compared it to "a dead rat in the wall,—an awful stink and no cure." Julian "*knew* that I didn't know he was interviewing me. To any sane man the shamble-shamble stuff he has made me utter is proof of it." Predictably, Julian proclaimed his innocence. While Lowell doubtless "believes every word that he has written in his letter to the *Advertiser*," Julian harbored "no doubt until this moment that Mr. Lowell knew I was interviewing him." Lowell replied in turn by questioning Julian's integrity: "If he shall assert that he told me for what he came and that I understood him, I shall feel obliged to leave the matter to those who know us both." In his final public response, Julian posed as the injured party: "Your letter was calculated to do me serious injury, both as a man and as a journalist, and to cast discredit upon the paper which employed me. . . . *I explicitly told you what I came for.*"[48] Rather than prolong the public debate, Lowell chose the better part of valor.

The brouhaha, like the controversy over Julian's publication of his father's comments about Fuller two years before, simmered in the press for weeks, a tempest in a Boston teapot. Many journalists publicly defended Julian as a brother reporter. His Harvard chum Bill Blaikie expressed his admiration for "Hawthorne's frank, open manner all the more it is placed in contrast to the pie-crusty style of Lowell. . . . Hawthorne is a gentleman and he is above deceit." Julian's friend Eugene Field, a satirical poet and columnist on the staff of the *Chicago Daily News*, defended him in a parody of Lowell's "Biglow Papers" titled "The Official Explanation" and narrated in Down East dialect by Hosea Biglow.

> One night aside the fire at hum,
>   Ez I was settin' napp n'
> Down from the lower hall there come
>   The seound uv some one rappin'.
> The son uv old Nat Hawthorne he—
>   Julian, I think his name wuz—
> Uv course he feound a friend in me,
>   Not knowin' what his game wuz.
>
> And ez we visited a spell,
>   Our talk ranged wide an' wider,
> And if we struck dry subjects—well,
>   We washed 'em down with cider.
> Neow, with that cider coursin' thru
>   My system an' a playin'
> Upon my tongue, I hard knew
>   Just what I wuz a sayin'.
>
> I kin remember that I spun
>   A hifalutin' story
> Abeout the prince uv Wales on' one
>   Abeout old Queen Victory.
> But, sakes alive! I never dreamed
>   The cuss would get it printed—
> (By that old gal I'm much esteemed,
>   Ez she has often hinted).
>
> Oh, if had that critter neow,
>   You bet your boots I'd larn him
> In mighty lively fashion heow
>   To walk the chalk, god darn him!
> Meanwhile, between his folks an' mine
>   The breach grows wide an' wider,
> And, by the way, it's my design
>   To give up drinkin' cider.

In the long run, however, the scandal indelibly scarred Julian's reputation. Many fellow authors thought him an unprincipled knave. The *Springfield* [Massachusetts] *Republican* declared that if he would only develop a conscience, "he would be one of the most charming men of letters in America." George William Curtis accused him of "the worst breach of faith I have ever known to occur in journalism." Howells characterized the interview in letters to Edmund Gosse and Henry James as "a most cruel betrayal" and "cruel atrocity." James judged Julian guilty of a "beastly and blackguardly betrayal" of confidence. He wrote Lowell that the episode proved "how dangerous & noxious a man may become when he is so discredited (as J. H. has been, I take it, for a long time,) that he has no further credit to lose. . . . He ought to be shot & that is the end of it." Julian's role in the scandal inspired James's portrayal of George Flack, an unscrupulous young American reporter in *The Reverberator* (1888), of whom another character declares, "He ought to be shot."[49] Though Julian's editors at the *World* publicly defended him against all allegations of impropriety, he was quietly fired five months later. But his warning shot across Lowell's bow served its purpose. Lowell never wrote a biography of Nathaniel, because he knew that if he did, Julian was lying in the weeds poised to attack.

1887–96
"The literary profession is no sinecure"

When Julian was fired by the *World,* he was thrown back upon his own resources. He had discovered during his stint with the newspaper the influence of the accounting room, or the extent to which expectations of subscribers, and especially advertisers, may shape the contents of a publication. "In reality the advertisers are the formers of our literature," he concluded. They "refuse to advertise" in a publication that "does not reach the class of people with whom they trade."[1] In tacit recognition of the point, he penned a pair of stories—"The Heart of Amunuhet" and "A Thousand Years Are but as Yesterday"—exclusively for *Strawbridge and Clothier's Quarterly,* an advertising circular, to the chagrin of critics. No serious author would stoop to such a scheme to sell his work, and the *Boston Herald* deplored "his prostitution of talents."[2] Julian was untroubled; after all, his father had been the target of similar accusations in 1852 when he wrote Franklin Pierce's campaign biography. Even as Julian pitched his prose to more general readers, he doubled down on its price, increasing his rates from fifteen dollars per thousand words in 1884, to twenty dollars in 1886, to twenty-five dollars in 1887. By comparison, Howells earned about one hundred dollars per thousand words.[3] Moreover, Julian averaged between five hundred and one thousand dollars in royalties on each of the books, no matter how poorly they were reviewed.[4]

A case in point is the series of five detective novels he wrote in collaboration with Thomas F. Byrnes, the New York City chief inspector, in 1887–88. Julian did all the writing, and Byrnes supplied the plots and some local color. Among the earliest "true crime" or police procedurals, these novels proved to be extremely popular. Each of them was syndicated by McClure in some twenty newspapers; they sold in aggregate over a million copies in cheap editions; and they were translated into German, Swedish, and Dutch.[5]

Julian considered Byrnes "the greatest detective in the world,"[6] although in the novels he seems more like Poe's commonsensical prefect of police than the shrewd Dupin. Byrnes is best known today for inventing "the third degree," what might be described as "enhanced interrogation techniques." According to Jacob Riis, he "was unscrupulous. . . . His famous 'third degree' was chiefly what he no doubt considered a little wholesome 'slugging.'"[7] Although he accepted no bribes, Byrnes made a fortune in real estate while in the New York Police Department by following the investment advice of Jay Gould and other financiers. He was finally forced to retire in 1895 by the new police commissioner, Theodore Roosevelt.

Each of the five novels recounts the events surrounding an actual crime— for example, *A Tragic Mystery* (1887) was based on the Mike McGloin murder case of 1881, and *The Great Bank Robbery* (1887) centered on the New York bank heist of October 27, 1878. Together they introduce a rogues' gallery of criminals and construct a hierarchy of crime, with forgery in *An American Penman* (1887) the most prestigious felony, followed by robbery, then blackmail in *Section 558; or, The Fatal Letter* (1888) and *Another's Crime* (1888), then murder. Byrnes is a dogged investigator—he solves one mystery, for example, by the simple expedient of placing 118 post office boxes under simultaneous surveillance. He would have discovered a purloined letter had it been dropped in the mail. Despite their commercial success, however, the ostensible thrillers were critical disasters. The *Kansas City Star* again accused Julian of "prostituting genius." The *San Francisco Bulletin* complained they introduced readers to "a good deal of very low-life society" and "bear every mark of mere hackwork." The *Literary World* considered them "unfit for the reading of young people," at best good stories "of a bad kind."[8] Julian's reputation had fallen so low by the late 1880s that he was no longer considered up-and-coming but down-and-going. A reviewer in *Current Literature* echoed a famous libel in its dismissal of his fiction. John Ruskin scorned one of Whistler's nocturnes in 1877: he had "never expected to hear a coxcomb ask two hundred guineas for flinging a pot of paint in the public's face." Whistler sued Ruskin and won. Yet *Current Literature* declared with impunity a decade later that Julian had "reached a point where he no longer has to write; he simply throws a bottle of ink in the public's face."[9]

Not that Julian refrained from hurling the same brand of insults. As book editor between June 1886 and June 1889 of the *New York World, American Magazine, America,* and *Bookmart,* Julian routinely skewered books and authors he disliked. In fact, the best parts of his reviews were his bon mots; for example, Lady Brassey, author of *The Last Voyage,* "had not the intellect of an ordinary chambermaid." Another author was "so determined to give plenty of mustard with his beef that he sometimes omits the beef." "The best feature" of a new biography of Lewis Carroll, he quipped, "is its brevity." Elsewhere he was unintentionally funny, as when he used the phrase "gratuitous verbosity" without irony.[10] Henry David Thoreau became a special target of Julian's ire, apparently because his body had been reburied on Authors' Ridge in Sleepy Hollow Cemetery; thus, the town fathers had elevated "the hermit of Concord" to the rank of Emerson and his father in the literary pecking order of the village. Julian asserted not only that Thoreau had an "ultra-bilious physical organization" and a "bitter, selfish, jealous, and morbid" nature but also that he was "the most dismal fraud of the New England transcendental group."[11] Julian's critical judgments were often suspect and sometimes wrong, as in his comments on George Eliot. She "was not an artist," he opined; "she was simply an interesting storyteller," and Charles Reade's *Very Hard Cash* was "a much greater book than *Daniel Deronda*."[12] He was especially critical of Eliot's relationship with George Lewes: "The less said about George Eliot's private life the better. She was guilty of a great piece of folly, which impaired her genius and bedeviled her career."[13]

By the late 1880s, after the publication of Howells's *The Rise of Silas Lapham* (1885), "the romantic-idealists found it time to strip off their kid gloves and go to war" against literary realism, as Edwin H. Cady has explained. As a writer of sensation stories, the son of the greatest American romancer, and a book editor, Julian rallied if he did not rush to the front lines. To be sure, he was not a systematic literary theorist. His attitudes were essentially market-driven: the best fiction was often the best-selling fiction. But he resisted the inroads of realism. As the *Spectator* put it, "If the tendency of modern fiction" is toward realism, "it cannot be said that Mr. Julian Hawthorne is in the slightest measure influenced by this tendency."[14]

He opposed both Comstockery, or censorship, and realism, which he equated with indecency. He argued that governments had "no right" to enforce arbitrary standards of decency, that "corrupt freedom is better than enforced virtue," and that the Society for the Suppression of Vice under "the opera bouffe leadership" of "the accursed jackal" Anthony Comstock had "done more to augment and nourish the rottenness of the community than have all the vicious and criminal classes put together."[15] Yet he also turned his guns on Howells. Julian ridiculed the "spectacle" of Howells "industriously and gravely manufacturing mud pies." He joked that there had been a rumor that as editor of the *Atlantic*, Howells would "reject his own contributions." He discouraged aspiring authors from heeding

Howells's suggestions: "Howells says: 'Stick to nature; describe only what you see and know.' There never was advice more wrong and foolish. The public does not want to hear what you see and know." Privately, Julian derided Howells, who was, he said, "a man of transparent sincerity and circumscribed intelligence" and "a wooden stick—a non-conductor—painted to look like a lightning rod, but incapable of exercising or comprehending its functions."[16]

He disdained Walt Whitman no less. Soon after he was fired by the *World*, Julian was commissioned to write a sensational novella by Joseph Stoddart of *Lippincott's* much as a tailor would receive an order for a suit. Stoddart paid him one thousand dollars for "Sinfire,"[17] and it appeared alongside an excerpt from Whitman's "A Backward Glance o'er Traveled Roads" in the January 1887 issue of the magazine. Two years later, on May 31, 1889, the editor introduced the two authors. Julian accompanied Stoddart to Whitman's seventieth birthday celebration at Morgan's Hall in Camden, New Jersey, across the Delaware River from Philadelphia, where he delivered a brief toast in tribute to the poet. Julian joked later that "a haze as of green chartreuse arises whenever I look back in the direction of Philadelphia" on account of the quantity of absinthe they drank during his visit. (Absinthe "makes the heart grow fonder," he punned.)[18] Unfortunately, this anecdote masks Julian's true opinion of Whitman. In March 1892 he told an interviewer that he preferred "to abstain from comment on Whitman's work" until after the poet's death.[19] Whitman died two weeks later. Julian was too wedded to tradition, too fond of controversy, or too devoted to a sentimental ideal of middle-class heterosexuality ever to praise Whitman again. Instead, he resorted to personal smears: he was "the great American hog of letters." Far from a true poet, with "no understanding of form, no instinct for rhythm," Whitman wrote "lawless verse" that was merely "a huge bluff."[20]

*   *   *

In the summer of 1889, Julian was hired to accompany fifty skilled artisans—silversmiths, glass workers, carpenters, shoemakers, and so forth—on an excursion to Europe sponsored by the Scripps League of Western Newspapers. The junket was billed as educational and philanthropic in purpose, featuring a visit by manual laborers to the Exposition Universelle in Paris, but it was also promotional: the Scripps papers in Detroit, St. Louis, Cleveland, and Cincinnati targeted working-class readers, and they published daily bulletins during the tour, most of them by Julian. On July 23, the day before his departure, he was introduced to Lorenz Reich, a Hungarian-born

New York hotel magnate and wine importer, whose top-shelf Tokayer Ausbruch was a favorite of President Garfield, Henry Wadsworth Longfellow, and Mark Twain. That evening Reich sent an entire case of it to Julian's stateroom aboard the *City of Rome,* and as he later put it, "the Atlantic Ocean was never more like the Sea of Dreams than on that trip." Until Reich's death more than forty years later, their friendship "never waned or cooled."[21] Reich even named two of his sons Nathaniel and Julian.

The *City of Rome* was the largest passenger ship in the world, but Julian also considered it one of the dirtiest. On the whole he considered the trip "the most arduous enterprise that I had ever undertaken." Each of the artisans he accompanied "was chosen for special proficiency in his or her industry, each representing a separate trade," as he explained. "None of them, as it happened, had ever been in Europe, and what little any of them knew of it was from scant hearsay." Julian was a glorified tour guide as well as a working reporter. On August 1 the group landed in Liverpool. It was hardly a sentimental homecoming, though he did knock on the doors of Mary Blodget's boardinghouse and Monsieur Huguenin's gymnasium, only to learn that each of them was long dead. Worse yet, he learned by telegram that his house in Scotch Plains had been flooded a day or two earlier and much of his private library ruined, including some of his father's manuscripts.[22]

After touring the docks of Liverpool, the workers inspected the cotton factories of Manchester, the textile mills of Delph, the cutlery manufactories of Sheffield, and the ironworks of Birmingham. Along the way they enjoyed a holiday in Matlock Bath and Bradford. In Leeds, Julian visited the Saltaire Institute and bragged later that its library held copies of almost all of his books. On August 6 Lord Ripon guided them around the grounds of Fountains Abbey in North Yorkshire, and three days later they were the guests of honor at a dinner at the Tavistock Hotel in London attended by Robert Lincoln, U.S. minister to the Court of St. James and son of the sixteenth president.

The delegation sailed for the Continent on August 12 to attend the exposition in Paris. Julian dined for a final time with Francis Bennoch, who "was as jovial and eloquent as ever," although Julian noted without irony that "he was surrounded by parasites to the day of his death."[23] The group attended a performance of Buffalo Bill's Wild West in Paris at William F. Cody's invitation. When the Parisian police chief learned he "was personally acquainted with Inspector Byrnes of New York," Julian was welcomed "with great cordiality." During these days at the exposition, he first realized "that the ladies of the Orient danced after another fashion than our own." The "spectacle" was so "new and unprecedented that the first effect of it" on Julian was utter astonishment. The dancer's "body sways easily between her haunches" with movement "from the breasts to the junction of the thighs." Compared to the can-can, this style of dance "was as the song of Solomon to the latest Parisian boulevard ditty."[24] On August 23 Julian ascended the Eiffel Tower with some of the other delegates in company with Whitelaw Reid, the U.S. ambassador to France, and the next evening the group, along with Cornelius Vanderbilt and William B. Franklin, the U.S. commissioner-general for the exposition, was honored at a dinner hosted by Reid in the ambassadorial residence. Julian was seated at a place of honor next to Franklin. In all, he found that in both London and Paris "Americans are more popular than ever. They are regarded as good spenders, and their custom is sought everywhere."[25]

The group left Paris on August 24 for Brussels, Antwerp, and Cologne. Julian was overwhelmed by the sight of the Cologne Cathedral, "a mighty cliff of carven stone" and "beyond question the most magnificent specimen of Gothic architecture that the world has ever seen." They boarded a train for Bonn and from there cruised up the Rhine to the Drachenfels. After a stop in Essen to tour the Krupp munitions factory, they traveled to Rotterdam and sailed to Scotland, where they toured the shipyards of Edinburgh and Glasgow. They returned to Liverpool and departed on September 4 on the *City of Rome* for New York, arriving on September 12.[26]

*   *   *

With the loss of his job with the *World,* Julian no longer needed to live within commuting distance of New York. Between July 1887 and June 1889 he split time between Scotch Plains and Sag Harbor, where he could live more economically. He leased a hundred-acre farm with a Queen Anne house on the main highway to the village with a mile-long frontage on Shelter Island Sound about half an hour from the train station.[27] Thirty of the acres were cultivated (though the soil was barren, being so close to saltwater), thirty acres were in grass, and the other forty were wooded. Not only did Julian help with the haying in summer, but he also built a tennis court near the house, and Minne founded the Sag Harbor Tennis Club.[28] They were so well known locally that in 1925 the farm was subdivided into building lots and christened "Hawthorne Manor."[29]

During the winter of 1889–90, back in Sag Harbor full-time, Julian compiled a "compendium of American literature," a textbook for use in secondary schools. Leonard Lemmon, a Texas high-school principal, presented him with the draft of "a book on the literature of this country from John Smith of Pocahontas down to Howells" and proposed that if Julian would revise it, "he would reward me by putting my name in front of his on the title pages" and share half the royalties. Julian "rewrote the whole thing, rod, line, and sinker," and Lemmon appended "to each section an array of questions for students." They circulated the manuscript to every major publisher in New York and Boston before it finally found "a place to uncoil its lazy length" with the D. C. Heath Company, which "paid us good royalties for many years."[30]

The volume is certainly flawed. It devotes only thirteen pages to Puritan literature, for example, and it entirely ignores the poetry of Edward Taylor and Emily Dickinson, neither of whom had yet been canonized. It neglects literature by women and ignores ethnic writing entirely. Like Julian's other histories, it is derivative, based on similar histories by Charles F. Richardson and Reuben P. Halleck as well as E. C. Stedman's multivolume *Library of American Literature.* Julian also expresses typically blunt opinions; for example, Joel Barlow's epic poem "The Columbiad" was "the most stupendous and unmitigated failure in the annals of literature"; James Fenimore Cooper's *Precaution* was "one of the stupidest books ever written"; *Moby-Dick* was "the most powerful" of Melville's romances; and his father was "the greatest of American men of letters."[31] The volume was controversial for its alleged Southern bias. Critics decried its lukewarm praise for Whittier, Lowell, Holmes, and Franklin and inclusion of such writers as Jefferson Davis, William Gilmore Simms, and Sidney Lanier. Some public-spirited citizens even tried to ban it from the Flushing, New York, public schools in 1896. Theodore Roosevelt promised to read it so that he could "revile it."[32]

In June 1890 Julian penned perhaps the finest and most heartfelt prose of his life in recounting the death of his ninth child, Perdita, named for the lost princess in Shakespeare's *The Winter's Tale.* Minne was expecting her confinement on June 10, 1890, but

> early in the morning of the 6th she came to my door and told me to send for the doctor. . . . The doctor got here about 7. He saw Minne, and thought she would take some time. He had breakfast with us. At nine o'clock, as I was sitting in my study, Cecilia came to the door and said that the baby was born—she had heard it cry. A few minutes later, I saw Agatha, the German nurse; she said, in answer to my question, that the baby was "ein Mädchen [a girl]." Soon after, I went upstairs. Minne was lying on the bed, looking flushed and exhausted: the baby was being washed on the couch at the other side of the room. Minne said, with a smile, "I have told the Doctor this is the last baby I will have." It appeared the birth had been difficult. I went down again, but was soon told by

Cecilia that the Doctor wanted to see me. I went up, and found him in Agatha's room, at the end of the passage.

The doctor explained that the child had been born with spina bifida.

"I said, will it live?" He said, "Oh, no: it may live a few days, or weeks: it might even for some months: but it must die." I went down and told Cecilia; we decided it was better to tell Minne at once. She had already told me that she wished the baby to be named Perdita. I sat on the bed beside her, and took her hand and said, "My dear, we cannot keep this little baby with us." . . . I told her what the Doctor had said. She said, "Is it anything I have done?" I told her no. Indeed, the thing was a mystery: for Perdita was otherwise an unusually vigorous and healthy child, weighing over 9 pounds. . . . Minne shed tears: I could say nothing: the Doctor came up and attempted to say something soothing. Meantime the nurse had dressed little Perdita, and she was put beside her mother. She seemed singularly intelligent for a new-born baby: her eyes were open, and she kept them on her mother's face. We did not know how long she could live: we could not tell her: the only thing to do was to love her and try to make her easy. She did not cry much, or seem to suffer pain on account of her deformity. We thought it best to send for the minister, Mr. Lewis, and have her baptized at once. . . . The christening took place in the bedroom. Agatha held the baby in her arms. . . . During the afternoon, Perdita was quiet and well and took milk from her mother's breast. She seemed to know it was her mother. All went on quietly till morning. When I went to her, about noon, Minne and Perdita were there side by side, and Minne said with a smile, "I think she is going to live: she has eaten, and has slept four hours, and seems so well." I said, "Do you?" fearing she was mistaken, and would be the more bereaved when the loss came. She said, "It will be all right, whether she stays with us, or is taken away." I went to bed. In the dark of the night I was awakened by a tap at my door. Agatha's voice said, "Klein kind ist so vehwach [The little child is so misshapen]." It was then about half-past two. . . . I got up and lit the lamp, and went into Minne's room in my pajamas and stockings. The light was low, but it was easy to see Minne and the baby in the bed; Perdita lay on Minne's left arm. . . . At intervals of a second she drew her breath, with a little sound in the throat. It was a plaintive sound, hardly a painful one, except to our hearts, that knew the end was soon to come. I sat by the bed, and held Minne's hand in mine. We sat so for an hour, Agatha silent on the other side. Once I got up and bent over and kissed little Perdita on the face—the first and last kiss I ever gave her. . . . Minne said once, "It is awful." I said, "It is solemn, dear, but not awful; it is beautiful: I have never felt the love of the Lord so much as now." . . . Perdita continued to breathe, more and more slowly and gently. It was as gradual as the coming of the dawn. I do not know when it came. But at last she was still. Minne's tears came. Agatha got up and came round and looked at the clock and said "halb vier [half hour 'til four]." In a few moments I put my head down on the bed and cried. Minne put her hand on me and said some comforting word. We sat together for a while longer. Agatha took the little baby and carried her to the couch on the other side of the room. About four, I kissed Minne and went back to my room, and went to bed, and fell into a deep sleep. It was just before dawn.

In the morning Imogen awakened me, and I dressed her, and myself, and went into the room. The little child's body lay on the couch in its white dress and shawl. . . . Henry Amelung went into the village and learned that we could have the child buried here on the place. We decided it should be done that afternoon. After lunch Henry went in again, and sent out Archibald to dig the grave and bring the coffin—a little white coffin, not thin but long, lined with white satin. We chose, at Minne's suggestion, a spot under some cedars, and close by a sweet-briar bush, near the drive: the grave faces the east and the bay. Archibald gave me the coffin, and I carried it up to Minne. Then, while I sat beside her, Agatha put the little baby in it, and fastened down the lid. When it was done, I took it up in my hands, and held it to Minne, who laid her cheek against it and kissed it, crying, and I too kissed it. I took it downstairs. The children had put a white cloth on the round table in the drawing-room, and had covered it with the great white daisies and the white clover from the field. I put the coffin there, and put some of the flowers on it. . . . After a chat with Lewis in my study, we came out, and stood round the table in the drawing-room. Lewis put on his official vestment, and stood up, and read the service and the prayer. . . . When the time came, I took up the little white coffin in my hands, with the daisies on it, and a sprig of sweet-briar, and went out of the house to the grave. . . . Mr. Lewis now read the conclusion of the service. . . . I had taken a sprig of sweet-briar from the lid of the coffin before lowering it down, and kept it to give to Minne.[33]

Julian later planted the grave in flowers and wrote a sonnet about his infant daughter.

> Though oft I pause by this small, grassy mound,
>> Gemmed with forget-me-not, shadowed by trees,
>> By soft rains moistened, swept by the sea-breeze,
> . . . well I know, not here—not underground—
>> Rests the innocent child whom Memory sees.[34]

Minne was pregnant ten times and gave birth to nine children during the first nineteen years of their marriage. That is, for nearly two decades she was pregnant more than a third of the time. During the fifty-three months between April 1878 and September 1882, she was pregnant more than half the time. Little wonder that at the age of forty-one, after the birth of Perdita, she chose to bear no more children. Without a reliable means of birth control, she was probably sexually abstinent the rest of her life.

*   *   *

During the 1890s Julian's wielded a pen for hire. He became a regular columnist for *Collier's Once a Week* and its successor *Collier's Weekly*, contributing more than 120 stories and essays to its pages; and he freelanced for the *New York Herald*, the *New York Commercial Advertiser*, the *Philadelphia Press*, and several newspaper syndicates. In 1891 he was paid one thousand dollars for a history of Oregon to be sold by subscription. He had never visited the Pacific Northwest, however, so he compiled the chronicle entirely on the basis of published sources, including histories by H. H. Bancroft and H. L. Wells. Half of the two-volume history consisted of biographical sketches of citizens of the state, who paid for the privilege to be included, so he hired a local researcher, George E. Yerger, to ghostwrite them. The 920-plus-page *Story of Oregon* appeared on schedule the next year. However, H. W. Scott, the editor of the *Portland Oregonian*, withdrew his approval of the project when he discovered it was "merely an advertising scheme of cheap and commonplace character," and many of the subscribers, particularly the Oregonians who were the subjects of the ghostwritten sketches, refused to accept delivery of the volumes on the grounds that Julian was not their actual author and sued to recovery their money. Yerger in turn sued Scott for libel in the amount of one hundred thousand dollars. In reply, Scott insisted he had been tricked into endorsing the work, because he "supposed that the person who was named as the author would do nothing to discredit or diminish the luster of a great ancestral name."[35]

Julian was just trying to earn a living. He had long since abandoned all pretense to the kind of literary success his father had enjoyed. Writing was "a trade," he insisted, or "a means of livelihood. You pass your imagination through the ink bottle, and it comes out in the shape of bread and meat, coats and shoes." Much as Melville had once described it as "sawing wood," Julian compared it to "making nails or horseshoes." Not only did he not enjoy writing, but he also discouraged aspiring writers from adopting it as a profession. "Even the leading authors barely make a living" by the pen—he estimated that "hardly half a dozen in 10,000 can expect to make a decent living"—"and for the others, the time employed in writing could not be spent in a less remunerative way.... The literary profession is no sinecure." Virtually everything he had published had "been written from necessity; and there is very little of it that I shall not be glad to see forgotten." He wryly joked, "Necessity is the mother of literature." Whereas Emily Dickinson had declared succinctly that "publication is the auction of the mind," Julian declared even more succinctly that "Pegasus must sometimes pull the plough." For all his trouble, he barely stayed ahead of his creditors. Julian's son Fred remembered that his father "was always hard-pressed to support" his family "by pen alone." Nor did he escape the "dun": "I still have indelible memories of tradesmen wearing out the 'Welcome' mats at our various residences, looking for payment for groceries, butchers and bakers, etc." The family became so desperate for money that Minne asked Rose and George to urge the editor Richard Watson Gilder to suggest to President Grover Cleveland that he appoint Julian to a diplomatic post. Julian lent his name, no doubt for a "consideration," to an enterprise called the Central Florida Phosphate Company, with offices in the Equitable Building on Broadway in New York, on whose letterhead he is listed as "secretary."[36]

He accepted virtually every writing assignment offered him, no matter how trivial, so long as it was remunerative. He followed the gothic excesses of "The Secret of the Were-Wolf" (1889) in the sensational *New York Ledger* with a pseudonymous tale—"A Mystery of the Campagna" (1891), a vampire story in the manner of his friend Bram Stoker's *Dracula*—in Cassell's Library of "unknown" authors. In November 1891, armed with letters of introduction from his philanthropist friend George W. Childs, Julian interviewed several federal officials, including James G. Blaine, the secretary of state; John Wannamaker, the postmaster general; and A. R. Spofford, the librarian of Congress. He was even invited to the White House to interview President Benjamin Harrison—"a short-necked, clumsy, inconsequential little creature, with the brains of an attorney and the manner of a village selectman." In July 1892 Julian railed to Mexico to meet members of the government there and to examine "some of the mining properties. My original profession was engineering, and it is a pity I didn't stick to it." The trip prompted him to bang out *The Golden Fleece* (1892), a novella about the gold and jewels of Montezuma hidden from the Spanish in the sixteenth century and recovered by a reincarnated Aztec priest in the nineteenth. The *San Francisco Call* considered the tale more evidence that Julian was "degenerating." The *Chicago Tribune* noted that to resolve the labyrinthine plot, Julian had introduced several *deux ex* creaky and contrived *machinae*: "magic arts, occultism, earthquakes, subterranean floods, and a few other phenomena."[37]

The next year he wrote an op-ed piece on the Homestead strike in which he defended Andrew Carnegie, the steel industry, and the Pennsylvania national guard in their clash with labor. An advocate of laissez-faire, he considered the strike "a spectacle but nominally distinguishable from anarchy. Indeed avowed anarchy took a hand in the battle, in the attack on one of the firm's managers," Henry Clay Frick. The discharged workers had been spanked by the Invisible Hand for continuing to live in company housing after they had been fired. That is, Carnegie was "in the position of a householder whose discharged servants bar him out of his own house and will only admit him on his promise to reemploy them on their own terms and to forever renounce all servants but them." The only mistake the company made, Julian insisted, "was in sending in Pinkerton guards." After killing seven Pinkerton agents, the strikers were "like burglars who fortify a man's house against him and shoot him down on his attempt to enter." Julian ignored the fact that nine strikers had been killed, too. Instead, he upheld the "sacred" right of employers "to conduct their business in their own way" and of scabs to replace union men—rights to be protected, if necessary, "by the whole force of the State." Nor did he have faith in the efficacy of compulsory arbitration. "The remedy for 'Homestead,' then, and solution of all else insoluble disagreements between Labor and Capital," was the so-called safety valve in the West: "give the underpaid laborer free recourse to the unused land."[38] Such a notion begged the question whether industrial workers could earn their living by farming.

By mid-1892 Julian worked more frantically and carelessly than ever. He cranked out a novella, "A Messenger from the Unknown," featuring a fair damsel in a trance for over twenty years, for *Collier's Once a Week*. To boost circulation (and thus advertising revenue) it was offered as a premium to every purchaser of the May 3, 1892, issue of the magazine. On July 11 Julian started a fifty-thousand-word story that was due to the editors of *Godey's* on August 1; that is, he procrastinated so long that he was obliged to average twenty-five hundred words of publishable prose a day for twenty days to meet the deadline.[39] The nightmarish novella—"Brabazon Waring"—betrays the haste with which it was written. The episodic plot is as fantastic as it is incoherent: the hero lives in a cavern on a four-hundred-square-mile tract of land in the mountains of northern California and imports five hundred European workers to sculpt the landscape and remodel his cave. The tale was accompanied by ink drawings by Dan Beard, best known today for illustrating the first edition of Mark Twain's *A Connecticut Yankee in King Arthur's Court* (1889).

That autumn Julian was instrumental in the founding of the Syndicate of Associated Authors. Attracting such members as George Lathrop, Eugene Field, Thomas Nelson Page, Frank Stockton, and Joel Chandler Harris, the group expected to supply fiction and feature stories directly to newspaper editors without working through agents or such established syndicates as Bacheller and McClure. It also planned to sponsor a voyage around the world led by Julian in search of literary material for the syndicate, a revival of his wistful fantasy fifteen years earlier. He would be accompanied by Minne and the children as well as passengers willing to pay sixteen hundred to five thousand dollars for the privilege. Within weeks, the scheme was so far advanced that Julian had letterhead printed for "The Literary

Argonauts"; selected a name for their ship (the *Sargasso*); and leased a "low, raking, piratical-looking craft." He was again forced to abandon the pipe dream, however, as a result of the Panic of 1893 and the ensuing economic depression.[40]

Like Howells, Theodore Dreiser, and other prominent American writers, Julian covered the Columbian Exposition in Chicago—the so-called White City in Jackson Park—during the summer of 1893. In fact, he toured the exposition in February while the buildings were still under construction. Accompanied by Hildegarde, Julian returned to Chicago in May and remained until July.[41] He contributed some undistinguished articles about the fair to *Cosmopolitan* and *Lippincott's* in which he remarked on the musical stylings of John Philip Sousa's band, the original Ferris wheel, and the "savage natives of the Fiji Islands" on the Midway Plaisance.[42]

Julian's more significant literary accomplishment during his sojourn in Chicago was his authorship of a parodic guidebook titled *Humors of the Fair*, a throwback to his satirical *Saxon Studies*. He described it as "an antidote to the various guidebooks which you will be compelled to buy, or have already bought," and he assured the reader of his "sustained effort . . . to divest its pages of anything that could be construed as Useful Information." He referred the visitor to an "equestrian figure made of corn-cobs, or some such material," in the California Building and a malfunctioning device "to manufacture cigarette wrappers" in Machinery Hall. The nude statues in the gallery were so poorly executed they apparently are "all portraits of the artist's acquaintance." Of course, he also recommended to the prurient the exotic dancing of Little Egypt and the Circassian girls at the Persian Café.[43]

❊   ❊   ❊

Rather than sail around the world on the *Sargasso*, Julian chose to emigrate to Jamaica. In October 1893 he finally completed the paperwork necessary to obtain clear title to the Chicago property once owned by Una and Rose, and he sold it immediately for seven thousand dollars. With this windfall he and Minne began to plan their move to the Antilles. P. F. Collier proposed that during his exile Julian contribute an article a week to *Collier's Weekly*. With the sale of the land, he had "become comparatively affluent" and anticipated "a long holiday. So I hesitated, but Peter kept repeating, 'A check every week—every week—every week'; and at last hypnotized me into assent."[44]

The family left New York on the *Ailsa* on December 2. After a stormy voyage the ship docked in Kingston on December 9, two days behind schedule. While Julian searched for a farm to lease, they resided in the fashionable

Kingston neighborhood of Cherry Gardens. He soon located a plantation with a house and a thousand acres of land on the northern coast of Jamaica eight miles from St. Ann's Bay available for $30 a month. The house, as Hildegarde described it, "backed against the soft rise of a green hill, with palms grouped about it, a lawn in front, and off to one side other, small houses, clustered together." Julian was convinced that—were it not for the native black population—he had discovered paradise on earth: Jamaica "was supreme above every other part of this world that I have visited" in climate and charm. The air was "of so pure a quality that meat and fish can be carried long distances, in spite of the heat, without spoiling." A single afternoon rain "filled a five thousand gallon cistern." "Jamaica rum, hot, with Jamaica pimento-leaves in it" was an ambrosial beverage "good enough for Olympus."[45] From his study window he gazed across the Caribbean to the cliffs of Cuba a hundred miles distant. Nearer at hand, he enjoyed verdant scenery. In the morning "the loudest sound that greeted his awakening ears was the buzz of hummingbirds." The payroll for seven servants was only $11.25 per week. "People grow young instead of old" here, he joked. "I am becoming quite a boy." "There was never a place or a climate better suited to my sort of industry," he decided, and he hoped the temperate conditions would have the same effect on Minne's health. She had escaped the brisk winds of Long Island for balmy Bermuda in the spring of 1889 during her pregnancy with Perdita, and Hildegarde agreed that her mother "needed a softer climate and an easier life" in order to recover her health. In the first entry in his journal for 1894, a month after their arrival on the island, in fact, Julian jotted, "Minne better."[46]

He also hoped to build a business in Jamaica "that would assure a future" for his boys. His father had saved part of his salary in Liverpool to pay for his tuition at Harvard, but Julian had failed utterly to plan for his own sons' educations. He expected to get rich by growing winter vegetables in Jamaica for sale in the eastern U.S. market, but the plan proved impractical—another burst pipe dream. He reveled in the details of the project, however, as in his story "The Tragedy of Peter Hackett" (1896): "Eight thousand [cucumber] plants to the acre; ten cents apiece, New York winter market; ten to a hill—say five; four thousand dollars an acre; crop matures in six weeks; three crops the season: twelve thousand dollars net in four months. Plant a hundred acres; allow ten per cent off for accidents; there's a million dollars clear." Hardly satisfied with a hundred acres, Julian expected his farm to grow to "ten thousand acres; from that I would have derived an annual income of ten million dollars net."[47]

But he underestimated the difficulty of hiring workers to clear the land and plant and gather the crops, and he had not realized that the harvest season coincided with the spring monsoons. In fact, he planted only twenty acres in cucumbers and potatoes the first winter. Even the few vegetables that his sons hauled to the docks were liable to languish there—Julian had no contracts to transport and distribute them, nor were the shipping companies obliged to carry his produce. His journal for all of 1895 reports exactly one shipment of vegetables: on March 4 "Henry & Fred went to St. Ann's with 95 doz. cucumbers for New York." In the end, according to Hildegarde, Julian's income from vegetables was little more than what he paid for the seeds. As the father figure remarks in her autobiographical novel, *Island Farm*, "Thought we'd roost here and raise spring vegetables and sell in New York for fancy prices. First-rate idea, only it don't seem to work."[48] The seven thousand dollars he received for the land in Chicago soon went the way of all vegetables. Once again he had miscalculated.

Undeterred, Julian decided to form a syndicate of West Indies vegetable exporters. "No doubt," he insisted privately, "were a syndicate controlling several millions and a line of fast steamers to take hold here, fortunes might be made in the winter vegetable business; but any private enterprise is doomed beforehand. The syndicate would have to own its own steamers, and its own wharves and warehouses in eight or ten Atlantic coast cities. Then they must import coolies from India to do the work, and experts in agriculture and packing to oversee it; and then, in two or three years, they would make a profit." If only ten thousand acres were cultivated between December and April "and the produce placed for sale in our seaboard cities, the profits, over and above all expenses and accidents, would be so enormous that I shall not state them." He discussed his scheme with Sir Henry Blake, the British governor of Jamaica, who, he claimed, was "enthusiastic about it, and says there is big money in it, and would himself take stock in the Company. He will also put us in the way of obtaining all the land and labor we want on the most favorable terms." Julian figured that "we should require about two and a half million dollars" to start, and "I might do it through an English syndicate, with the help of Sir Henry; but I particularly wish to keep it in American hands if possible."[49] Nothing came of these ambitious plans.

Instead, he harbored naïve hopes of wealth easily earned in Jamaica. After a year near St. Ann's Bay he moved his family in March 1895 to a plantation called "The Gardens" near Gordon Town, "an even more lovely place a little way up the hills, nine miles from Kingston." It consisted of "180 acres of first rate land, with an annual yield of $1000 worth of coffee, and several small tenants." He figured he could buy the property for twelve thousand dollars after three years, and "whether or not the syndicate materialises," it would "always be a good place to own and live in—healthy, accessible and beautiful."⁵⁰

Meanwhile, he was no more productive as an author than as a gentleman farmer. He ghosted a few pieces under Minne's name for *Youth's Companion*—sketches on shopping for yams, "Farming in Jamaica," and "Thanksgiving in Jamaica"—and knocked out a Sherlock Holmes parody, "The Adventure of the Lost Object," for the Bacheller syndicate. Though Bacheller paid him one hundred dollars for the story, Julian allowed that after a year on the island he had not "sold more than $1,000 worth of stuff since coming here—literary stuff, I mean." During the economic depression of the mid-1890s, "Nobody wants to buy anything; and as all the magazines have an immense quantity of material on hand, which they have bought and have not been able to use, they are using it now, and so keeping along until the storm is over; without reflecting that if meanwhile all the authors starve, they will ultimately starve, too." Not that he was liable to starve in Jamaica even if he never sold another article. These were his salad days, or his tropical fruit salad days. "I begin every day with fifteen oranges and a bunch of bananas," he reported, and his other meals included such delicacies as pineapples, peaches, grapes, mangos, honey, and coconuts. In addition, he finally had time to write at a normal pace. "I have been hard at work ever since coming here on a book and finished it this week," he explained. "It is a very short book after all, but I wrote it with some care—a thing I have not been able to do for a good many years past."⁵¹

Love Is a Spirit was a new departure for Julian—a psychological romance comprised largely of internal monologues. He read Henry James's *The Princess Casamassima* while writing it, and not surprisingly it is the most Jamesian of all his works. It features another love triangle: the poltroon Strathspey is married to Vivien but loves the innocent Jamaican native Yolande. On the one hand, Vivien "had ruined him, by the only means that can ruin such a man; sapping the sources of his energy, destroying the roots of his self-respect, stabbing the vitals of his aspiration." On the other, Yolande is erotic and exotic, with "fragrant lips of flesh and humid, gleaming eyes" and a "pliant body undulating in touch with his." The unabashed eroticism of the novel frightened editors, and it was rejected by *Harper's, Century*, the *Atlantic, Scribner's*, and *Cosmopolitan*.⁵²

The fictional Strathspey was not the only character in Julian's life at the time with relationship issues. Rose and George Lathrop had converted to Roman Catholicism in March 1891 to Julian's profession of approval. "Had you entered the Mohammedan, or even the Mormon church," he assured his sister, "I should still have rejoiced in the fact that you are consumed with your creator." (On his part, he added, "My personal salvation does not concern me," because he believed "no morality or immorality . . . could either increase or diminish the love of God towards me.") Two months later he assured her that he hoped "this first Catholic year of yours will be as happy as all the previous ones combined." But in February 1895, Rose finally left George for good. She sailed for Jamaica on the ninth, and as soon as she reached Julian's house, they "had a long talk . . . about her affairs." She admitted to her brother that George had behaved like "a maniac" and that she had asked an ecclesiastical court "to meet next autumn to pass on her case." She had suffered verbal if not physical abuse, and the court sanctioned their separation. Fortunately, she was financially independent, with an income from Houghton Mifflin of about two thousand dollars a year. Still, as Julian observed in his journal, "It is all a wretched business, and made ten times worse by her being a Catholic."[53] The family quarrels ended in April 1898 with George's death at the age of forty-six of complications from alcohol abuse.

Hildegarde almost made an unsuitable match the very next month. Jack had taken a job in the local American consulate and introduced her to H. C. Poundstone, a young naval officer aboard the USS *New York* anchored in Kingston Harbor. Julian was unimpressed. On March 11, 1895, he noted in his journal that he had "dreamed Hildegarde was married to that ass Poundstone, or someone like him." The nightmare nearly became reality. Three weeks later, "Poundstone drove home with Hildegarde, proposed to her, & she accepted him—like the vain little fool she is." For the next several days she could "think of nothing but Poundstone," and Julian was resigned to the officer's request for her hand. He "entirely disapprove[d] of the match, which is preposterous from any point of view: but she must do as she pleases and suffer the consequences at leisure." She was twenty-four with a promising literary career, having already published a few poems and stories. Poundstone called on Julian on April 2 and announced, in fact, that he did "not desire an engagement." The flummoxed Julian did not approve of this course, either: "I do not like his style. He does not act in the proper way." By the end of the week, Hildegarde "decided she had better break off with Poundstone" because he was indecisive. She was brokenhearted, but Julian maintained that "she has had a very lucky escape, as she will realize some day."[54] She traveled to Europe that summer to recover from her disappointment. In the meantime, Poundstone enjoyed a long and distinguished naval career, retiring twenty years later at the rank of commander.

*   *   *

In February 1895 James Gordon Bennett Jr. tried to entice Julian back to New York to become managing editor of the *Sunday Herald*. Julian replied with his terms: a salary of three hundred dollars a week guaranteed for one year. Bennett had a reputation as a tyrant with "a trick of getting drunk, and discharging his employees, or changing them around," and "I was not going to subject myself to contingencies of that kind," Julian reasoned. After "struggling with the question" for two months, Bennett finally declined. He "could go the $300 a week," according to Julian, "but the year's guarantee stuck in his crop."[55]

Ironically, on February 3, 1895, only days before Bennett contacted Julian about the job, the *New York Herald* announced a novel-writing contest, the winner to receive ten thousand dollars. Manuscripts were to be submitted anonymously by July 1, after which a committee of three readers would select the best. The *Herald* declared, with pardonable hyperbole, that it was "the greatest prize contest known to literary history." At his home in the Jamaican hills, Julian read the announcement and "marked it for a time when I should feel more disposed to industry." After a false start in February on a novel titled "Esau: The Natural Man," the moment finally occurred on May 26. He worked for seven hours a day for the next twenty days on a novel eventually titled *A Fool of Nature*. As he noted in his diary for June 6, "Wrote from 4 to 6:30. I write about 7 hours a day, and finish about as many pages. I am now at the 75th page—26250 words. I have to write 50000 in all (or more if I choose) so I am more than half through. I have been writing since May 26th—12 chap. I have till June 20 to finish—14 days. So I am two days ahead of time." He finished the manuscript at the stroke of midnight on June 15 and mailed it the next morning to Lorenz Reich. Not surprisingly, given the haste with which it was written, the novel is utterly forgettable: part roman à clef, part novel of manners, part murder mystery featuring such well-worn plot devices as mistaken identities, secret affairs, and lost treasure. He gleaned the names of his characters—such as the Reverend Christopher Plukerose Agabag, Murgatroyd Whiterduce, and Polydore Seamell—from "the lists of jurors in the 'English State Trials' reports."[56]

In his version of events, Julian was visited some weeks later by "an old negro woman striding up from the town" with a cablegram from New York. "I opened the envelope and read, 'You win prize on condition of abandoning anonymity.' 'Anonymity,' indeed! I hate to think what I wouldn't have abandoned for ten thousand dollars. I wired my consent later in the day." He soon left for New York and was met at Grand Central Depot by a "confidential friend" who conducted him first "to the newspaper office, where they actually gave me a check for the money," and afterward to the Hoffman House on Madison Square, where they "fared sumptuously." Of the three judges, he later learned, one "was drunk all the time and couldn't function. The second was a woman novelist" who "was so offended by the queer names given to the characters that she refused to give any verdict." The third judge, "the leading literary critic of the period, . . . accepted it with enthusiasm: of the three thousand and odd competitors it was my tropic-born progeny that landed the bacon; the cable was sent to me asking who I was; and you know the rest."[57]

Unfortunately, Julian was neither so innocent nor as deserving of the prize as he pretended. In fact, there is circumstantial evidence aplenty to indicate the contest was fixed. He orchestrated the conspiracy without allowing any of the other conspirators to know who was involved. He warned Reich on June 10, "Do not tell anyone that I have even competed for the prize—not Stoddart . . . it would go against my chances were the fact to leak out in any way." A week later, in his letter to Reich accompanying the manuscript, he expressed confidence in his submission: "The Book (value $10000) goes to you by port by the Morris steamer. Heaven grant it safe arrival!" Reich acknowledged receipt of the manuscript "on Tuesday the 25th June, & his delivery of it at the Herald Office on the 26th," and he notified Julian two weeks after the deadline for submissions with the names of ten potential judges, three of whom would make the final decision. Among them were Mayo Hazeltine of the *New York Sun*, Julian's friend for more than a decade; Joe Stoddart of *Lippincott's*, his friend for half a decade; and his brother-in-law George Lathrop. Despite Julian's earlier admonition, Reich asked in his letter "whether he should give a hint to Stoddart" about Julian's entry in the contest.[58] The fix was beginning to take shape.

Though not a final judge, Stoddart was instrumental in Julian's receipt of the prize. Either Reich contacted him about Julian's submission to the contest as he had proposed or (more likely) Julian contacted him directly, because Stoddart was soon privy to a secret: Julian had signed his manuscript with the pseudonym "Judith Holinshed," preserving his initials in the nom de plume. All Julian needed to do, if the judges wanted to award him the prize, was to reveal his authorship of the story—and by late July he had two agents (Reich and Stoddart) working on his behalf. The readers of the *Herald* selected the final judges: Hazeltine, Lathrop, and Amelia Barr. Of the three, only Barr was not an intimate. Hazeltine and Lathrop, it may fairly be said, were predisposed in Julian's favor. George could hardly oppose Julian's receipt of the prize so long as he hoped to reconcile with Rose.

The machinations of their deliberations during the summer and fall of 1895, and Julian's influence on them, are now impossible to trace in detail. The pages in Julian's diary for August 23–27, October 18–22, and November 23–27, 1895—the last days before he was notified that he had won the prize

Etching of Julian Hawthorne
(*New York Herald*, December 1,
1895, VI, 1).

and his name announced—have been excised. But as early as mid-September
Julian presumed he had won. Expecting the announcement by the end of
the month, on September 17 he sent an "order" for the prize check signed
with the name Judith Holinshed to Stoddart to present to William Reick,
city editor of the *Herald*. Stoddart replied on October 30 that because the
final decision had not yet been announced, "of course there was nothing to
do further about this. The moment the announcement is made and I hope
to God that it will be in your favor, I shall act promptly you may be assured." The remainder of Stoddart's letter, preserved in Julian's scrapbook
in the Bancroft Library, has been mutilated or pasted shut. Certainly Julian
became familiar with their deliberations. Again, as he later reported, Lathrop
was "drunk all the time"; Barr was "offended by the queer names"; and
Hazeltine was "the leading literary critic" who read his submission "with
enthusiasm" and awarded it the prize.[59]
    Julian was informed by cablegram on November 26, 1895, that he had
won the ten thousand dollars not by Reick of the *Herald* but by Stoddart.
Of course, Reick wanted to know the identity of "Judith Holinshed." Julian
was forced to abandon his pseudonym as a condition of the prize—but only
after the judges had named him the winner. Meanwhile, Stoddart continued
to work behind the scenes to arrange for payment of the prize money. "You
may depend upon it," he wrote Julian on November 28, that "I am doing all
that I can to get you the money as soon as I can, if for no other reason than
to enable you to come home and be with us again." Edward W. Bok, editor
of the *Ladies' Home Journal*, publicly applauded Julian after his receipt of

the "rich plum" was announced on December 1. "It is but stating an open secret," Bok added, "that of late years the fortunes of this once favorite novelist have not been of the rosiest character. Hawthorne at one time had practically everything his own way in his profession. His early work was strong, and he found a ready market for his novels and stories. But he soon lost sight of his art and produced too much, and not of the best at that."[60]

Julian received dozens of congratulatory letters and telegrams—one from Ben Ticknor, another from his co-conspirator Lorenz Reich, still another from the lecture agent James B. Pond. Julian replied to Pond by ridiculing the contest. He had "rattle[d] off two hundred pages of glittering rubbish" in three weeks "and lo!—he wins the $10,000 prize." Upon its serialization in the *Herald* between January 1 and 12, 1896, the reviewers of the novel largely expressed an opinion of it similar to Julian's. The *New York Times* complained it was "a highly spiced and utterly indigestible, romantic potpourri" with "voluminous" padding. The reviewer for *Bookman* insisted he would not have presented "even a ten-cent prize" to the novel. William Morton Payne asked in the *Dial*, "If this story was the best of the hundreds entered, what must the others have been?" Six years later, the novel was banned by the Evanston, Illinois, public library.[61]

Nevertheless, the award threatened to rejuvenate Julian's writing career. On November 30, 1895, he calculated that he had "already written enough things to make $17,000 at least the coming year (including the Prize)." Though they had earlier rejected *Love Is a Spirit* for serialization, the Harpers accepted it for publication in cloth covers that summer. It was the last of his novels to be issued by a major publishing house. He offered another serial novel complete in manuscript to Frederick Macmillan "to begin 1897 in [his] magazine, price $15,000," but having once been burned on *Fortune's Fool*, Macmillan was twice shy. In the first blush of his success, Julian offered four other finished stories to the American newspaper syndicates for ten thousand dollars. They were "to comprise all I shall publish in 1896."[62] None of them was ever printed.

Julian waited until early February 1896 to claim the prize money, though it was available to him a month sooner. He wanted to play the part of the literary lion upon his arrival in the United States, so he had to stage a triumphant return. In late January he sailed alone to New York, where he was feted by Collier, Reich, the Aldine Club, and the Authors' Guild and initiated into the Masonic Lodge. He traveled to Washington to see friends and accompanied the Stoddarts to Atlantic City. He visited Westchester County to scout for a new house, and when he found one in New Rochelle, an artists' colony, he summoned Minne and the children to join him. He was the guest of honor at a breakfast hosted by his new neighbors, among them painter and sculptor Frederic Remington and E. W. Kemble, best known today for illustrating the first edition of *Adventures of Huckleberry Finn*. In an interview a year later, he admitted that he had been surprised by the success of *A Fool of Nature*, "but one may sometimes do his best work without knowing it."[63]

*　*　*

William Randolph Hearst, the ostentatious owner of the *New York Journal*, immediately recruited Julian to be a type of roving "super-reporter" or reporter-at-large dispatched on the spur of the moment to the sites of breaking news. Julian joined a stable of Hearst journalists that included Damon Runyon, Walter Camp, Dorothy Dix, Ella Wheeler Wilcox, and Ambrose Bierce. His first assignment, however, was utterly banal: a series of feature articles about Atlantic City, Long Branch, and Saratoga resorts. Coincidentally, a train wrecked near Atlantic City while Julian was there, and he filed a story about the disaster exactly suited to Hearst's brand of sensational, or "yellow," reporting—an omen of things to come.[64]

For the next decade he was at the height of his fame, a mercenary with a byline, brandishing not a pistol but a pen. He contributed almost exclusively to the yellow press and hewed the Hearst party line. He was an unapologetic defender of so-called advocacy journalism, what Hearst termed "government by newspaper." Yellow papers represented "the incarnate civic virtue of the nation," Julian insisted, and were "the most effective discouragers of vice in the world." He conceded that they were "often open to abuses, and guilty of them," but he contended that on the whole they exercised an ameliorating influence in a democracy. All articles in yellow newspapers were signed, Julian pointed out, so there was no pose of objectivity in slanted reporting as in the mainstream press. In other words, Julian became a political hack no less than a literary one. As a Hearst *apparatnik*, he was again accused of prostituting his name, exactly as had been the case ten years earlier when he published his fiction in advertising circulars.[65]

For a period of several years around the turn of the twentieth century there were few high-profile murder trials in America that Julian did not report for the *Journal*. He was the designated "crime reporter" for the paper, but he didn't cover the police blotter. On April 26, 1895, Maria Barberi (aka Barbella) killed her fiancé, Dominico Cataldo,[66] who had drugged and raped her, according to sworn testimony. Her first trial, in July 1895, ended in a conviction for murder but was overturned on appeal. Julian covered her second trial in November and December 1896 for Hearst. In the interim Maria had learned to speak halting English, and, more to the point, the

New York Journal, New York World, and other yellow papers had aroused public sympathy on her behalf. Julian's job was to rouse the public even more.

Maria at first seemed "rattled" by the prosecution. "She seemed to me like a child who is severely scolded and fears a whipping," Julian reported. "Her mental faculties were confused and numbed." The explanation was simple: at her first trial she had been questioned in Italian, but at the second the questioning was done in English. Julian was not surprised "that she should fail to recognize" her earlier testimony when it was read to her in translation. She expressed no remorse for killing Cataldo; he had promised to marry her without telling her that he already had a wife and children in Italy. Her "only distress" was that she had been "disgraced before her family" by her loss of virginity. Her lawyers tried to mount an insanity defense. It failed, but it was also unnecessary. Her lead attorney delivered a powerful defense summation justifying her violent behavior, and Julian reported that, in his opinion, "no one could have stated the case more ably, more movingly, and more effectively."[67] The jury deliberated for only half an hour. Although the prosecution expected a conviction for manslaughter in the first degree, Maria was acquitted and released.

Julian was next assigned to William Jennings Bryan's presidential campaign. He met Bryan, the thirty-six-year-old Democratic/Populist candidate, in Lincoln, Nebraska, on August 7, 1896, and accompanied him intermittently on his whistle-stops for the next three months. As a "sound money" Democrat, Julian opposed free silver, but the Great Commoner won him over. "Bryan made an agreeable impression on me when I saw him for the first time," he remembered. "His manner of greeting a stranger is very quiet and courteous," though in arguing for his policy positions he could be "as undiplomatic as a hedgehog." Julian joined the army of journalists traveling with the candidate, most of them "increasingly pro-Bryan; for he turned out to be a very good fellow, friendly, simple, unpretentious." From Lincoln they railed to Chicago, overnight to Pittsburgh, then to New York. "I was not myself prepared for the unmistakable sincerity and almost passionate enthusiasm" that greeted Bryan "at every town and village along our route," Julian admitted. Most folks at these rallies "were poor people—men in dirty shirts and bad hats, hairy-armed, rough-handed farmers, small storekeepers, day laborers, clerks, and their wives, sisters, and children. Bareheaded and barefooted many of them." This was a national canvass unlike any other—in many respects, the first modern presidential campaign—and Julian contrasted Bryan's speeches to crowds of thousands in the open air with "the little gilded, pinchbeck" William McKinley, the Republican candidate, "peeking and piping his complacent platitudes" from the porch of "his

Canton cottage." On August 12, when Bryan rose to speak to his supporters at Madison Square Garden, "the last restraints of emotion were thrown aside and for many minutes no power of chairman or police could quiet or moderate the tumult." Julian later claimed credit for persuading Bryan to deliver this "crowning address" of his campaign extemporaneously rather than read it from a script because "a read speech is a dead speech."[68]

During the final week of the campaign, Julian accompanied the so-called Boy Orator of the Platte on the stump across Illinois, Wisconsin, Iowa, and Nebraska. He was convinced not only that Bryan was "our greatest public man" but also that he would be elected. The "entire population" of towns such as Elgin and Rockford, Illinois, gathered to cheer Bryan. At Pacific Junction, Iowa, a thousand farmers turned out. "Never can I cease to be affected by those outstretched, upreaching hands, crowded together, striving to touch" the candidate, Julian reported. "Never did I see, or shall see again, such a spectacle. To those crowds, he was a Messiah." Julian predicted that "many a man, years hence, will recall" as a boy seeing Bryan's "stalwart figure" just as he remembered Louis Kossuth's visit to West Newton, Massachusetts, in 1852. On November 2, the day before the election, Bryan delivered seven speeches in Omaha and was never "more unaffectedly his simple self."[69]

Julian spent most of Election Day at Bryan's house in Lincoln awaiting the results along with the candidate, his entourage, and other reporters. "The house contained four or five pleasant little rooms with nothing conspicuous in the way of furniture or decoration," he noted. "It was the home of an honest and useful American citizen of small means." He was present when Bryan received a telegram from the Democratic National Committee informing him that he had lost, although he received more popular votes—over six and a half million—than every presidential candidate before 1896, including all those who had been elected. As he was leaving, Julian tried to console Bryan: "You fought well, but the fight is over." Bryan replied, "The fight for free silver has just begun." Julian admired him unconditionally. "Bryan is a man, standing plumb on his own feet," he later wrote. It was a judgment that colored his political opinions for the next twenty years. "McKinley is a wraith propped up on the feet of other persons," nothing more than "a piece of affable putty," "a timid, plastic, grateful, moralized person, sure to be favored by old women and respectabilities everywhere." Julian laughed off the fears of some citizens that McKinley might be assassinated: "There is something almost comical in the notion of his joining the army of political martyrs. It would establish beyond cavil the asinine stupidity of the martyr-makers."[70] Soon enough he would eat his words.

PART III
THE SHADOW

1897–1907
"I did a few things for them
and gave them some sage counsel"

The publisher of *Cosmopolitan*, John Brisbane Walker, believed the British were guilty of genocide in India, where millions of people were dying of starvation. But he had no proof, so in late January 1897 he commissioned Julian to find it. "I would fear to risk your life," Walker wrote him on January 24, but "these relations of Great Brit[ain] to India" needed to be investigated.[1] At a farewell dinner for Julian at the Waldorf-Astoria the evening of January 30, attended by Archbishop Michael Corrigan of New York; Samuel Pierpont Langley, secretary of the Smithsonian Institution in Washington; and about thirty other guests, Walker delivered a brief speech: "Mr. Hawthorne, at the hazard of his life, will expose the hideous crimes now being committed by our blood-brothers in the Antipodes: if he survives, you will read the tale in the magazine." Julian replied with false bravado, "the do-or-die sort of thing."[2] Before his departure, Julian visited Rose at the hospice she had opened the year before in a tenement district on the Lower East Side. She brought dying men and women to the three rooms and, Julian explained, "nursed them with the care and tenderness that a mother bestows on her children until they died. Then she buried them and took others to fill their places." She sought to safeguard her brother, too. She placed around his neck "a tiny metal effigy which had, she said, been blessed by the Holy Father and would shield me from harm."[3]

He left New York on the *St. Paul* on February 3, arrived in Southampton on the twelfth, and dallied a week in London before leaving Gravesend on the *Australia*. After stops in Gibraltar, Malta, Brindisi, Port Said, Suez, and Aden, he arrived in Bombay on March 12. For the next several days he strolled the city. "The narrow streets were thronged with half-naked Hindus and turbaned Mohammedans, and every few moments a stretcher would pass carrying a corpse," he reported. "The city of Bombay is dead. Of its population of 900,000 only 300,000 are left. All those who could go hurried out of the city."[4] In company with General William Forbes Gatacre, British commander of the Bombay district, he toured hospitals in the Mandvi quarter and Parel to his horror. "We went into places which would make Tophet seem like an airy summer resort at the seaside,"[5] and he had not yet reached the disaster area.

"Discarding pessimistic reflections as best I might," Julian "left the pestilent atmosphere of Bombay" the night of March 27 for Jubbulpore. There he visited an orphanage that sheltered hundreds of children, most of them under ten years old. A few days later he toured a poorhouse in Allahabad, in the center of the famine district, where "utterly destitute and helpless" men and children were warehoused. From Allahabad he railed to Agra, the northernmost point of his journey, before detouring to Jhansi, returning to Bombay on April 12, and sailing for London aboard the *Peninsular* on the seventeenth. He traveled for a total of five weeks in India and, with side excursions, visited "hundreds of villages" as well as such sites as Malabar Hill in Bombay, the Rani fort outside Jhansi, and the Taj Mahal in Agra, for Julian a "symbol of wealth amid the reality of want." He filled a notebook with enough information to "make articles aggregating about 50,000 words," but in the end he could not offer "a detailed account of what I saw," because "there was a monotony underlying it all; the experiences of one day resembled those of another," days and nights alike punctuated by funeral pyres. He estimated that eight and a half million people had died of famine and disease due to famine, many more than the official death toll.[6]

Nor could he suggest a simple palliative to ease the suffering. To Walker's dismay, Julian concluded that the colonial government was not to blame. The Brits were "doing all that wisdom and experience can devise, and heroic energy and devotion execute, to combat and diminish this stupendous calamity." The underlying problems of plague and drought were exacerbated by greed, he concluded. The Bunniah caste, "the capitalists of the country," had cornered the grain market, reducing farmers to sharecroppers. There was sufficient grain in India to feed the starving, but dealers sold it "at the highest possible price." What could be done? Julian believed there was only one practical alternative: capitulate to the thieves by sending money to American missionaries to buy food to feed the starving. A single dollar "will keep a human being alive in India for a month." The "worst thing" would be "to send grain to India for free distribution," because "the native grain merchants would immediately shut down." In his view the missionaries were key to addressing the problem, because "there were no harder working people in India the year round than the American missionaries." The orphans in Allahabad, for example, "would have died of the famine had not the mission found and saved them."[7]

Leaving Bombay on April 17, the *Peninsular* reversed Julian's outbound route back to London. But his life would never again be the same after these three weeks aboard the ship. He yielded to temptation by deliberate choice. Her name was Minna Desborough, and she was thirty-three, eighteen years younger than Julian, when they met aboard ship. She hailed from Australia, probably from the region around Adelaide in New South Wales, and she was traveling to England to visit her family. She was an aspiring writer, once publishing a piece about the Kelly gang of bushrangers that operated in the vicinity of Victoria. Julian was immediately drawn to her; he later declared that all the Australians he ever met were "exceptionally attractive." He also believed that women raised Down Under were more sexually liberated than women in the northern hemisphere; or, as he crudely put it, below the equator a woman "loses the key of her cunt." In a later story he depicted a "ravishing" beauty named "Minna Daventry," whom he compared, as was his wont, to classical sculpture. She is adorned in "soft, clinging white, on a figure that might pose for the Winged Victory; the severe loveliness of that face, crowned with midnight hair, saddened with the fathomless eyes of Fate, to win a smile from which a man would spend his soul; the flexible ivory of those hands, delicate, yet strong enough to draw a man to perdition; those diamonds—a river of light flowing round the neck of a goddess."

They consummated their affair on May 10, the day after they landed, in the anonymity of a London hotel. Unfortunately, Minna has left relatively few other traces in the record. No letters she and Julian exchanged have survived. Nor did she did accompany him when he embarked for New York aboard the *St. Paul* on May 15.[8] In fact, there is no record of the date and place she entered the United States. She may have sailed to Canada, a country that, as a citizen of the United Kingdom, she might have entered without difficulty, and traveled overland across the border. In any event, she soon followed Julian to New York.

After the *St. Paul* docked on May 21, 1897, Walker contacted Julian in Sag Harbor to ask when his articles about the trip would be ready. "The journey was certainly an arduous one," Julian replied. "People out there warned me of many dangers which I 'must avoid.' . . . But I could not avoid them, and do the work I had set out to do." He would compose the essays as soon as

Minna Desborough, ca. 1897. (Courtesy of Tiffany McFarland.)

he recovered from "a most tremendous cold" he caught, ironically, at the very end of his travels while the *St. Paul* was in quarantine off Sandy Hook, New Jersey. He had purchased commercial photos in Bombay and Jubbulpore to illustrate his essays. In all, he published five pieces about India, one in each issue of *Cosmopolitan* between July and November 1897, three of them lead articles. They appeared in the magazine alongside installments of H. G. Wells's *The War of the Worlds*, and they were arguably his proudest literary achievement. According to the editor of *Frank Leslie's Illustrated Newspaper*, they were "of worldwide importance" in their description of a famine that surpassed "all the horrible fears of the reading public." "Probably no write-up of the famine in India was so widely read as was the Julian Hawthorne account," according to the *Dallas Morning News*. "The man's name is his capital."[9]

* * *

Julian in his Sag Harbor study in 1898 (*Shapes That Pass*, opposite p. 340).

In May 1897, the same month Julian returned from India, Adolph Luetgert, a Chicago butcher, was charged with killing his wife and dissolving her body in a sausage vat. Without a corpus delicti the State should have had no case. Luetgert was nevertheless prosecuted on the basis of bone fragments and a couple of rings found in the thirty-one pounds of slime at the bottom of the vat, and Julian was convinced virtually from the start of the trial that he was guilty. In his news reporting he betrayed his anti-German bias—Luetgert was a type of "clumsy, coarse, uneducated" German American—and he exhibited a flair for amateur phrenology: Luetgert's "chin is sharp and aggressive, not broad and ponderous. It is the chin of a man with a savage temper, not under good control." Julian's dispatches, as several critics observed, were less reports of the proceedings than "a quasi-editorial attempt to hang the sausage man." As the *Waukegan* [Illinois] *Gazette* observed, "The author of 'The Scarlet Letter' must rest uneasily in his grave at the spectacle of his less skillful son's lapse from the ways of grace."[10]

Luetgert's lawyers contended that Louisa Luetgert was still alive, probably in her native Germany, although during the trial she was reportedly sighted in both Kenosha, Wisconsin, and Wheaton, Illinois. They also argued that the Chicago police had planted the rings and that the potash stew in the vat was simply the product of their client's failed attempt to manufacture soap. In the end the trial was reduced to a duel of expert witnesses quarreling over the definition of such terms as "sesamoidal," "distal," and "ungual," and Julian complained that he felt as if he were "in a schoolroom, not in a criminal court." The lawyers were like dogs fighting over bones—literally bones of contention. The prosecution team contended that there were no duplicate bones in the vat, suggesting that all of them were from the same person. The defense argued that the bones were nonhuman and stumped the experts for the State by asking them to identify femurs of a gorilla, a hog, a sheep, and a human. They "knew so little about human anatomy," Julian reported, that they mistook "pieces of half a dozen quite distinct and different bones for the broken pieces of a single bone."[11] The forensic evidence was inconclusive and the trial ended on October 21, 1897, with a hung jury, although Luetgert was eventually retried and convicted and died in prison.

The next month, Martin Thorn was tried in Long Island City for the murder of Willie Guldensuppe, whose head and decapitated body had been discovered in June 1897, and again Julian was assigned to cover the trial. Thorn had allegedly shot his romantic rival, Guldensuppe, in the back of the head, stabbed him with a stiletto, encased his severed head in plaster, wrapped it in brown paper, and dumped it in the East River. Julian again tested his phrenological powers on the murderer: Thorn "has a cold and re-pellant aspect," and he eyed each of the jurymen "as a weasel eyes a chicken." His yellow skin was "like that of a mummy," and when he laughed in court "a more ghastly spasm I never looked upon. Had the headless fragments of Guldensuppe's body assembled themselves in a hornpipe the spectacle would not have been more grewsome." Called to testify on his own behalf, Thorn confessed to the crime—according to Julian, "the most revolting and cowardly murder on record." Thorn told his story on the witness stand "with a frigidity and quiet deliberation that seemed strange, in view of the repulsive horror of the details."[12] Thorn was convicted two days later and electrocuted on August 1, 1898.

Even before the Thorn trial was over, Julian was assigned—along with his New Rochelle neighbor Frederic Remington and Richard Harding Davis of the *Journal* and Stephen Crane of the *World*—to report from Cuba on the plight of the *reconcentados* or rebel patriots there. For several months the Spanish overlords on the island, led by General Valeriano Weyler (aka "the Butcher"), had starved hundreds of thousands of civilians; the crisis had reached a flashpoint, and Hearst wanted his reporters on the scene. When Remington complained there was nothing to draw, according to legend, Hearst cabled him to remain in Cuba: "You supply the pictures and I'll supply the war." Like Remington, as Kenneth Whyte has remarked, Julian was deployed "less as a political analyst than as a sketch writer or scene setter."[13]

Julian joined in relating the tale according to Hearst's exacting specifica-tions. He countenanced the mythology constructed at Hearst's direction around the rescue of Evangelina Cisneros from a Cuban prison by the *Journal*'s "gallant correspondent" Karl Decker. It was, Julian asserted in a front-page story, "the most romantic and daring episode of modern times," with beautiful Evangelina the damsel in distress and Decker "the Prince of the Fairytale." He later conceded that "when news is slack, the paper creates news," as in the case of the "rescue of Miss Cisneros." In fact, he factiously proposed in *Collier's Weekly* that an unnamed yellow sheet feature a "head-ing over the first column of the editorial page": "This War is copyright by the Editor of this Paper; any infringement will be strictly prosecuted."[14]

Julian sailed from New York for Cuba aboard Hearst's private yacht, the *Buccaneer*, on February 1, 1898. Upon arrival in Havana Harbor on February 7, the ship was boarded by Cuban police, who confiscated some small artillery pieces and quarantined the vessel. They suspected it was a privateer, and its name did not dissuade them. Julian appealed for help from the U.S. consul in Havana the next day. The Spanish government had "no just cause" to detain him, he insisted. "I have done nothing against the peace or law. I therefore respectfully request that you notify the Spanish authorities to let me proceed upon my affairs, in this yacht *Buccaneer*, forthwith: and to inform them that I consider myself injured by this enforced delay, and that I estimate my damages at the sum of five thousand dollars per day beginning at six o'clock on the evening of Feb. 8, 1898."[15] Eventually a deal was struck: the Spanish government would ignore Julian's demand for compensation and waive the fine levied on the ship as soon as it left Havana Harbor.

Meanwhile, he surreptitiously investigated the situation ashore. "Under the guidance of a gentleman who knew where to take me," he beheld "the saddest sights that earth can show." The shelters and orphanages around Havana were death camps, with hundreds of women and children succumbing every day. The children were "murdered"—"there is no other word for it"—and buried in mass graves. "I have seen famine in its awful form in India, but there it was not accompanied by the brutality, willful cruelty, and wanton insult that have pursued its victims here." Whereas "the Indian disaster was, to a large extent, an act of nature," the Cuban calamity was wanton and deliberate. If the British were innocent of the deaths by starvation in India, the Spanish were certainly guilty of the deaths by starvation in Cuba. Julian's pleas for American intervention on humanitarian grounds resonated with the public. According to Hearst's biographer Ben Proctor, Julian's reports from the camps "triggered public sympathy and shocked American sensibilities." William E. Mason of Illinois read Julian's account of the atrocities in Cuba aloud on the floor of the U.S. Senate on February 18, and upon finishing the two columns of newsprint, Mason identified him as a journalist "well known to many of us personally" and a man with "a national reputation."[16] He was considered a credible witness to events in Cuba.

The *Buccaneer* anchored near the USS *Maine* in Havana Harbor. After the yacht was released from quarantine, Julian was escorted around the battleship by its navigator, Lieutenant George F. W. Holman. He "chatted with the officers, and with some of the men," and reported to Hearst's readers that the vessel was "an "up-to-date battleship in perfect condition, bristling with polished guns, and populous with three hundred athletic tars." His inspection of the ship proved to him "the impossibility of anything in the way of an accident, due either to carelessness or to natural causes, ever occurring on board." Still, "in a half jesting way but with a certain underlying seriousness," many of the sailors "spoke of the possibility of being blown up where they lay." Julian also reported a rumor that the *Maine* was "lying over a torpedo, which can be exploded from the shore by touching a button."[17]

So he wrote after the catastrophe. The night of February 15 more than five tons of powder in the forward magazines of the *Maine* detonated, killing three-fourths of the crew—264 seamen and two officers—and sinking the ship. Only 89 sailors survived the blast. The cause is still debated, though it was probably a fire on board, because the hull burst outward. Not that it mattered to Hearst and his minions. "Hearst overreached in defense of the external explosion theory," according to Whyte, and "took refuge in nativist demagoguery." He offered a fifty-thousand-dollar reward "for the detection of the perpetrator of the *Maine* outrage." Daily circulation of both the *Journal* and the *World* increased to over a million during the run-up to war. By the end of April, Congress had approved a war resolution, and "Remember the *Maine*" became a national call to arms. Julian asserted that "a more disinterested and honorable war was never undertaken."[18]

Certainly he was complicit in Hearst's warmongering and jingoism. He sent the *Journal* a "pen picture" of the explosion aboard the *Maine,* published under scare headlines and designed to inflame public opinion. "At twenty minutes before ten," according to his report, one of the watchmen "fancied he saw a black object approaching silently. . . . It seemed to him that smoke issued from one end of the object, and that there was a glow as of flame." Suddenly, "the heaven of peace and repose" was transformed into "a hell of destruction and human agony." The ship sank "into a wild boiling of maddened waves," and most of the crew, "human flotsam and jetsam," were "grievously wounded," some to die, others "to live lifelong cripples." All of them "knew that an enemy had done this" and "that their country would avenge them." It was "a coward's blow" and "one of the darkest crimes of history." The ship was destroyed according to "a secret plot hatched in the town whose harbor she was a friendly visitor." He trumpeted news of the disaster as if he were at the scene. Rival newspapers enviously reported that Julian had been "an eyewitness" to the sinking of the *Maine*.[19]

But he wasn't. The *Buccaneer* had hoisted anchor and sailed to Florida the evening of February 11 after only four days in Havana Harbor. Julian and his cadre had received a cablegram "recalling us to Key West and incidentally preventing us from sharing the Maine's fate; but what a chance for a scoop was lost, had any of us survived." He was on a train "somewhere in North Carolina" when he learned the news. "I alighted at the next station" and sent "a dispatch to my paper affirming my conviction that the deed was deliberately committed." He failed to mention in the dispatch that he had no firsthand knowledge. The *San Francisco Call* carped once that Julian "sees nothing even when he is paid to observe." In this case he reported something even when he did not see it. According to Proctor, Hearst's "reporters and editors scripted their own stories of exciting historical fiction," and Julian was one of the sanctimonious "apostles of venom and make-believe."[20] Or as Stephen Crane put it: "A newspaper is a market / Where wisdom sells its freedom."

*   *   *

Though nonpartisan most of his life, like his father in his essay "Chiefly about War Matters" (1862), Julian became a gadfly in the political ointment after American troops returned from the Cuban war in the summer and fall of 1898. His son Jack, who had left his job in the U.S. consulate in Jamaica at the start of the war to join the Seventy-first New York Volunteers, had contracted yellow fever in the field and was near death when his regiment arrived at Montauk Point. Minne visited him at Camp Wykoff in late August and was stunned by the conditions there. After only fifteen minutes in the camp, a civilian was "quite familiar with the look that means starvation," she was dismayed to find. The soldiers "were restricted—sick, wounded and well alike—to food unfit to eat, such as rotten canned beef, mouldy hardtack, and bad and insufficient water; and for some time they were obliged to lie without blankets or tents on the bare ground."[21]

Years earlier both Jack and Henry had aspired to attend military academies. Julian asked George Childs in fall 1891 to help arrange their appointments. The following February, Minne wrote the retired army officer Charles King to ask him to intervene on Jack's behalf, but King was no help. In the summer of 1892 Jack was named an alternate to the U.S. Naval Academy. When he returned from Cuba in late 1898, Julian expressed relief that he "could not get a son of mine into West Point" and that Jack had instead enlisted as a private.[22] As an officer he would have been in an impossible position: responsible for soldiers betrayed by their country.

Although the captain of Jack's company insisted that Jack was not sick, the medic told Minne later "that if [she] had not brought him home [to Sag Harbor] that day it is quite probable" he would have died. Julian was livid when Jack told him about the cowardice of the officers of the Seventy-first during the Battle of San Juan Hill in July. When the soldiers were mustered out, Julian promised, "We shall hear who were 'missing' on that day of San Juan, and why. We shall discover who were the officers who systematically robbed the men under their charge, and treated them, not like soldiers, but like dogs and beasts of burden." On November 28, three months after returning from Cuba and immediately after his honorable discharge, Jack spoke out. During the battle he saw several regimental officers cowering in the underbrush "near where the wounded were being cared for by the Red Cross." He mentioned by name Colonel Wallace A. Downs, Lieutenant-

Colonel Clinton Smith, and Major John H. Whittle. Despite the spinelessness of their officers, as Julian later recounted the story, the "men of the 71st New York kept side by side with the regulars and fully shared their glory" in the "desperate charge up San Juan Hill."[23]

Julian's claim contradicted Crane's account of the battle, however. According to Crane, the soldiers in the regular army kept their distance from the orphans of the Seventy-first who tried to join their ranks, because the puffs of smoke from their antiquated black powder rifles drew fire from the enemy. Crane's report may explain an otherwise inexplicable blind spot in Julian's biography. He doubtless was acquainted with Crane, because they both published articles in the February 1897 issue of *Century*, the June 1897 issue of the *Pocket Magazine*, and the June 1900 issue of *Harper's*, and they were colleagues on the staff of the *New York Journal*. Julian even conceded that "everybody who knows Stephen Crane has liked him." But they were never friends. Julian considered Crane too much a realist. He thought *The Red Badge of Courage* was "dreary" and "The Monster" an "outrage on art and humanity." Crane had "a keen sense of the queer, the bizarre, the morbid," Julian concluded in characteristic fashion, but "he is anything but an artist." He also damned Crane's war reporting with faint praise: "What a very moderate ripple in the news columns was caused by the work in Cuba and Greece of the author of the 'Red Badge of Courage.'"[24]

Julian believed that the incompetence of the War Department and its mismanagement of the Cuban war—a "carnival of malfeasance in office"— warranted the impeachment of the war secretary, Russell A. Alger, an aging Civil War general and former governor of Michigan. Julian knew Alger's cousin Horatio from Harvard Club dinners in New York, but he considered Secretary Alger inept if not corrupt. Rather than procuring army rations in Cuba or Florida, in or near the theater of war, he insisted on buying meat from Chicago packinghouses and shipping it to the Caribbean. Much of this meat was spoiled and injected with preservatives. As W. A. Swanberg explains, the War Department had "sent troops to the tropics in woolen winter clothing, given them inferior arms, and fed them rotten beef." Upton Sinclair refers in chapter 9 of *The Jungle* (1906) to the tainted or "embalmed beef" that killed more American soldiers in Cuba than "the bullets of the Spaniards." Julian went so far as to accuse Alger of treason for the "irreparable injury" he had inflicted on the nation and proposed to hang him "at least once for every soldier whose life was lost through sickness during and after the Cuban war." If not sentenced to death, Julian suggested, Alger should follow the example of Colonel Hubert-Joseph Henry of the French army, convicted of falsifying evidence in the Dreyfus affair, and slit his own throat with a razor.[25]

There was such public outcry over the lack of accountability in the government that McKinley finally appointed a commission of military officers to investigate allegations of abuse. From the first, however, Julian suspected a cover-up. If Alger was guilty of killing hundreds of American soldiers in Cuba and Puerto Rico, McKinley was complicit in their deaths by appointing Alger and failing to remove him. The commission would whitewash the scandal, Julian feared, so he warned his readers not to be misled into placing any confidence in its inquiry. The sessions were held in a small room in a building near the White House to which only a handful of reporters were admitted. Julian petitioned to be one of them, but his request was denied. Instead, he was forced to rely on stenographic reports of testimony that were approved before their release. The commission began its work in late September, though the witnesses were officers, not the "haggard and pallid" foot soldiers who had actually suffered in the camps and on the ships, and during the first three days only two of them were heard. The rank and file were ignored, Julian believed, because they would have testified to "the bitter truth, and the bitter truth would not advance the Republican cause at the polls" the next month. As he predicted, the inquiry exonerated Alger "and recommended that no further proceedings be taken against anyone," although the scandal continued to simmer until Alger was forced to resign from McKinley's cabinet two years later.[26] Julian helped drive him from office.

*   *   *

Sometime between the spring of 1897 and the spring of 1898 Julian and Minna resumed their affair. Most of what is known about their relationship can be gleaned from Julian's memorandum book for 1899 archived among his papers in the Bancroft Library at Berkeley. Though his papers have been sanitized, this memo book apparently survives because Julian's entries are in an elementary code that his heirs and executors failed to decipher.[27] While Minna is nowhere mentioned by name, she is everywhere present. Julian refers to her in the book variously as "Australia," "the Club," "93" (because she lived on Ninety-third Street), and "Ashton" (perhaps her hometown near Adelaide). As with Minne, he entered an X in the book each time they had sex. His entries thus become simple to interpret; for example,

Jan 16 X Dinner in Ashton. Fine night.
Jan 22 Dreamt I was in Australia. Went out at four, going by Madison Ave to 93rd street.
Feb 3 Ashton. Left $37.

Mar 15 Came up to 93, and left $125.

Mar 24 Got cheque for $115. Cashed by aid of Grave's banker & took it up to 93.

May 2 At 7.30 I went to Ashton Club, and had a new sensation. XX

May 11 The Park was deliciously lovely, & I saw what was loveliest at 93.

Occasionally Julian confided to his memo book their most closely guarded secrets, including the precautions they took to hide their affair. On March 31 he "walked up 5 ave past 93 & saw a blueness in the window" (the all-clear), whereas on April 10 he "saw the grey in window," a signal that Minna had visitors.

Even more significantly, on March 5, 1899, he entered these words: "Born at 2.30 am. She has dark hair." On this day Julian's tenth child was born to his mistress. If he could not give her his name, he could at least christen her with the name of a shrub in the same genus as the hawthorn: Mayflower. Thus these subsequent entries:

Mar 6 Went to Ashton & saw M[ayflower]. All well.

Apr 19 There was a time like old time till May awoke.

May 10 The second anniversary.[28] I went up from the Library & was there from 4 to 6. May[f]l[ow]er was awake all the while.

May 30 Decoration Day. Sat in Park for an hour with the M's.

How was Julian able to maintain the ruse? He resided with his family in New Rochelle but worked in Manhattan. A co-worker on the staff of the *Journal*, Walt Macdougall, remembered that he was not only "an extremely handsome man, a perfect athlete," and "a connoisseur in gastronomy," but he was also a prodigious walker. When Julian lived "beyond the upper boundary of New York," as the newspapers reported, it was "no uncommon thing for him to make his daily walk reach from his home to his office in lower New York," some twenty miles. He doubtless walked the distance on occasion, but he more often took the train to or from the city and spent the time he saved at Minna's apartment.[29]

In late June, Julian and Minna managed to spend a weekend together when Minne and their two youngest children traveled to the country.

June 22 My 53rd birthday. Minne, Imogen & Fred went to Garrison at 3.57. I went to A[shton] at 3.55. Arrived at 6 & drove up with A[shton]. All heavenly Delicious first night. XX

June 23 Another lovely night. X

June 24 There was never anything like it. Read and lounged about. Each night is better than the last. XXX

June 25 What a Sunday! The last night.

Two weeks later, when Minne embarked for Bremen, Julian and Minna slipped away for a weekend tête-à-tête near Nassau in upstate New York. Taking a hint from Whitman, for whom the phallic-shaped calamus leaf symbolized "manly love," Julian referred to the phallic-shaped Japanese tea-leaf Kaihua, short for Kaihua Long Ding, to describe fellatio.

> July 11 Minne . . . sail on *Lahn*. Took train at 3.45 on Harlem Road. Arrived at 6. All well. A lovely night. [Illegible] Pushed down her ~~throat~~. XX
> July 12 Walk under the maples. Another lovely night till 4. But Kaihua did not speak.
> July 13 Walked to Nassau. A heavenly day from first to last, & a [illegible] night. K[aihua] down her throat. XXX

Late in 1899, perhaps because she suspected or had learned of the affair, Minne and Julian moved to Philadelphia, where he joined the staff of the daily *North American*, and Minna moved with Mayflower across the East River. But Julian continued to visit them surreptitiously in Brooklyn as often as possible.

The affair lasted for years. Julian and Minna's second daughter, Joan, was born on January 3, 1903. He defended his infidelity on the grounds that he was a free-born pagan unbound by convention. In a tale titled "A Pebble from India" (1905), the hero falls in love with an enchantress named Inda (Minna), who bears his child. He justifies his behavior by invoking a kind of transcendent authority: their love, he explains, was "unreservedly primitive, like a glorious wild animal, and yet so exquisitely spiritual and human; tender, with a beautiful fierceness in it—flesh transmuted into a soul." In some of his private writings around the turn of the century, Julian expressed the same defiance, as in this scrap of purple prose:

> On the little hill, under the pine tree; the roots, spreading arm wise, made a chair for you. You wore a skirt of grey woolen, a white shirt waist: you had taken off your hat, and the breeze was stirring your brown hair. I sat near you: we talked of indifferent things. A song thrush came—and sang from a thick-leaved tree hard by. It was as if no music had ever before been made in the world. . . . Our voices faltered and my eyes, lifting in a sort of fear, rested on your face; but you did not look up. . . . My eyes burned upon you. . . . For we knew that our souls would then meet in naked truth and music. . . . What we had been till now was a cast off garment.

What Minne knew about Julian's affair and when she knew it is now impossible to tell. Their marriage had been floundering for a decade or more. He suggested as much in his poem "The Trilogy," published while they lived in Jamaica.

By strife disheartened (half a lifetime since),
   The fretful consequence of wayward wrongs
      Done each to each, or fancied to be done,
There fell a day, we scarce knew how or whence,
   When (that sweet reverence which to love belongs
      No longer rendered), Love himself seemed gone,
And we, lovers no longer, needs must part.

Still, Minne refused to grant Julian a divorce.[30]

Instead, they maintained the semblance of a marriage. There apparently was no decisive break, though their gradual separation began no later than 1903. They shared a home in Cornwall-on-Hudson in the spring, but Minne moved to Yonkers in July. She alone announced the engagements of Beatrix and Gwendolen that month. She and Julian can last be placed in the same room together at a social event in December 1903, although he continued to receive mail at the Yonkers house until 1907. In any case, both his marriage to Minne and his relationship with Minna seem to have dissolved around the same time. On July 23, 1908, Julian acknowledged paternity of his last two children in his will.

> This is to certify that the two girls, Mayflower and Joan, daughters of Minna Desborough, are also my own daughters, born to Minna Desborough and me during our life together in New York City. Had I lived, and had I been free to marry, I should have married her, and given her and our beloved children my name. But my wife, Mrs Hawthorne (who knows the above facts) and I decided not to apply for a divorce, out of regard for the seven children, now living, who were born to Mrs Hawthorne and me during our married life of thirty-eight years. . . . I ask the forgiveness and charity of these two women, whose lives I have injured, and of my daughters Mayflower and Joan, and of my other children.

Both Minna and Minne almost entirely disappear from the record after Julian signed this will. According to census records for 1910, Minna lived in Union, New Jersey. In 1913 her address was Germantown, Pennsylvania. According to the New York City directory for 1915, she resided on West 152nd Street and was the "w[idow of] Julian." When she sailed from London for New York in March 1925, she listed her occupation as "widowed factory worker." She died in New York on May 14, 1927, at the age of sixty-three. Julian sued for "emancipation" from Minne—that is, he was released from all obligations to support her—in December 1915.[31]

* * *

In 1899, with two families to support, Julian needed to double his income. While the prices he received for his short fiction and essays remained fairly stable—between twenty-five and thirty dollars per thousand words, about the same rate of payment Stephen Crane commanded—he became more prolific than ever. In 1896 he published about 45 items in newspapers and magazines. In 1897, the year he began his affair with Minna, the number swelled to 114, by 1900 to 187, and by 1905 to 250.[32] Julian contributed to *Collier's Weekly* the same time Henry James's "The Turn of the Screw" and Crane's "The Blue Hotel" appeared in its pages and to the *Saturday Evening Post* the same time Charlotte Perkins Gilman contributed to it.

His support of a second, shadow family explains many of his otherwise inexplicable literary and financial decisions around the turn of the century. He never again published a novel, because he could no longer afford the investment of time a novel required. He began to liquidate even trivial assets in 1903. As Darrel Abel observed, "Julian knew the value of his father's autograph manuscripts and made as much money as he could out of all of them he could lay hands on." He sold the originals of Nathaniel's American notebooks in 1903 to the collector Stephen H. Wakeman. Between 1904 and 1907 he repeatedly contacted the author and editor George S. Hellman with offers of Hawthorniana, including the originals of his father's love letters to his mother; two hundred "autographs from distinguished persons," most of them "intimate & characteristic letters from the writer to my father and to me"; and thirty-seven books from his father's library. He hawked his father's fourteen-volume edition of Shakespeare for $100 per volume, or $1,400. He offered Houghton Mifflin and Harper and Brothers his copyrights to *Nathaniel Hawthorne and His Wife* and *Love Is a Spirit*, respectively—his royalty on the novel in 1904 was a whopping $1.13, and he offered to sell the copyright for $5.00.[33]

Julian continued to exploit every opportunity to earn money by his pen—or if not his pen, then by his name. His friend P. F. Collier persuaded him to write "a 'History of the United States' in three volumes [1898]—and for years afterward" paid him royalties (Julian claimed two hundred dollars a week) "and finally a lump sum for the surrender of my copyright." His popular histories were in the same vein as his father's *True Stories in Biography and History* and *Universal History*. Like Julian's earlier histories of American literature and Oregon, they were entirely derivative, based on earlier works by Bancroft, James Schouler, and Samuel Adams Drake. Despite their epic sweep, these narratives are no less romantic than his romances. "History is today at least as much a fine art as is the writing of imaginative fiction," as Julian had observed in his *Story of Oregon*. He staked no new claims; on the contrary, he expressed with little nuance a providential view of history, a germ theory of democracy, and conventional notions about American exceptionalism. "The American nation is the embodiment and vehicle of a Divine purpose to emancipate and enlighten the human race," he insisted in his introduction, and the Puritans "implanted" the "immortal soul" of the American ideal. He graphed the whole of American history, read through a rose-colored prism, onto a template of simple generalizations: Walter Raleigh and John Smith "were Americans before America"; the "blood of the farmers who drove England out of America flows in our veins still"; and the Constitution incarnates "that principle of the freedom of the individual which had its first expression in the emigration of the Pilgrim Fathers." The "great men" in this story of colonization and conquest are all Anglo-Saxon males, including Ben Franklin, George Washington, Thomas Jefferson, Andrew Jackson, and Abe Lincoln. Its 1,200 pages cover four centuries, but more than 200 pages are devoted to the years 1775–1783 and 150 to the years 1852 to 1865. He singled out for particular praise presidents Zachary Taylor, who appointed his father to the Salem Custom House, and Franklin Pierce, who appointed him to the Liverpool consulate. Then there are thumbnail characterizations: Millard Fillmore was an "amiable nonentity," Charles Sumner "very egotistic and supercilious," Preston Brooks "a young ass," Stephen Douglas "an ingrained demagogue," and John Brown a "monomaniac."[34] Still, according to Gregory M. Pfitzer, Julian's work contains "some of the most memorable descriptive writing in any popular history of the United States."[35]

With his credentials now established, the next year Julian composed a popular history of Spanish America for Collier, who paid him one thousand dollars, or about two dollars a page. Based on earlier writings by Bancroft, William H. Prescott, Adolph Bandelier, Susan Hale, Theodore Child, and others, it is thematically similar to his *History of the United States*. It presumes that the Spanish colonists were evil or incompetent and that after four centuries the Anglo-Saxons favored by God were able finally to "oust Spain from the lands she cursed with her presence." Julian's prose was again lively if thesis-ridden: the Aztecs, for example, "wished to kill and eat" the conquistadors according to their "laws of religion and gastronomy" or "to make a ragout of Cortes and his men and horses." The Spaniards and their descendants were, according to Julian, constitutionally incapable of self-government, so the benevolent despotism of Porfirio Díaz was the best the Mexicans should expect.[36]

Between 1899 and 1902, Julian was also nominally the editor of a sixty-one-volume compilation of "the World's Great Classics" published by a New York subscription house. The series was a forerunner of the fifty-one-volume Harvard Classics, or "five-foot shelf," edited by Charles W. Eliot, the president of Harvard. In Julian's case, however, he seems neither to have selected the texts nor even to have read all of them. As he admitted, "at the outset, I did a few things for them and gave them some sage counsel; and my name as managing editor is on their paper, though I seldom see the correspondence that is going on under my name." Julian was so well known at the time that he was paid to endorse Funk and Wagnalls dictionaries and a line of men's clothing.[37] Though he had long traded on his name, during these years for the first time he began to sell it.

In August 1899 Julian received another bonus as the result of his celebrity. As a publicity stunt to build circulation, Harry Bonfils and Harry Tammin, flamboyant publishers of the *Denver Post*, invited him to join the staff of the paper for four weeks at a salary of $250 per week. Julian eagerly agreed, left New York the morning of September 3, arrived in Denver the afternoon of September 6, and registered at the Brown Palace, the finest hotel in the country between Chicago and San Francisco. It was his first trip west of Lincoln. The stretch of road in western Nebraska was "terrible," he reported, with cities of prairie dogs just as they had been "described in Mayne Reid's 'Boy Hunters' forty years ago." But he was favorably impressed with Denver, a prosperous city located in a veritable Garden of Eden. There was a dearth there "of the foreign and mongrel rubbish which flagitious immigration laws have allowed Europe to dump into this continent and which chokes up and degrades our Eastern cities." Instead, "Denver is populated by actual bona fide Americans." Women had voted in Colorado since 1893, and Julian speculated that suffrage was the source "of the municipal superiority of Denver; at any rate it has done no harm." As usual, too, he had an eye for the ladies: "Denver women are intelligent and attractive. I have been told that not all of them are beautiful, and I believe it; but among the several thousand I have thus far seen, the ugly one has not yet happened to present herself."[38]

For most of the month Julian toured the countryside in a private rail car with Bonfils. He contributed to the *Post* a series of travel essays boosting some of the major towns and tourist sites in the state as well as the railroads linking them. In mid-September he rode the Denver and Rio Grande Railway across Colorado to the Peach Festival in Grand Junction, returning on the narrow-gauge Denver South Park and Pacific via Gunnison and the Alpine Tunnel. "I came reeling to Leadville . . . with its lure of gold and its lack of oxygen . . . like a giddy waltzer whose partner had run away with him," he reported. He and Bonfils next stopped in Como to fly-fish the trout streams there.[39] In all, Julian wrote only nine articles—an average of only two per week—but he had been hired for the splash of publicity he would bring the paper, not for what he would actually add to its pages. Before he left Denver on October 1, he agreed to serve as literary editor of the *Sunday*

Post through 1900, a position that required him merely to mail a weekly column to the paper.

*   *   *

Julian returned to Lincoln in early July 1900 to interview William Jennings Bryan during the Democratic National Convention two hundred miles away in Kansas City. He covered the campaign in 1900 not for Hearst's *New York Journal* but for the *Philadelphia North American*—that is, he no longer needed to skew his reports to please his employer—yet he was even more enthusiastic about Bryan's campaign that year than he had been in 1896. His affection for the candidate was genuine. He joined the dozens of correspondents who gathered on Bryan's veranda for five days awaiting bulletins from the convention. When Bryan received the news on July 5 that he had been renominated by acclamation, "there was a general and hearty expression of gratification." Julian again expected Bryan to be elected. He was "formidable enough four years ago," he wrote, "but it is my belief that he is thrice as formidable now." In 1896 Bryan had been defeated by "the most nearly perfect political machinery ever constructed," but in 1900 "no man was better known than he" and "no statesman . . . so passionately loved."[40]

Julian and William Jennings Bryan, July 4, 1900 (*Philadelphia North American*, July 10, 1900, 3).

*   *   *

Whereas he had defended the rights of employers and criticized the role of labor in the Homestead strike in 1892, Julian switched sides in 1900. He had changed his mind about laissez-faire, perhaps because he had witnessed how the greed of the capitalist class in India had exacerbated the famine there. In any case, he traveled to the Pennsylvania coal fields in early September to cover a miners' strike for the *North American*. He suspected "that the state of things could not actually be so bad as had been represented. I found it to be worse than had been told, and much worse than I had expected." The miners were "compelled to submit to a system of tyranny and extortion" by their bosses. He reported from Shamokin on September 3 that the "average miner gets about a dollar a day," lives in a company-owned house and shops in a company store, and is liable to be blacklisted if he protests any of these practices. In Wilkes-Barre the next day he met Mother Jones, "a dauntless champion and encourager of labor in its long battle against injustice." On September 9 he compared the town of Hazelton to "the ruins of the castle of the Giant Despair" in his childhood favorite, *Pilgrim's Progress*. Children "as young as 7 years old" worked in the mines, received "from 25 cents to 35 for ten hours' labor," and "[slept] like sardines in a box" so that "coal barons and railway kings" might "live well."[41]

Early in the new century Julian became a convert to socialism, at least the parlor variety advocated by the so-called millionaire socialist, Gaylord Wilshire. He contributed to Wilshire's magazines at the same time as Eugene V. Debs. In his first submission, in February 1901, Julian wrote: "When [the socialists] are ready to strike they will know exactly where to aim their blow. Mr. Morgan and Mr. Rockefeller have only one neck apiece, and there are millions of lampposts at hand." A year later he insisted that his ancestral New England Puritans were socialists "in the full sense of the term."[42] He continued to write for *Wilshire's* until March 1908, only weeks before he began to tout Canadian silver mines to would-be venture capitalists.

*   *   *

On September 8, 1900, a hurricane pounded Galveston, the busiest port in Texas, with estimated winds of 135 miles per hour and a storm surge of over fifteen feet—more than twice the average elevation of the barrier island. It literally dashed the city to splinters, destroying some thirty-six hundred houses and killing about a fifth of the forty thousand people who lived there. It remains the deadliest natural disaster in U.S. history. Julian was recalled from the Pennsylvania coal district to supervise the relief efforts of the *North American*, specifically to supervise the distribution of food and clothing packed into four freight cars—a "quarter of a million pounds of solid succor," as he put it—and, of course, to interview survivors and report from the scene. He was accompanied by eight doctors and nurses, two other journalists, and a staff photographer. The train left Broad Street Station in Philadelphia on September 12, and Julian filed his first dispatch from "Camp North American" in Texas City, across the bay from Galveston, on the seventeenth. En route to the devastation, the relief train "passed through a dozen smitten villages" and stopped "at each of them to "hand out a few barrels and bags of goods." Twelve miles inland for thirty miles along the coast, he marveled, "the waves swept nine feet above the surface of the prairie." Many of the bodies that had been recovered were naked, literally stripped by the force of the storm, and they were cremated en masse in bonfires that reminded him of funeral pyres in India. Martial law had been declared to discourage looting, and disinfectants had "put an end to the death stench." The supplies collected by the *North American* fed and clothed some eight hundred victims of the storm. Passing through New Orleans on September 21 on his way back to Philadelphia, Julian allowed that not only would he "not go to Galveston to live" but that he did not expect the city ever to be rebuilt.[43]

Julian (left) in Texas City, Texas, after the Galveston hurricane (*Philadelphia North American,* October 4, 1900, 8). (Courtesy of the Bancroft Library, University of California, Berkeley [72/236 vol. 2, p. 8].)

*   *   *

Julian joined Bryan the next month on a campaign swing from New York to towns along the Hudson and the Mohawk Rivers. They left Grand Central Depot on October 16, and Julian wrote from Ithaca on the nineteenth that he doubted "if there has ever been a political orator in our time who so promptly inspires his audiences with complete trust, not only in his intelligence, but in his honesty and moral elevation." Julian stayed with the campaign until Bryan spoke in Philadelphia on October 25,[44] two weeks before the election that returned McKinley to office.

Ironically, just as he opposed Bryan's silver policy in 1896, Julian opposed his anti-imperialism in 1900. That is, he admired Bryan despite their political differences. He believed the Treaty of Paris had conceded too much authority to Spain in the Philippines. Whereas Bryan wanted to curtail the U.S. presence there, however, Julian wanted to preserve it. "Every acre of the Philippines must remain ours, and their every inhabitant be governed as we are governed," he asserted. Like Mark Twain, he considered immoral the demand of victorious countries for indemnities paid by defeated nations. "A delicately nurtured and normally non-productive American girl, by simply being outraged [raped], and then slowly tortured to death, may earn more money than a dozen factory-fulls of female operatives could earn in twenty years," he fulminated in a tone similar to Twain's sarcasm in "To the Person Sitting in Darkness."[45] The differences were that Julian favored annexation of the Philippines—and that he published his comment seven months before Twain.

*   *   *

At the turn of the century Julian was a respected workaday journalist. He had admired Oscar Wilde's *The Picture of Dorian Gray* when it appeared in *Lippincott's* for July 1890—he had a short piece in the same issue—and he favorably reviewed the novel two months later. After Wilde's conviction on a charge of "gross indecency with other male persons" in May 1895, however, Julian rarely mentioned him again. In "One of Cattermole's Experiments," printed in the inaugural issue of the *Smart Set* in March 1900, he implicitly criticized Wilde, though not by name, for his testimony at court. Like Wilde at Old Bailey, Cattermole argues that the artist is a superior being, that whatever he may do "he can never be charged with crime, baseness or selfishness, because his motive is always culture, which aims to create the immortal good and fair." The purity of the water lily—a transparent allusion to Wilde, for whom the flower was iconic—is "born of the black mud of the river bottom." Julian summarized Wilde's line of defense in order to ridicule it. He did not mention Wilde again until December 3, 1900, a couple of days after the writer's death in Paris. Much as he had assailed the dead Margaret Fuller for her loss of maidenly virtue and the dead Walt Whitman for his decadence, he derided the dead Oscar Wilde for his homosexuality. "Men will forgive any crimes but those against nature," Julian fumed, "because these murder more than the body." Of all Wilde's writings, he thought only "The Ballad of Reading Gaol" would survive. His plays were "harmless except as they are false representations of life," his stories "carefully and gracefully vicious," and his essays and poetry generally "clever but shallow." But in this poem "the inmost note of sincerity is sounded. Nothing that I know of in modern literature is more appallingly true."[46]

Julian also hailed Frank Norris's *The Octopus* upon its publication in the spring of 1901. The author "shows many indications of being, or at least of becoming, a really great novelist," he judged. Norris dropped a note to Julian to thank him for his "kind and extremely discriminating review." Yet Julian was not always so generous. He inexplicably ignored Theodore Dreiser entirely, though he and Dreiser both contributed to the July 1898 issue of *Cosmopolitan*; he dismissed Elizabeth Stuart Phelps Ward's *Life of Christ* as "a mess of emasculate slipslop"; and he questioned whether the actress Olga Nethersole "could draw a corporal's guard to see her in a decent play."[47]

Meanwhile, he continued to sniff out feature stories. Julian had known Thomas Edison since 1886 and interviewed him at his lab in Orange, New Jersey, in May 1901 about his most recent invention, the alkaline storage battery. In fact, the interview appeared in the *North American* the same day the Edison Storage Battery Company was incorporated. He also interviewed Edison's rival Nikola Tesla. In February 1901 he took a train to Detroit for the sole purpose of interviewing Hazen ("Potato") Pingree, the former Republican governor of Michigan who had sparked a controversy by pardoning dozens of prisoners in the waning days of his administration. Julian was impressed with Pingree as they chatted in the St. Claire Hotel. He "would have been President of the United States," Julian thought, had he not unexpectedly died of peritonitis four months after their meeting.[48]

In his articles during this period, Julian regularly discussed matters of race, though in truth he was not particularly enlightened on the issue. While planning to emigrate to the Caribbean in 1893, for example, he had expressly avoided Haiti, a nation he believed had been "polluted" by the "black-skinned rascals" who lived there. Julian and the editorial cartoonist Homer Davenport covered the Alabama state Democratic Party convention in Montgomery in late April 1900 on assignment from Hearst, who was trying to build a constituency in the South. Julian praised the Southerners' "sense of civic duty"

Homer Davenport caricature of Julian
Hawthorne (*Birmingham Age-Herald*,
April 21, 1900, 1).

and determination to enforce Jim Crow laws and to rescind the voting rights
the Fourteenth Amendment guaranteed to black men.[49]

His most sustained commentary about race, however, appeared in a series of articles in April 1901, when he accompanied a delegation of seventy
"educators" on a junket to the South. During the tour he attended graduation
exercises at the Hampton Institute, the meeting of the Southern Educational
Conference, and the dedication of some buildings at Tuskegee Institute. On the
basis of these "investigations," Julian extolled the type of industrial education
or manual training that black Americans received at Hampton and Tuskegee.
"If you teach a Southern negro arithmetic, bookkeeping, political economy
and English literature," he reasoned, "you may be doing him an ill service;
you will widen his intellectual horizon, without at the same time giving him
judgment and a remunerative occupation." He echoed here the argument
of Booker T. Washington, and in fact he paid a backhanded compliment
to Washington while visiting Tuskegee: "The white man is in him, and has

probably had an influence on his intellectual quality as well as on his color, but the negro strain of thousands of years back dominates all his contours; it has swamped the white man out of sight." Julian reiterated his belief that "the enfranchisement of the negro" after the Civil War had been a grave error, and he abhorred the idea of integration: "The two races cannot live together under the present laws. The negroes cannot be either exterminated or deported. They must then be disfranchised." He opposed lynch law, but for a peculiar reason—not because hundreds of black people were tortured and killed, but because the public spectacles had a demoralizing influence or "dehumanizing effect" on the white folks who witnessed them.[50]

* * *

In a review of Theodore Roosevelt's *Ranch Life and the Hunting Trail* (1888), Julian had predicted "a future of some good sort" for him. But reminiscing about TR the day before he was elected governor of New York a decade later, Julian was dismayed that such "an honest egoist of limited experience and intelligence, a short-tempered and obstinate boy, easily controlled and hoodwinked through his vanity," had become a political heavyweight. Not until the Battle of San Juan Hill "was this innocent catspaw discussed as a possible governor" of the most populous state in the Union. Julian thought him better qualified to be "administrator of Porto Rico."[51] Less than two years later, Roosevelt was elected vice president on the Republican ticket with William McKinley, and the following fall, at the age of only forty-two, he became the twenty-sixth president of the United States.

On September 6, 1901, in the Temple of Music at the Pan-American Exposition in Buffalo, New York, McKinley was shot twice at point-blank range by Leon Czolgosz. The second bullet lodged in McKinley's back and his surgeons were unable to locate it. Julian arrived in Buffalo on September 8 to report on the assassination attempt for the *North American*, and, from the first, he cautioned against a rush to punishment, because Czolgosz's crime was "too grave to be dealt with otherwise than by due and solemn process of law." For three or four days, McKinley seemed to recover, at least according to the statements of his doctors, but by September 12 he had taken a turn for the worse. In an editorial typed on *North American* letterhead and titled "Anarchy and the Terror," Julian again argued that Czolgosz "ought to be under the strict protection of a mighty nation, which is in duty bound" to protect him "for the sake of the national dignity and honor" until he could be tried. In his view those who advocated the immediate lynching of Czolgosz were the real anarchists. The editorial was never published; instead, it was quashed when McKinley died of an infection in the early morning of September 14. In his subsequent reports, Julian lamented the murder of "this good man" whom he had so often ridiculed, although when Czolgosz was executed in October he also questioned whether the assassin was as morally culpable as "the man who picks a pocket or wrecks a railroad" and expressed doubt that his electrocution would deter future capital crimes.[52]

*   *   *

Julian left the *North American* in April 1902 to freelance and work part-time for Hearst's rechristened *New York American*. He devoted his time during the remainder of the year to writing some pieces for the Bacheller syndicate and reviewing books for the *American*, and he also covered the autumn murder trial of Roland Molineux in New York City. During the first six months of 1903, he contributed book reviews to *Wilshire's*; essays to *Booklover's*; fiction to the *Olympian*; articles to *Smart Set, New Metropolitan, Cosmopolitan*, the *North American Review*; and he reported on the Edwin Burdick homicide in Buffalo, a crime compared at the time to the Lizzie Borden case. The more murder trials he depicted, the more he presumed to know about criminology. In "Legal Penalties and Public Opinion" in the *North American Review*, he tore a page from *The Scarlet Letter* by proposing the branding of felons "with a letter or other mark indicating the nature of the crime" they committed. Lest it seem cruel and unusual punishment, Julian assured his readers that "the mark need not be branded on his flesh with a hot iron; it might be tattooed." He also wrote a piece for the *Atlantic*—"English Lawns and Literary Folk"—about some of his experiences in England in the 1870s. It was his last article to appear in the magazine. As usual, he had trouble with the accounting departments of the magazines. "I have as yet received nothing but promises from the Book Lover folks," he complained to Joe Stoddart. "I need the money, and I need it next Thursday. If I don't get it then, I am going to attach their property, if they have any. . . . Thursday is my ultimate and unalterable limit. If they don't pay then, I will give them a publicity which they may find inconvenient. I have their letters promising to pay."[53]

During the second half of 1903 Julian wrote another biography of his father, a sort of sequel to *Nathaniel Hawthorne and His Wife*. In *Hawthorne and His Circle*, however, he skipped the chance to correct his earlier mistakes. Rather than comment on Margaret Fuller, he disregarded her entirely. Rather than credit James T. Fields with saving his father's career, he praised him with faint damns. "Having at that time no notion of the fame the romance was to achieve, or of the value that would attach to every scrap of Hawthorne's writing," he suggested, Fields had failed to prevent the typesetters from destroying the original manuscript of *The Scarlet Letter*. Annie Fields was disturbed by this characterization of her late husband, and she urged Julian to delete it from subsequent printings. True to form, he refused. "What I wrote and have often said," he replied, "was that Mr. Fields did not at that time anticipate the value that would attach to Hawthorne's mss."[54]

Annie Fields was not the only one distressed by the book. Sarah J. Lippincott, aka Grace Greenwood, filed a libel suit against Harper and Brothers for fifty thousand dollars in damages based upon the publication of an anecdote Julian copied from his father's English notebooks. While listening once to the actor Charles Kemble read Shakespeare, the story went, Lippincott had expressed "her good taste and depth of feeling by going into hysterics and finally fainting away upon the floor." One of Sophia Hawthorne's best friends, Lippincott had read fairy stories to Una and Julian at the Wayside and dedicated her book *Recollections of My Childhood* (1851) to the Hawthorne and Mann children. "My relations with the whole Hawthorne family were always of the pleasantest," she recalled. "Julian, who has such vivid and unpleasant recollections of me, it seems, was then not more than five years old, and was my most earnest and admiring listener. I don't understand his attitude toward me." As for Julian, he was stunned to learn she was still alive.[55] In fact, Lippincott died two months later and the suit was dropped.

Despite these minor controversies, critics generally lauded *Hawthorne and His Circle*. As the *Washington Post* put it, "Happy rest the ashes of the man of genius who finds his Boswell in his own son." W. D. Howells praised it in the *North American Review* as "a picture of one of the most fascinating and important literary men who ever lived, as his own family knew him, and as the lovers of his books will be glad to know him." Though he had scorned Howells's critical judgments in the past, Julian thanked him for this one. "Nothing could have been spoken more fitly to my sensibilities, filial or literary," he avowed. Still, as he admitted, the book "was written at the request of the publishers and I didn't much care for it, except as a record of odds and ends. I don't think it was a good seller."[56]

*   *   *

In January 1905 Julian was summoned to Los Angeles by his editorial friend Sam Chamberlain, a longtime managing editor in the Hearst chain, to help him boost circulation of Hearst's newest paper, the *Los Angeles Examiner*, with a series of feature articles touting Southern California as a mecca for tourism and commerce. He left New York on January 1; traveled via the Southern Pacific across "the level, mountain-bounded stretches" of New Mexico and Arizona; arrived in Los Angeles on January 6; and registered at the Angelus Hotel downtown.[57] It was his first trip west of Denver.

Julian crossed paths with Jack London his first week in the city. He had panned London's *A Daughter of the Snows* in *Wilshire's* two years earlier, and London complained to George Brett at the time that Julian "slated me good & hard." On the evening of January 8, Julian attended London's lecture on "The Scab" and reviewed it in the *Examiner*. He admired London's physique and his "big, hearty, healthy nature" but not his ideas. As a fellow socialist he should have been sympathetic to London's politics, but instead he patronized his fellow novelist. Julian was always more an impoverished plebian than a genuine proletarian. Incredibly, he took London to task for his condemnation of the scab and those who employ him and even wished he "had said something about the despotic tyranny over their members of labor unions." His solution to class conflict? Workers should surrender to the capitalists and trust to providence. Little wonder London reported later that "the whole trouble with Hawthorne is his *conventional* mind. He cannot understand things that are not, but which might be, or ought to be."[58]

The two men met personally for the only time at a California Club luncheon in their honor on January 11, the day after publication of Julian's review of London's lecture. Julian long remembered their encounter "and the erectile clams which [London] declined to devour." Afterward they chatted and Julian wrote up their conversation for the *Examiner*. He regarded London with grudging respect gusting to qualified admiration. He assured his readers that London inspired affection "from first to last. If I dissent from some of his views, I somehow like to have him hold them." He figured London would eventually outgrow his more vulgar ideas.[59]

Over the next four months, Julian sang the glories of such towns and villages as Redlands, Riverside, Ojai, and Pomona. He wrote these articles in effusive chamber-of-commerce prose and the imperative mood of a real-estate shill, as in these comments about Riverside: "It is a healthy, clean, active, American community, one of the sort that makes this country great. . . . Riverside is the richest town in the world, each man, woman, and child in it averaging twelve thousand dollars of live property!" George F. Babbitt could not have said it any better. In early March Julian left L.A. to tour the California missions by automobile—"a White steamer, the newest and best of its kind"—and his articles about his trips to such towns as San Diego, San Luis Rey, San Juan Capistrano, and Santa Barbara were more temperate. He also interviewed the novelist H. Rider Haggard at the home of Major Frederick Russell Burnham in Pasadena and the astronomer E. E. Barnard at the observatory on Wilson's Peak.[60]

Julian literally stumbled into Henry James in the lobby of his hotel one day in late March. Neither of them knew the other was in Los Angeles,

Julian Hawthorne (right) upon starting his tour of the California missions along the Camino Real from San Juan Capistrano in a White steam car (*Los Angeles Examiner*, February 27, 1905, 3). (Courtesy of the Bancroft Library, University of California, Berkeley [PIC 1981.103-ALB, p. 41].)

and they had last seen each other twenty-six years earlier and half a world away. (They had stayed in a kind of indirect touch, however, as they both published articles in the same issues of *Century* and the *Atlantic* six times between May 1884 and December 1888.) James was touring the United States, a trip he partly chronicled in *The American Scene* (1907). They spent the day together, and during their conversation James touched on a variety of topics: the threat to privacy posed by modern celebrity; the rigors of travel across America; his move to Rye, near Hastings on the southern coast of England; even the unfortunate success of their mutual acquaintance Theodore Roosevelt, with whom James had dined in Washington. They took a trolley to Playa del Rey, where Julian "had the pleasure . . . of introducing Henry to the Pacific Ocean." According to Julian, James "strolled along the beach and filled himself with its splendor and immensity." But was James aware that Julian would report their meeting and conversation? It's highly likely. He was, of course, familiar with Julian's infamous interview with James Russell Lowell in 1886, so he was effectively forewarned if he had wanted the interview to remain off the record. And there is internal evidence as well: James steered the conversation to the subjects he wished to discuss. As Richard Salmon explains, while "James privately complained about the journalistic attention which surrounded his return to America, he clearly consented to much of it."[61] That is, James apparently agreed to Julian's interview because he thought it would burnish his public image.

*   *   *

Though he was no Damon Runyon, Julian left his mark as a sportswriter. His ideas about sports were catholic, encompassing such forms of athletic competition as sailing, rowing, and bicycle, horse, and auto racing. He covered college regattas on the Hudson and the Charles Rivers, bicycle meets on Manhattan Beach, America's Cup yacht races in New York Harbor, horse races at Saratoga, and the Vanderbilt Cup car race on Long Island. Given his initiation to fisticuffs as a Harvard freshman, he was predictably infatuated with the "sweet science." He reported the heavyweight bouts at the Coney Island Athletic Club of Jim Jeffries and Bob Fitzsimmons in June 1899, Jeffries and Tom Sharkey in November 1899, and Jeffries and James J. Corbett in May 1900—all won by the "giant unbeatable" Jeffries. In August 1900 he reported the Corbett vs. Kid McCoy prizefight at Madison Square Garden. Soon afterward, however, he concluded that gambling had ruined the sport and he never again covered a live bout. But in May 1905, upon his return from California, Julian was appointed sports editor of the *New York American*. A proponent of every form of physical exercise, he immediately launched a weekly advice column on health and hygiene that appeared in all Hearst papers, including the *San Francisco Examiner* and *Chicago Examiner*. While many of his recommendations were banal—chew gum rather than smoke tobacco, avoid red meat, "masticate thoroughly"— he also broadcast some quack ideas, such as that gravitation causes aging and that "proper breathing prevents baldness."[62]

As another measure of his versatility, Julian left the sports desk in December 1905 to report the Fifty-ninth Congress for the *American*. For the next six months he "journeyed through the canyons, caverns, and tunnels which intervene between the House and the Senate" on Capitol Hill. As a factotum in the employ of Representative William Randolph Hearst of New York, who "alone stands between us and the menace of anarchy," he was, of course, critical of the Republican majority and the "moneyed oligarchy" it represented. Like Hearst, Julian championed the Hepburn railroad-rate bill opposed by the "the coal-railroad combine" and the "pot-house politicians" in its hire. He campaigned against the Beef Trust, skewered the Senate as a "huge parasite of corporation greed and tyranny," President Roosevelt as a "flibbertigibbet" and a "pettifogging lawyer," and cautioned against both his election to a third term and the election of William Howard Taft to succeed him. A Taft presidency would amount "to continuing the Roosevelt regime under another name" and turn "the clock of progress back about one hundred and fifty years."[63] Little did he know that one day he might want a favor from Taft, who would be ill-disposed to grant it.

*   *   *

On February 22, 1906, seventeen-year-old Josephina Terranova stabbed and killed her uncle and aunt in Williamsbridge, New York. She had been routinely molested by her uncle since the age of eleven, and her aunt aided and abetted his crimes. Josephina was indicted for the murders on March 21 and her trial began on May 14. As Jacob M. Appel notes, "Jurors and the public were subjected to a harrowing account of incest, torture, murder and madness." A front-row observer of the trial, Julian heard a "story that can never be retold in print." Despite her distressed adolescence, she struck him as "somehow, truth and purity. There was no shadow of insincerity on her forehead, no guile on her lips, no indirection in the frank unself-conscious look of her eyes. All about her was childlike, and childlike was her voice." Both prosecution and defense called "alienists" to testify, and to Julian's dismay, the trial, like Luetgert's, dissolved into a duel of expert witnesses. Still, he expected Josephina to be acquitted and he was right. The jury deliberated only fifteen minutes before returning a verdict of not guilty. Her acquittal, according to Appel, significantly influenced the way "future lawyers, courts, and even journalists handled 'crimes of honor.'"[64] In effect, the Terranova case was a rehearsal for the Harry Thaw trials, and several of the same experts testified during both proceedings.

On June 25, 1906, the millionaire playboy Thaw murdered Stanford White on the rooftop theater of Madison Square Garden, which White had designed, by firing three bullets into his face. The most famous architect in America, White had also designed the Washington Square Arch; the new Boston Public Library on Copley Square, in partnership with William Rutherford Mead, the brother-in-law of W. D. Howells; and the *Cosmopolitan* building in Irvington, New York, thirty miles north of Manhattan. White's apartment on West Twenty-fourth was a notorious boudoir with a mirror room, and Thaw believed that White had raped his wife there. When arrested, Thaw reportedly said, "I shot him because he ruined my wife." In truth, Evelyn Nesbit Thaw, a beautiful former chorus girl and Gibson Girl, likely had engaged in consensual if underage sex with White. He was no doubt an "elderly rake" and sexual predator, but he was never charged or convicted of a crime; and Thaw was a drug-addicted paranoid, Harvard dropout, and reputed inventor of the speedball. The trial was ready-made for Hearst's brand of sensational journalism, and Julian was only too willing to accede to his demands. He reported the story of the love triangle as if it were a modern version of *The Scarlet Letter*, with White in the role of the satanic Chillingworth, Thaw as the weak-kneed Dimmesdale, and Evelyn as the soiled dove Hester Prynne. Once destined to become "a great novelist" like his father, as the *Boston Journal* opined on the eve of the trial, Julian was now writing "queer stuff for the 'yellows.'"[65]

Thaw's first murder trial was one of the most sensational courtroom disputes in American legal history. It pitted District Attorney William Travers Jerome against Delphin Delmas, the so-called Napoleon of the Western bar, the second most famous defense attorney of his generation after Clarence Darrow, and it lasted from January 23 until April 12, 1907. Julian remembered the victim as the "intelligent and good-natured little son" of his friend Richard Grant White, although he was quick to assure his readers that he was "not prejudging the case." But of course he had. Even before the jury was seated, Julian was convinced that Thaw deserved to be acquitted on grounds of the unwritten "primal law": a husband may kill anyone who violates his wife. Insanity would be "the pretext for acknowledging the unwritten law's supremacy," what came to be known as the "Dementia Americana" defense. Julian was sympathetic from the first toward Evelyn Thaw, with her "soft, graceful, and regular features," and he objected to Jerome's "Penelope tactics," the procedural delays of the prosecution. In particular he protested Jerome's attempt to smear Evelyn's character by suggesting "she was already corrupt when White first met her."[66]

On February 7, the day Evelyn testified on her husband's behalf, some ten thousand New Yorkers gathered outside the Criminal Courts Building to catch a glimpse of her. Irvin S. Cobb of the *New York Evening World* thought Evelyn was "the most exquisitely lovely human being I ever looked at," and E. L. Doctorow writes that she was "the first sex goddess in American history." She has been portrayed in such movies as *The Girl in the Red Velvet Swing* (1955) by actress Joan Collins and *Ragtime* (1981) by Elizabeth McGovern. Julian considered her "one of the tragic figures of our day."

> Undoubtedly such another story has never been told in a courtroom in this country. It was one of those things that seem impossible to tell until they have been told; one cannot picture in his imagination a young girl relating before a public audience the sequel of events that led up to her ruin. . . . The story was that of the entrapping and ruin of a child of sixteen by a man of more than mature age, a man of the world, of reputation and social consideration. No element was lacking in it which could alleviate in any respect the guilt of the betrayer. . . . After this part of her life history had been told, no man in the jury box would have hesitated to justify Thaw's act.

At the conclusion of her testimony, Julian turned to his colleague Dorothy Dix and said, "If Thaw had missed White, after hearing that story every other man would have taken a shot at him!" Thaw's first trial was, he later contended, "the greatest human document which has been published in our generation."[67] It ended in a hung jury. In a second trial in 1908, as he had predicted, Thaw was found not guilty by reason of insanity, but his legal travails for killing White lasted until 1915.

*   *   *

All the while Julian worked for Hearst early in the new century, he tried to carve out a niche in the magazine market. He began to experiment in science fiction, an increasingly popular and potentially lucrative genre in light of the successes of Jules Verne and H. G. Wells. In "Hearn's Romance" (1902), a tale about time travel, the hero returns through the "fourth dimension" to prehistory. Julian revivified zombies and monsters in "The Men of the Dark" (1906). But he was most intrigued by the idea of space travel. As early as 1896 he had speculated about the possibility of extraterrestrial life, and in 1898 he conjectured that the surface of Saturn resembled the American West, a "beautiful but wild" region where "people live much as our Indians did." Julian imagined life there in his short story "Our Ambassador to Saturn" (1907), which features interplanetary communication and a scientist-hero who discovers laws of physics that enable him to soar through space.[68]

Even before he became sports editor of the *New York American* in 1905, Julian had been assigned to the college football beat. He was never an enthusiastic fan, however. That "football players are armored like medieval knights, from head to foot, is a sign that there is something wrong," he editorialized in November 1897. The first game he covered for the *American* was the Yale-Columbia contest on October 31, 1903, and the second was a classic: the Yale-Princeton contest in New Haven two weeks later with thirty thousand people in the stands, won on a late field goal by the Princeton captain and future college Hall of Famer John DeWitt. But by 1905 he had concluded that football was a blood sport. Eighteen high school and college players died that year from injuries. On November 28, 1905, three days after watching the Yale-Harvard contest in Boston along with forty-three thousand other spectators, Julian publicly urged the extirpation of the sport. It "cannot be purged of its evil features; for, if this were done, no game would be left," he argued. "The only alternative . . . is to abolish it altogether."[69] After the season, Theodore Roosevelt, apostle of the strenuous life, saved football. TR helped found the organization that evolved into the National Collegiate Athletic Association and introduced rule changes that took effect in 1906. The flying wedge was outlawed and forward pass legalized, opening the game to skilled players instead of only brutes, and Julian was mollified. He covered the Ivy League in 1906–07—the Yale-Harvard, Yale-Princeton, and Yale-West Point games in fall 1906 and the Yale, Princeton, Penn, and Harvard training camps in fall 1907.

Those practices were among his last assignments for the *New York American*, however. Though he had been reappointed sports editor of the paper in April 1907, he was fired in November "on account of the impossibility of accommodating my system to that of Mr. Hearst." After the most productive decade of his career, Julian rarely mentioned Hearst again—this despite his habit late in life of reminiscing about virtually every famous person he had ever known. Out of a job at the age of sixty-two, he took a vacation. Publicly, he merely stated that he "was tired of New York and suddenly decided to visit Cuba." After a decade of deadlines, he spent the winter in the port city of Matanzas.[70]

At the height of his fame, when his name was both a byline and headline, Julian was an A-list celebrity and man about town. He was a coveted guest and moved in the same social circles as Howells, Woodrow Wilson, John Jacob Astor, and General Nelson Miles. He was invited to Mark Twain's seventieth birthday celebration in the Red Room at Delmonico's and Henry Alden's seventieth birthday celebration at the Harpers headquarters on Franklin Square.[71] Unfortunately, he was soon embroiled in a scandal that would forever tarnish his reputation.

Julian Hawthorne (third from left) at Henry M. Alden's seventieth birthday celebration at Delmonico's (*Harper's Weekly*, December 15, 1906, p. 1839).

1908–14
"Whatever disgrace attaches
to this affair belongs not to me"

When he returned from Cuba in January 1908, Julian commenced a desperate job search. At first he accepted piecework: He was hired to ghostwrite a book for the author and editor Seymour Eaton, although there is no evidence he finished it or received more than a hundred dollars for his work.[1] He began to hype a vanity press called "The Thinkers Club" that Eaton founded to print short books on topical issues for a fee,[2] though the club failed to issue a single volume. He penned a promotional brochure for Jamaica Estates, a real-estate development in Queens. At the end of March he begged Mayo Hazeltine for a regular job with the *New York Sun*. "I would take a position at any reasonable salary," he pleaded. City reporters typically earned from forty to sixty dollars per week, and Julian considered "$100 liberal, these times; and would take half of that without winking. I can do all manner of work; but my own idea is that I would be at my best with a daily column or half column of my own comments on the daily news, or on any topic of interest that might turn up. But I can also describe earthquakes and murder, or even interview eminent persons."[3] But there was no opening on the staff of the *Sun*. Julian claimed later that during this period he was working on a biography of W. S. G. Morton, Will's father. He ostensibly was to be paid twenty-five hundred dollars for it, a thousand of which he had already received, although not a shred of such a project survives.[4] That is, Julian had no apparent source of income. Down on his luck, he was nearly on the street.

At this juncture, on July 10, 1908, Will invited Julian to his office in the Cambridge Building to discuss "a business proposition which may turn out to be of considerable value to you" and "will cost you nothing." They had been out of touch for most of the quarter century since the death of Julian's daughter Gladys. Julian called on Morton the same day he received his note and found him "lounging about." Morton had spent the past two summers in the Temagami region of northern Ontario, and being struck "by the glitter of the mining discoveries" there, he had invested fourteen thousand dollars in twenty-one claims totaling eight hundred acres.[5] Professional assayers, he told Julian, "have found rich indications of values quite equal to any that have been found in the Cobalt region,—silver, gold, copper, and cobalt"— but he needed money to develop the mines. Morton proposed that Julian front the operation, "become a director in the company," "accept a block of stock" for his trouble, and "draw your dividends as they fall due."[6]

Julian was overwhelmed at Morton's generosity. "I was very glad of all this because it makes the future, financially speaking," he conceded. "Though my name will be of some value the returns will far exceed any possible good I can be to the enterprise." Julian accepted Morton's invitation because it would both "benefit me" and "cost him nothing."[7] He joined a company whose officers included Albert Freeman, an Austrian-born operator of dubious reputation who had been suspended from the Consolidated Stock Exchange in 1892; Josiah Quincy III, former mayor of Boston and former undersecretary of state in the Cleveland administration, who had declared bankruptcy in 1907; and James B. Hanna of Cleveland, nephew of former Republican political boss Mark Hanna. However, Julian's name was the most prominent among them and "seems to have been the great drawing card" for investors.[8] He volunteered to write the promotional circulars and manage the office to earn his dividends. According to Freeman, "He said he had no money and must live, but it was against his principles to borrow money from the company. So he suggested that he should pledge his stocks with me in return for loans as he needed them." By his estimate, Freeman loaned Julian about $21,500 over a period of sixteen to eighteen months."[9]

The first circulars promoting the mines over his signature were mailed within a month. Between August 1908 and March 1910, in fact, Julian's name was appended to some seven hundred thousand letters sent to potential investors, a "sucker list" of names and addresses mostly gleaned from a mailing list bought from the commercial reporting agency R. G. Dun and Company and from college alumni directories—the early twentieth-century equivalent of spam. They targeted "persons of intelligence, but of limited means, such as teachers and army officers."[10] Although the texts of these letters varied over time, they all contained the essential appeal of a carnival barker: buy now before it is too late. While he qualified his spiel with reminders of the risks, he emphasized the probable rewards with "safe, sane, sober" businessmen in charge and assays that indicated upward of twenty thousand troy ounces of silver per ton of ore—fully five-eighths of the thirty-two thousand ounces in a ton. ("If they had discovered all they advertised," the government prosecutors later charged, "railroads would be making rails out of silver, and the steel corporation would be put out of business." An independent assayist discovered only trace amounts of silver in the Temagami ore, worth mere pennies to the ton.)[11] Julian predicted the mines would "make immense profits for many thousands of people" at nominal cost "for at least fifty years to come." He claimed that the engineering firm of Ricketts and Banks had submitted an offer to purchase the mines and that the agent William F. Wilkinson had tried to buy them on behalf of Gold Fields Limited of London; and he cited testimonials to their worth by such experts as Louis D. Huntoon, retired professor of mining engineering at Yale University, and Woodford Brooks, president of Temagami-Cobalt. "Wilkinson talks of 500% dividends without a change in his voice," Julian asserted. Not least, Julian mentioned his own engineering training and experience, his spotless reputation, his personal investigation of the mining sites, and his own investments in stock: "I have not only put every dollar I was able to get hold of into this company, but I advised every member of my family to do the same." (There is no evidence he invested any of his own money.) His letters were usually accompanied by enclosures: for example, maps, prospectuses, pledge cards, or exhortatory stories such as *The Secret of Solomon* and *Julian Hawthorne and Company*.

Freeman spent about seventy thousand dollars on these mailings. "I did not care how much I paid if the letter was perfect," he explained. "The trouble was to get the different names put into the letters in such a way to make those who received them think they were personal letters from Hawthorne and not mere circulars."[12] From his perspective, the investors deserved to be fleeced for their gullibility and greed. The "Hawthorne Companies" employed a circulation manager and eight typists to insert names and addresses into the multigraphed letters, and they were trained to forge Julian's signature at the bottom. Dozens if not hundreds of these letters are archived today as if the signatures were genuine. Julian once joked that they so resembled his real signature "he wouldn't want to leave a checkbook" around the office. When the operation was in high gear, as many as ten thousand letters were mailed in a single day.[13] Nikola Tesla received one of the letters, prompting a sarcastic response to Julian: "If your success in mining is commensurate to the gray matter you are burning up in writing your prospectuses, you should be congratulated."[14]

Mark Twain also received one of the circulars, and his first instinct was to trust the message because he trusted the messenger. Twain dictated his reaction to Isabel Lyon, his secretary, who penciled it on the letter: "I'm not gambling on the mines, because I know people sometimes say things about mines that are not true. I used to do it myself when I had mines to sell—But I am gambling on Julian Hawthorne's integrity & levelheadedness."[15] While there is no evidence that Twain actually bought stock in the mines, he was a sucker for such boondoggles as James Paige's typesetting machine and the dehydrated egg product called plasmon. If he did invest, the money he spent was never a cause of friction between them; they remained friends until Twain's death in 1910. "I knew him well and loved him; I have laughed and grieved with him; he was as genuine and simple as an honest boy," Julian attested, and he attended Twain's funeral at the Brick Church in New York.[16]

Edith Garrigues Hutchins also received one of the first circulars Julian wrote, along with a cover letter so ambiguous or disingenuous that it fails to resolve the question of his culpability. The daughter of the eminent surgeon Henry Jacques Garrigues, Edith was a debutante, socialite, and student of the impressionist painter William Merritt Chase. In 1895, at the age of nineteen, she had married the architect Harry C. Hutchins. Julian met her through Will Morton in July 1908, the same month he began to tout the stock, and he addressed her as his "beloved and revered friend" in a letter the next month. He warned her in a jocular tone "against paying any attention to the enclosed prospectus. No one can go up against it with impunity, and it would be a shame for me to take your money. If you want to make money—*save it*; don't do any risks on chances of making six hundred per cent. You would be lucky if you made 500." Had he not appended the final sentence he would have seemed to be cautioning her. Is he recommending the stock sincerely, if slightly tongue in cheek, or is he admitting the investment is a scam? "There are many cases of desperate men being reduced to Congress or to the Court of St. James by less money than you would get in a year by subscribing to the stock of this mine," he added. "I hope what I have said may influence you; but if not, a check to the above address will be appreciated. No subscriptions are received for less than Three Hundred Dollars."[17]

Edith was no ordinary mark. She became Julian's lover and divorced Hutchins in October 1909. Edith and Julian took a two-week cruise to Cuba together aboard the *Saratoga* in January 1910. Under Edith's influence, moreover, he became a member of the Woman's National Progressive League along with Jack London and Charlotte Perkins Gilman, and while she was in Reno awaiting her divorce, he signed a petition in support of women's suffrage along with W. D. Howells, Julia Ward Howe, and Dorothy Dix.[18]

Edith also inspired some of the only writing Julian completed during this period apart from mining circulars. In his story "The Amazon" in *Lippincott's* (1911), the type of racy tale that had begun to appear in pulp magazines like *Argosy*, he portrayed a strong, independent woman whose grass skirt is always askew. He also addressed poetry to her, including such erotic blank verse as the unpublished "Intercourse," with its tortured syntax, clichéd allusions, and idiosyncratic rhyme scheme.

> Words there may be for what you are to sight,
> But none to clothe my seeing;
> Your speech of eyes, mouth, hands, and motions light
> Or grave—of voice too, sometimes murmurous
> Clear-toned now and proudly resolute,
> Mean this or that, but not the meaning of your being.
> But, bellying-out my sail adventurous,
> An air, divinely eloquent and mute,
> Flows from your seas unsailed and trackless shores,
> Keen snow-lit heights and valleys verdurous:
> And ever toward that realm
> I set my eager helm,
> Dreaming of golden doors
> Of the enchanted palace of my hope
> Yonder aloft, oh, high beyond the scope
> Of my possession—though my soul and yours
> Ever have dwelt there and shall ever dwell.
> The Infinite in your guards our treasure well:
> The Gift of gifts is never given,
> That so the rich economy of Heaven
> May substance lost transmute to vision that endures.[19]

He also published a trio of love poems to Edith, one of them titled "Monarch and Mendicant": "All that deep noon of day / Heart to beating heart we lay, / And oh, love had his way!"[20] It appeared in the same volume as the first printing of Edna St. Vincent Millay's "Renascence."

*   *   *

The U.S. Post Office received the first complaints about the sale of Hawthorne mining stock in October 1908, and its inspectors immediately launched an investigation. According to rumors that swirled at the time, the inquiry was instigated by Senator Elihu Root of New York, whom Julian had known socially since the mid-1880s and who had gotten wind of the flim-flam.[21] In a letter Julian sent to Post Office Inspector F. A. O'Brien on October 23, 1908, he assumed a tone of injured innocence. All promotional literature mailed by his company was approved by its directors, he insisted. His reputation should have shielded him from inquiry, and with more than a little chutzpah he appended a list of character witnesses O'Brien might contact, including Theodore Roosevelt, William Jennings Bryan, Mark Twain, Howells, Hearst, Joseph Pulitzer, and Whitelaw Reid.[22] He admitted confidentially to his sister that he was in the crosshairs of a team of lawyers. Rose, who had taken the name Alphonsa when she was invested as a lay nun, replied that she would not contact "Imogen or Beatrix, or even Hildegarde, until you should tell me that 'silence' was no longer necessary."[23]

Julian's responsibility in the sale of the worthless stock—what he knew and when he knew it—is still difficult to determine over a century later. Did he join a fraudulent business with malicious or criminal intent? Did he plan from the first to bilk investors? No. Was he too gullible? Duped? A patsy? Probably. Was he guilty of the crimes for which he was convicted? Yes. In 1908, unemployed and his marriage in shambles, with two young daughters by another woman to support, he was desperate enough to sell his surname just as he had traded it to the Central Florida Phosphate Company and the World's Classics years before. He was lured by Morton and Freeman into touting worthless silver mines for a share of the booty and with no investment. He ignored the red flags that flapped in his face, like this one Morton mailed to him from Bear Lake, Ontario, in mid-September 1908: "It is a perfect circus & a three ring one at that—you—Freeman—I. But where does the public come in—they do come in. And, now you see them—and now you don't—that is by & by. . . . that bare rock chunk of land . . . erected into a $20 000 000 fairy tale. Yet who shall say there is *not* $20 000 000 worth of silver in it from here down to China?"[24] On the surface, this letter reads like the admission of a con man. Yet neither Morton nor Julian profited much from the wildcat scheme. Morton received a total of only fourteen thousand dollars, the same amount he invested, and stock. In lieu of a salary, Julian borrowed against the six hundred thousand shares of stock in the Hawthorne Silver and Iron Mines, Ltd., that he was given.[25]

That his circulars were balderdash, filled with false and exaggerated claims, is beyond dispute, however, and mining authorities were quick to expose them. In the issue of the *Engineering and Mining Journal* for October 3, 1908, the editor Walter Ingalls noted Julian's misuse of the name of Ricketts and Banks but initially dismissed the problem as a mere misunderstanding. Julian soon proved otherwise. When Ricketts and Banks warned Julian that his letters "misrepresent[ed] the facts," he sent in reply "a feeble letter of apology in which he said 'I could easily have gotten along without mentioning any name. In order to avoid any criticism in this regard I shall certainly be careful in the future.' He promptly showed how he would get along without the mention of any name by bringing out a new circular, in which he substitutes for his original phrase 'the firm of Ricketts & Banks of New York' the following: 'a prominent firm of engineers of New York.'" Ingalls pronounced the revised circular "a willful deception" and regretted that he had been forced "to waste our space upon such a miserable attempt" at fraud.[26]

Similarly, W. F. Wilkinson, the supposed agent of Gold Fields Limited, was "astonished" to read in one of Julian's circulars that he wanted to buy the Temagami mine. As he protested to Morton on October 7, 1908, he had written the *Engineering and Mining Journal* "to deny that I ever made an offer for the mine, as Hawthorne makes out. I do not remember him, but I called on someone, who, I suppose, was he, in New York, and discussed Cobalt." He referred to Julian's claims of wealth as mere "moonshine" and added that he had never so much as "examined the property." He demanded to know "what has been going on" and that Morton "explain how Hawthorne could use my name in such an impudent fashion." Professor Huntoon complained "angrily" that he, too, had been misquoted, that he had described to Julian the rich ore of the Cobalt silver mines, not "Hawthorne's properties at Temagami," which he had never seen.[27] As for the testimonials by Woodford Brooks: "He never was in a mine except once, when at the age of five he was taken into a coal mine," according to another employee at Temagami. Rather than a mining expert, Brooks "was a clerk in Freeman's employ until Freeman made him Vice President" of the company.[28] Only after the Post Office launched its investigation did Julian finally visit the Diabase peninsula personally, and then only for a few days. Little wonder that the *Canadian Mining Journal* in April 1909 referred to him as "a sublimated ass" and in September 1910 declared that shares in his mines were "worth about as much as Confederate paper money."[29] Caveat emptor.

Federal prosecutors convened a grand jury on September 1, 1911, to consider indictments of Julian and his fellow company directors, who immediately suspended operation of the mines and halted the mailing of circulars. That is, in fall 1911 Julian again lost his only source of income. Within weeks he was in a state of "acute destitution." Though a bon vivant and snappy dresser most of his life, by November he was "not even decent to look at now; my laundry is in an unpresentable state, and my outside clothes cannot much longer present even an illusion of respectability." He planned "to keep as much as possible out of sight of my friends until an end of some sort comes to my predicament," even if it required "the aid of the District Attorney." The state prison at Sing Sing "may solve the enigma for me." Meanwhile, Minne could "be kept in food and lodging by her children; and for myself I care very little."[30]

After subpoenaing witnesses and company ledgers, the grand jury returned indictments of Julian, Morton, Freeman, and Quincy on December 28. Hanna slipped the noose—probably with political pull. The government alleged—claims never in dispute—that the mines had yielded no paying ore and the companies had paid no dividends to stockholders. Freeman, the brains behind the scheme, was the chief target of prosecutors. The defendants were arraigned on January 5. All of them pleaded not guilty and were released on bail pending trial—twenty-five thousand dollars for Freeman, ten thousand for each of the others.[31] Julian somehow scraped up the money, probably by borrowing it from his children.

Jury selection began on November 25, 1912. While twelve men had been seated in the jury box by the close of the first day, the defense still had nine peremptory challenges and the prosecution had six. By the close of the second day, five of the original twelve had been replaced. The New York Times reported at the time that "a somewhat unusual method of obtaining a jury was followed." The final juror selected on the second day, after the defense had exhausted its challenges, was Michael Kehoe. With Judge Charles M. Hough presiding, the first of dozens of prosecution witnesses,[32] most of them irate investors, took the stand on November 26. The trial was held in the same courthouse in Lower Manhattan where Julian had covered the murder trials of Maria Barbella, Josephina Terranova, and Harry Thaw.

While the defendants claimed they had collected about $400,000 from the sale of mining stock, the prosecution insisted the amount was nine times greater, about $3.5 million. In either case, both sides agreed that as sole stockholder in a holding company that owned the Hawthorne companies, Freeman pocketed most of the money. Both sides also agreed that the Hawthorne mines had been worked during the summer of 1911. More than a hundred men were employed in extracting ore, and each of them was paid between $2 and $5 a day. The companies paid the Canadian government royalties on the ore extracted. But, the prosecution added, none of the ore was shipped to a smelter. The company had constructed a dock to transfer the ore to barges at Collins Bay on Lake Ontario, some ninety-five miles from the mine, but it had "no visible means of shipping the ore" to the dock.[33]

During the first seven weeks of the trial, the prosecution laid out its case, detailing the half-truths and lies of the accused. The Hawthorne companies purported to own five thousand acres of iron ore and six thousand acres of silver and gold ore, had estimated its daily output of pig iron at one thousand tons and an annual profit of $3.45 million, and promised to pay dividends of 100 percent on its stock. According to their circulars, Ricketts and Banks "had made determined and persistent efforts to buy the mine" and "brought forward one of the Tiffany firm who was willing to give a large sum for a three-fifths interest in the Temagami mine." The so-called mining expert Woodford Brooks had, "after an investigation of the mines, invested in them every dollar he had in the world." None of these claims were true. The prosecution characterized the defendants as "green goods men" and "bunko steerers."[34] On January 7, 1913, the government rested its case.

Freeman's lawyer promptly moved for the dismissal of all indictments against all the defendants, and Quincy's lawyer rested his case on the lack of evidence brought by the prosecution implicating his client. Hough dismissed most of the charges against Quincy and the trial continued. The defendants' case was a simple one: they "believed absolutely in the value of the properties they sought to promote," and had the government not interfered, the mines "would be paying properties now." Julian's lawyer, addressing the jury on behalf of his client, reminded them that Julian was the son of Nathaniel Hawthorne; that he had written some fifty books; that he earned on average ten thousand dollars a year as "novelist, historian, biographer, and journalist"; and that he was sixty-seven years old. He had joined the mining enterprise with the hope of making a better life for his "large family of children and grandchildren."[35]

Freeman then took the stand and laid all the blame on Julian. He blamed Julian for writing virtually all of the circulars mailed to potential investors. He protested that "it was none of his business" what Julian was writing to his college classmates and friends. He had no knowledge of criminal behavior, or else he would have prevented it. When he received an inquiry from one of the recipients of Julian's letters, he testified, "I told Mr. Hawthorne that he had better confine himself to urging inquirers to go to Temagami to make personal investigations. I told him I did not like what he was writing." According to Freeman, Julian was the single troublemaker among the defendants. During lunch recess this day, Hough was rushed to New York Hospital with abdominal pain. He was unable to continue to preside at what was nearly declared a mistrial after eight weeks, more than a hundred witnesses, and legal expenses on both sides of the aisle totaling tens of thousands of dollars.[36]

The defendants at this critical moment agreed to continue the proceedings under the supervision of a different judge. The trial lasted another two

192 PART III: THE SHADOW

months with Julius Mayer presiding. Julian reminisced later that while he "was sitting in the courtroom being tried on charges sworn to by certain post office officials, the dull and sordid scenes would sometimes vanish before me, and I would say to myself, 'It is an illusion—what is really taking place is very different from this appearance.'"[37] Whereas the prosecution called 106 witnesses, the defense called only six, including Freeman and Morton, and rested its case on March 6. Julian did not testify in his own defense because he did not think it was necessary. During cross-examination, more-over, he might have been forced to reveal the reason he had been desperate for money: that he had an even larger family to support than he publicly acknowledged. The situation was bad enough that he was an accused thief. How much worse would it have been to be both an accused thief and an adulterer?

In his closing argument, U.S. District Attorney Henry A. Wise described Julian as "a member of one of the most dangerous band of crooks and swindlers that ever infested New York." Wise contended that Julian was guilty of a "greater crime" than a run-of-the-mill thief because he had "prostituted" an "honorable name." Had he said "writer" rather than "thief" he would have echoed many a book critic.[38]

The prosecution of the Temagami Five was one of the trials of the twentieth century, at least in length. It lasted four months, or seventy court days, and cost the government seventy thousand dollars. It was the second longest trial to that date in the history of the New York federal courts, and the transcript of it fills some eight thousand pages.[39] On Wednesday, March 12, 1913, the jury began to deliberate. At 5:45 PM on March 14, the defendants were summoned back to court. After twenty-seven hours, the jury had reached a verdict.

*   *   *

The jurors walked into the courtroom without glancing at the defendants. "Up to the very last minute I had no doubt as to the outcome of the trial," Julian later told the reporters. "I fully expected to be acquitted." Instead, he and Will Morton were each convicted on seventeen counts of fraudulent use of the mails, Freeman on twenty-three counts, and Quincy was acquitted on a single charge of conspiring to defraud. The convictions were handed down almost exactly one year after their arrests. After Judge Mayer dismissed the jurors, Julian's lawyer, Herbert C. Smyth—a cousin of Beatrix's husband, Clifford Smyth—appealed for mercy on behalf of his client. "He is not a business man," Smyth said, "and his fault is rather one of judgment than of evil intent. His attitude throughout the trial has shown his supreme confidence in his own innocence, and he has never had the slightest fear of the result. He bears an honored name, and surely to a man of his age it should be sufficient punishment that he has knowledge that he has sullied this name in the eyes of the world. He made no profit whatever for himself from these mines, and he was carried away by enthusiasm for the enterprise." He added that Julian was "penniless." Morton's lawyer, Joseph H. Choate Jr., made a similar appeal, and the prosecution offered no rebuttal. As Mayer imposed sentence, he announced that it was "an extremely painful duty; I think the most painful I have ever been called upon to perform." He expressed the wish that he "might be able to follow the inclination of my heart as a man" and "suspend all the indictments" against Julian and Will "on account of their ages," "but I cannot do it; I must do that which I conceive to be my duty." He added that, in his opinion, "the brains of this situation" was Freeman. Because all the defendants had agreed "to continue the trial after Judge Hough was taken ill," moreover, he had decided to be as lenient as possible. He sentenced Freeman to five years in federal prison and both Julian and Will to a year and a day dating from the start of the trial. Under federal law, inmates of the Atlanta Federal Penitentiary sentenced to more than a year in jail were eligible for parole after serving a third of their sentences. "In imposing that extra day," Julian explained, "the judge could hardly have been motivated by anything except the intention to open this door to us." Julian and Will could file for parole as early as March 26. As his sentence was read, according to a reporter, "a slight frown crossed Hawthorne's brow."[40] The defense lawyers obtained a ten-day stay while they considered whether to appeal.

Julian remained defiant, even as a federal marshal "with the look of a turkey buzzard" locked him in handcuffs. "I felt the steel close round [my wrists] with a solid snap," he remembered. "I was a manacled convict, and the community was saved." "Our only mistake was a commercial one," he insisted to the press in the marshal's office a few minutes later. "We did not develop fast enough, and did not realize how deep the mining must be up there." To the end of his life he refused to admit he was guilty of a crime and expressed confidence that the mines would eventually pay. As he returned from the courthouse via the Bridge of Sighs to the New York Halls of Justice and House of Detention, commonly known as the Tombs, on the evening of his conviction, he saw his son-in-law Clifford Smyth, editor of the *New York Times Book Review*, "pale in the electric light," wave to him "in greeting and farewell."[41]

*   *   *

The three men spent the next ten days in the Tombs, Julian and Freeman cellmates on the third tier, Morton alone in a cell on the seventh. The morning of August 15 Julian figuratively thumbed his nose at his captors by comparing his first night in jail to a holiday aboard a ship. "The illusion was so perfect I soon passed off into sleep and had a very restful night," he said. "This morning a man came to my cell with a big pail of coffee. Of course it wasn't served just as coffee is served on shipboard, but the serving of coffee in my 'cabin' heightened the illusion of my being on shipboard."[42]

At the end of ten days, Freeman had decided to appeal his conviction and was released on $150,000 bond. Julian and Will opted not to appeal, because they planned to apply for parole the day after they arrived in Atlanta. The joke went around that they might return to New York with the guards on the same train that carried them to jail. "We were led to understand," Julian later said, "that we would have to spend only a day in the Atlanta Prison. It was understood that we should not appeal our cases. They told us to be good boys and then we could be back in New York almost immediately. Well, we were good boys and went to Atlanta." Escorted by a federal marshal, Julian and Morton left New York on March 23 and arrived in Atlanta the next day. Julian's mustache was shaved before he sat for his mug shot—the only photograph of him as an adult without facial hair. Upon entering prison he surrendered a pocket knife and $70 in cash. He listed his religion as "Swedenborgian" and was assigned the number 4435.[43] He joined a prison population of 830 men.

A coda to the trial: Freeman's conviction was overturned on appeal in March 1914. Michael Kehoe, a member of the grand jury that indicted all four men, also sat on the petit jury that convicted three of them. The method of their selection, or, more correctly, the method of stacking the jury by limiting the number of preemptive dismissals permitted the defense, had allowed Kehoe to be seated. Was the prosecution aware of this irregularity? Probably. As Julian mockingly noted in an unpublished manuscript, "The Government Attorney who addressed [Kehoe] as a member of the Grand Jury failed to recognize him when he appeared as a petit juror." Kehoe was a "professional juryman," having served on five federal panels in two years, a "lifelong gambler," and a "keeper of a house of ill fame." Freeman's attorney declared in his opening remarks that he would prove Kehoe was installed on the jury by the prosecution to ensure there would be no acquittal of his client. Judge Mayer, who heard the appeal, ruled that at the least Kehoe harbored "a prejudicial bias," that Freeman had not been tried before an impartial jury, and thus he was entitled to a new trial. Julian and Will attended the hearing and told reporters afterward that if Freeman was entitled to a new trial, then so were they—even after they had already served their sentences.

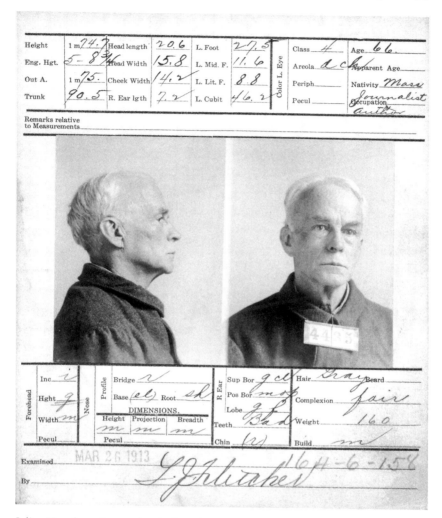

Julian Hawthorne's mug shot in the Atlanta Federal Penitentiary, March 23, 1913. The photo was taken three days before it was "approved" and filed. (Courtesy of the National Archives—Atlanta Region.)

Freeman's second trial ended in a hung jury and he then plea-bargained. In exchange for a guilty plea he was fined three thousand dollars and walked free.[44] His ten days in the Tombs pending his release on bail while appealing his conviction in spring 1913 were the only days he spent behind bars.

A second coda: Morton received a presidential pardon in December 1913 that enabled him to resume his medical career. Hawthorne was not pardoned, because, as a White House official put it, the "necessity was not acute."[45] Of the five principal suspects targeted in the original investigation of mail fraud, one was not indicted (Hanna), one was found not guilty (Quincy), one successfully appealed his conviction and paid a fine (Freeman), and one served his prison term and was subsequently pardoned (Morton). That is, Julian suffered the most severe punishment of all the company officers, though he was hardly the most culpable.

*   *   *

Unknown to his lawyers or to Morton, Julian began to angle for a presidential pardon while in the Tombs during the ten-day stay. He was convinced beyond a reasonable doubt that "the men whom our country had deputed to handle the machinery of law had blundered, and had convicted and condemned those who had done no wrong." He dictated a letter to Edith to be sent to his friend William Jennings Bryan, soon to become Woodrow Wilson's Secretary of State. "I am here," he explained, "because a jury brought against me a verdict of guilty using the U.S. mails to defraud investors in a mining company of which I was president. . . . The statements as to the mines which I made I believed at the time to be true and I believe so still and were the thing to do again I would act as I did then. My position therefore is that whatever disgrace attaches to this affair belongs not to me but to the government which found me guilty." The "obloquy" the nation risked by imprisoning him might be assuaged, he suggested, "by giving me a free pardon through the instrumentality of the President of the United States. I apply to you to lay the matter before him."[46] There is no record of a response.

Meanwhile, Mother Alphonsa campaigned for a pardon for her brother. She had no doubt he was innocent. The day after his conviction she urged him to be strong. "Your brave soul is what comforts us all in seeing you insulted," she avowed. He was simply the victim of "a human blunder." He had not been tried by a jury of his peers, because "there was not even one man among the Jury who knew well your career, or had the culture necessary to comprehend your mental processes." And as for the Canadian mines, "the gold & silver are laughing at us, from the great depths, & someday others will grow rich on them, & think of you with a gesture of gratitude." Four days after his conviction she sent a woeful message to former president William Howard Taft, during whose administration Julian had been indicted: "Oh, Mr. Taft, what have you done—what have you done?" and signed it "the sister of Julian Hawthorne." Taft jotted on the letter: "I have not done anything. The machinery of the law has caught Julian Hawthorne and he must stand the penalty." She mailed an appeal to President Wilson, then on April 4 visited the White House uninvited and unannounced, asking to speak with him in person. She was intercepted by Joseph Tumulty, Wilson's secretary, who assured her he would present her case to the president. She had traveled to Washington, she explained to Julian, not to ask for a normal pardon "but for an exoneration from a new mind, which I thought clear and noble . . . but the President was occupied with the Cabinet, & I could not talk with him." She had hoped "to avoid newspaper mention; & should have done so, but that the White House was fully armed with newspaper men," and so her attempt to meet Wilson became national news. Though Tumulty assured her "he would do all he could," she correctly surmised that Attorney General James Clark McReynolds, "who does not look like a good or brave man," was the stumbling block. She referred to Taft as "the Golf Pig" and, several months later, Julian referred to Wilson as a "strutting Pedagogue" and "unctuous Charlatan."[47]

He had been naïve. He didn't expect to be investigated. When he was, he didn't expect to be indicted. When he was, he didn't expect to be convicted. When he was, he didn't expect to be sentenced to prison. When he was, he expected to return from Atlanta on the next train. Nothing happened as he expected. The Department of Justice denied his request for a pardon in April on the grounds he had been in prison less than a month. Though the federal pardon board as well as Judge Mayer recommended that Julian and Morton be freed in August, the paroles were denied because officials in the Justice Department (that is, McReynolds) believed "that enough leniency has been shown them."[48] They would serve their entire sentences, less time for good behavior.

*   *   *

Julian was not exactly a soul on ice. Within two weeks of his arrival, he was assigned the job of editing the monthly prison magazine *Good Words*. The warden had founded it a few months earlier "as a medium for advertising and gaining credit for the penitentiary," and Julian did not initially realize "how fortunate . . . this accident was." For the duration of his sentence, the magazine gave him "constant occupation and interest." He contributed most of the articles, including a column titled "Philosophy of the Ranges" and some of the most astonishing book reviews ever to appear in a prison publication; for example, of Emerson's *English Traits*, *Plutarch's Lives*, and Thomas De Quincey's *Confessions of an Opium Eater*. He compiled a list of 330 books he recommended to the other inmates, including *Walden*, Ben Franklin's *Autobiography*, and *The Scarlet Letter*. Mostly he composed poems and inspirational essays for the magazine, signed with his convict number, much as Oscar Wilde had signed his number to his prison writings. (Julian later pasted a copy of "The Ballad of Reading Gaol" into his scrapbook.) That is, Julian was "sandpapered" by prison, and an editorialist for the *Washington Post* noticed: he was "giving cheer and comfort as well as moral education to all the other prisoners. . . . In forgetting himself and aiding others, Hawthorne has given to his punishment an air of heroism."[49]

For the first time in his life, Julian had a captive readership, and he carefully cultivated it. In the pages of *Good Words* he referred to incarceration as a "long, living death." He argued, in chorus with the lawyer Clarence Darrow against the Italian criminologist Cesar Lombroso, that there are no natural-born criminals, no essential difference between folks in and out of prison, and when a crime is committed, "heredity and circumstances are guilty." Either "build jails big enough to hold the entire population" or "abolish jails altogether," he declared. "The chief difference between the man in jail and the man in the Sunday pew" is that "we are the scapegoats." He condemned unpaid prison work: "In the contract labor jail" inmates are "mere slaves driven literally to death by a merciless and insatiable bloodsucker." He alluded none too subtly to the use of violence to maintain discipline: "Shooting and clubbing prisoners and subjecting them to torture have proved unsuccessful in leading them toward sweetness and light." Instead, "teach the prisoner to look upon his past as a mistake to be corrected, not as an irremediable and unforgivable sin." In one piece he envisioned the jails of the future: they will be transformed from "hells to a kind of antechamber to Paradise," with a waiting list to enter them, and only "the very best men of the community" will serve as guards and wardens. In another piece he promised his readers that such articles "are but a faint suggestion of the treatment" he planned to give these topics upon his release. After all, in jail "we write under supervision." He understood, like Michel Foucault, that the criminal, like the leper, is always subjected to the "disciplinary gaze" of police and prison guards.[50]

Good Words was so professionally produced and controversial it attracted subscribers from outside the prison, and its contents were sometimes reprinted in newspapers across the country. For example, Julian's poem "Footfalls" appeared in the *New York Times* the day after the release of the May 1913 issue.

> In the cell over mine at night
> A step goes to and fro,
> From barred door to iron wall,
> From wall to door I hear it go,
> Four paces heavy and slow,
> In the heart of the sleeping jail,
> And the goad that drives I know.
> I never saw his face nor heard him speak;

He may be Dutchman, Dago, Yankee, Greek;
But the language of that prison'd step
Too well I know;
Unknown brother of the remorseless bars,
Pent in your cage from earth and sky and stars,
The hunger for lost life that goads you so
I also know.

Some bureaucrats in the Justice Department were alarmed. Julian's writings disparaged the Atlanta prison and embarrassed the attorney general. On one occasion, Julian was censored by the department. In the July 2, 1913, issue of the *New York American*, his friend Arthur Brisbane urged the president to pardon Julian and "relegate as soon as possible" the scandal "to the generous domain of the forgotten." The editorial was reprinted in the *Atlanta Georgian*, where Julian read it, and he replied in a letter to the editor of the *American* dated July 8. Julian claimed (falsely) that he had not sought a pardon and would refuse one if granted.

> At my trial I pleaded not guilty. Nothing that took place at the trial, or in my own mind, has altered my attitude on that point; the conviction and sentence have not altered it, nor the months of my imprisonment here. . . . I would rather serve out my full term here than be placed in the attitude of accepting from the Government a clemency that would imply that I have in fact been guilty of any wrongdoing. . . . I do not wish, or intend, that what I have done shall be "relegated to the generous domain of the forgotten."

Julian waited a week in vain for his letter to appear in the paper. Then he wrote Brisbane again. "In holding back the letter I sent you dated July 8th," he observed, "you are doing me harm that cannot be easily or soon repaired." He was not a supplicant for a favor from his government. He did not learn until after his release that his July 8 letter had been confiscated at the prison and forwarded to Washington. An assistant attorney general had returned it to Warden William Moyer of the Atlanta Federal Penitentiary on July 12 and advised him "that it is not deemed expedient to allow this article to be sent out by Mr. Hawthorne for publication purposes."[51]

According to the records of his incarceration, he maintained a lively correspondence from behind bars with members of his family. He exchanged letters with Edith, whom he addressed as his niece, at her parents' home in Tryon, North Carolina, several times a week. Once a month he contacted and received letters from his "legitimate" children. Once or twice he wrote Minna. He received no visitors except for a local minister, and he routinely refused all reporters' requests for interviews. He declined one such request with this curt note: "I must ask you to excuse me. I have, as you know, not a name but a number. If anything I have written for 'Good Words' has done good or has caused interest, I am glad, but have nothing to say about it."[52]

He gradually earned the confidence of the other inmates. "They came to me freely, and either by laboriously penned or penciled letters written on surreptitious scraps of paper in ill-lighted cells, or by circumspect word of mouth mumbled into my ear on the baseball ground of a Saturday afternoon," they told him about their lives. Their stories were "the most important gift that he ever received." "There were men there who had committed merciless robberies, cruel murders, heartless swindles, abominable depravities," he allowed, but "I have felt greater temperamental aversion from many highly respectable persons than I did from them. Their crimes were one thing, they were another." When the Italian tenor Enrico Caruso sang for the prisoners on April 23, Julian welcomed him with a poem in which he compared his "brothers" to Lazarus in the tomb. During Caruso's performance he sat near the stage with the notorious mobster Ignazio Lupo (aka Lupo the Wolf). Among Julian's closest friends in lock-up was Sam Moore, an African American who in 1892, at the age of seventeen, killed a man in self-defense and spent the rest of his life in jail. "I knew no man in the prison more intimately than I did him and respected none more," Julian wrote. "A week's detention would have been ample penalty for what he did."[53]

By virtue of his age and notoriety, Julian enjoyed more privileges than a normal inmate. He was never treated harshly, and he was permitted to smoke and exercise in the prison yard. His encounters with the warden and his deputies, though "seldom and brief," were "uniformly suave and smiling." He was allowed to write as many letters as he wished, some of them for other inmates. Nevertheless, he was exposed to the brutality of prison life. The guards, with rare exceptions, were "petty tyrants of the worst type, sulky, sneering, malignant, brutal, and liars and treacherous into the bargain." Worse yet, the inmates were fed "at the rate of from eight to eleven cents per head a day." As a result, Julian nearly starved the first two months he was in Atlanta. He literally could not stomach the prison fare. He stopped eating, "unwilling to poison myself with the rancid grease and garbage." He lost so much weight that the prison doctor put him on a special diet of oatmeal and milk twice daily. When he was released, his physical condition was "quite as good as when I went in," and he had even gained a few pounds.[54]

The evening before they were freed, Julian and Will received a visit from Edith. She arranged to meet them the next day with their train tickets north.[55] When Julian walked out the prison gate the morning of October 15, 1913, to meet her, he was sixty-seven years old, disgraced, unemployed, and broke again though unbroken.

8

1915–34
"I am an old man and I know the world"

After publication of *The Subterranean Brotherhood*, Julian needed a job. He
pitched a series of essays on "Love Stories from the Bible" to the Wheeler
syndicate, the same outfit that serialized his prison memoirs. The syndicate
marketed the series without mentioning him by name, merely that he was
"an American author of national reputation." Two of the articles survive
in proof among Julian's papers—"Abraham and Hagar" and "The Story
of the Nazarite Who Betrayed the Secret of the Lord for the Sake of a
Woman"—but not a single newspaper seems to have subscribed.[1] Then his
friend Sam Chamberlain intervened. Like the *Los Angeles Examiner* in 1905,
the *Boston American*, another Hearst newspaper, was in financial trouble,
and Chamberlain was charged with reviving it. So "to Boston he went . . .
taking me with him" as a feature writer.[2] Julian was back in harness with
the Hearst chain—or back in Hearst's chains.

His first assignment was a plum—covering the 1915 spring training of the
Boston Braves in Macon, Georgia, and the Boston Red Sox in Hot Springs,
Arkansas. Julian was an avid baseball fan—he thought the game "exactly
suits our national temperament" because it "unites physical prowess with
quickness and accuracy of brain, science with athletics, mind with body."
He had also covered the World Series between the Philadelphia Athletics
and New York Giants as sports editor for the *New York American* a decade
earlier. But in 1915 Boston was the hub of the baseball universe. Julian
interviewed George Stallings, manager of the defending world champion
Braves, at his home in Haddocks, Georgia, in late February 1915, and he
accompanied Stallings and several players to Macon on February 28. For a
month Julian rubbed shoulders with such stars as Johnny Evers and Rabbit
Maranville of the Braves and Tris Speaker and Honus Wagner of the Red
Sox. But the player who most impressed him was a Red Sox rookie named

Babe Ruth. "He is a born pitcher, no doubt; but he can hit, too," Julian reported, and "he is only twenty years of age." He compared Ruth to "a rangy, loose-jointed colt ambling about the pasture. . . . What he will be at twenty-five need not now concern us; but we shall hear a good deal about him during the next five months."[3] At Julian's request, Ruth stripped to the waist and posed for photos that ran in the *Boston American*.

In April Julian accepted another assignment—a series of photo essays chronicling his sentimental journeys to old haunts in Boston, Salem, Cambridge, and especially Concord. There he posed outside Apple Slump and the Wayside, added a pebble to Thoreau's cairn at Walden Pond, and interviewed the eighty-three-year-old Frank Sanborn, whose "voice and bearing were hardly altered" after half a century. He was disturbed to discover, however, that the village was overrun with tourists. He complained that he was "expected to step softly around the place" and speak in a "hushed" and "reverential" voice as though it were hallowed ground.[4]

During the summer and fall Julian contributed several articles to the *Boston American* along the lines of Bartley Hubbard's "Solid Men of Boston" series in Howells's novel *The Rise of Silas Lapham*. He conducted interviews with such pillars of the community as Joseph Lannin, the owner of the Red

Julian at Thoreau's cairn, Walden Pond, May 1915. (Courtesy of the Bancroft Library, University of California, Berkeley [72/236 vol. 3, p. 113].)

Julian and Frank Sanborn, May 1915. (Courtesy of the Bancroft Library, University of California, Berkeley [87/23c scrapbook 2, p. 93].)

Sox; industrialist Theodore Vail; and Samuel W. McCall, governor-elect of Massachusetts. In June he profiled the poet and "sob sister" Ella Wheeler Wilcox—"no American woman is more widely loved"—who declared that the European war raging at the moment was "God's housekeeping," one of Julian's few references to the Great War. Wilcox thanked him a day or two later, saying his sketch was "the finest thing ever written about me."[5] Most significantly, Julian interviewed the lawyer Louis Brandeis, who would become an associate justice of the U.S. Supreme Court the next year. Brandeis, a leading American Zionist, compared the movement to "the Pilgrim inspiration and impulse. . . . The same ideas of government which emancipated the Colonies and created the United States were held by the Jews many centuries ago." The interview with Brandeis appeared on Independence Day 1915.[6]

Julian resigned from the newspaper in November—Sam Chamberlain was in failing health and died the following January—and he and Edith fled the East for a fresh start in the West. When he was first released from prison, they had maintained separate domiciles for the sake of appearances—he near Bryant Park, she on Madison Avenue just off Central Park East. In California they shared a home, although to forestall gossip, Edith posed as Julian's "nurse" or "aide." They initially settled in a bungalow adjacent to

Julian and Louis Brandeis (*Boston American*, July 4, 1915, 2:1). (Courtesy of the Bancroft Library, University of California, Berkeley [87/23 vol. 2, p. 64].)

an orange grove on Howard Street in Pasadena. Gaylord Wilshire bought a house next door and often came over to "recline on the sofa, smoking cigarettes and chatting, discussing innumerable projects."[7]

At the age of seventy Julian tried to resume his writing career, but without much success. The first week of December 1915 he contributed a couple of articles to the *Los Angeles Herald* about the trial of Matthew Schmidt, a Wobblie who had been implicated in the bombing of the Los Angeles Times Building in 1910 and spent five years on the lam. It was Julian's last murder trial. He peddled a screen treatment titled "The Vanishing Elephant" to the Universal Film Company in July 1916 for six hundred dollars, but it was never produced.[8] He claimed in 1920 to have had "movie people on my trail for the last six or seven years" to buy rights to his father's fiction "but never saw my way to accepting their propositions." Besides, he derided "the liberties which the film companies take in remodeling a novel" and haughtily claimed that "the Birthright-for-the-mess-of-pottage thing does not attract me."[9] The companies did not need his permission to adapt his father's novels to film, in any case—a major studio production of *The Scarlet Letter* starring Lillian Gish was released in 1926. Still, he wrote his own screenplay of it, titled "Lure of Youth," and tried his hand at adaptations of several of his own tales, including *Archibald Malmaison*, *Fortune's Fool*, and *Beatrix Randolph*, but sold none of them. He planned eventually to collect "some of my novels and to issue them in a uniform edition," though he conceded such a project might "never materialize" and it didn't. "I am getting to an age when I begin to doubt whether my projects will be carried out," he allowed. Nor was he "an addict of posthumous publication." He preferred "sweeping my debris out of the studio with my own broom, before finally closing the door and calling it a day."[10] He never entirely stopped writing stories, but editors stopped accepting them. He collected rejection letters during his last years from *Woman's World, Sportsman, McCall's, Good Housekeeping, American Mercury, Harper's, Poetry,* and the *Saturday Evening Post.* In the spring of 1924 he penned a final novel, "Letter of Credit" or "Companions of the Sun," but it was never published. In his journal for the same year, he listed the titles of more than a dozen stories he had failed to place, including "Letter from an Insane Woman," "The New Heart," and "The Doctor's Brains."[11]

His occasional triumphs were modest. In 1917 he published a crude, four-part science fiction serial titled "The Cosmic Courtship" in *All-Story Weekly,* the pulp magazine in which Edgar Rice Burroughs introduced Tarzan of the Apes and John Carter of Mars. Julian hung his hat on a rung of the literary ladder only a step or two above a penny-a-liner and far below the rank of his debut novels of the 1870s. This domestic romance set on Saturn (again!) eighty-four years in the future features ray guns and such extrasensory phenomena as mental telepathy and bodily transference, yet the characters still write with pens on paper and operate machines containing gears and dials. Julian's version of utopia is both classist (rich people own airplanes, but the poor travel on subways) and racist (pure Saturnians are superior to Nature people). He published three other stories in *All-Story Weekly:* "Absolute Evil" (1918), "A Goth from Boston" (1919), and "Sara Was Judith" (1920)—all narrated by Martha Klemm, Julian's only woman narrator, an innovation that enabled him to titillate readers with scenes in which, for example, Martha watches her pretty young niece undress.

Predictably, he enjoyed his greatest literary successes during his last years as a memoirist. His "Jocasta's Romance" (1917), a short story based on his prison experience, appeared in the *Smart Set* soon after H. L. Mencken and George Jean Nathan assumed its editorship. In it, he reiterated some of the charges he had leveled earlier (for instance, "the hash not only smelt bad, but had a beetle in it").[12] He received five hundred dollars from the *Ladies' Home Journal* for an essay about Louisa May Alcott in 1922—his largest payment for any project during the final eighteen years of his life. He contributed four autobiographical essays to the *Literary Digest International Book Review* between February 1925 and August 1926, edited at the time by his son-in-law Clifford Smyth, and twenty-nine essays, many of them about the Concord circle in the 1850s, for the *Dearborn Independent* between October 1925 and December 1927. His tenure with the *Independent* ended badly, however, after he fell out with its egomaniacal publisher, Henry Ford. "Beginning half a century ago as a sane human being," Julian griped a year after he stopped writing for the paper, Ford "has long since ceased to be human, while believing himself to be an epitome of whatever in humanity is best and most enlightened."[13] *Shapes That Pass*, a memoir of his life in England during the 1850s and '70s and the last book he published before his death, was issued by Houghton Mifflin in September 1928. It was welcomed in a sterling notice in the *New York Times Book Review* as "undeniably one of the most entertaining books of reminiscence by an American. And for a man of over 80 to write with so much humor and so much vigor is a feat to be appreciated."[14] He was either blessed or burdened with a prodigious memory.

Beginning in 1923, a relic of a generation more completely lost than the expatriates of the 1920s, Julian contributed a weekly column to the *Pasadena Star-News* in which he reminisced about dozens of famous men and women. He wrote more than 550 of these pieces for the paper and was paid twenty-five dollars a month for them. Combative to the end, he sometimes took a last lick at an old enemy. After ignoring her for over forty years, for example, Julian returned to Margaret Fuller like a dog to an old shoe in two of his weekly columns. Fuller could not have been the model for the heroine in his father's *The Blithedale Romance*, he had concluded, because Zenobia was "beautiful and mysterious" but "poor Margaret was plain and obvious." Intellectually she was on par with Bronson Alcott. Never one to tolerate uppity women, he scorned the new biography of Fuller by Margaret Bell—"the very worst biographer that ever lived"—and even its preface by Eleanor Roosevelt, "whose husband was foredoomed to become the President of this country."[15] Thus he aligned his critique of Transcendentalism with his condemnation of the New Deal. He recorded his final impressions of the good gay poet Walt Whitman, again in the form of ad hominem attack: "His intellect was immature and probably diseased. He was personally unclean and smelt so." He was also guilty of "such indiscretions as sufficed to send Wilde to jail."[16]

On the other hand, Julian ruthlessly defended his father's reputation, often in patronizing accents. He never praised a biography of his father other than his own. The family history still belonged to him seventy years after Nathaniel's death. Of Lloyd Morris's *The Rebellious Puritan: Portrait of Mr. Hawthorne* (1927), he remarked, "I can't reconcile myself to the tone of this fluting and harping composition: I long for an axe and a sledgehammer." He ridiculed the editions of his father's journals edited by Newton Arvin and Randall Stewart. The title of Arvin's volume "might have been 'Hawthorne Blue-Penciled,'" and Stewart's contention that his mother had sanitized his father's journals as she edited them for publication in 1868 was simply wrong. The professors "could not have barked up a more barren tree," Julian insisted, "but my time for spanking children is long since over."[17]

He was puzzled by the Melville revival in the '20s, though decades earlier he might have predicted it. He corresponded with Raymond Weaver, Melville's first biographer, in December 1919 and commended him for "undertaking the work of bringing out a complete account of Melville's life and writings," but he sounded an entirely different note after the book appeared. Weaver had taken unconscionable liberties in eulogizing Melville, and such reviewers as Carl Van Doren and Carl Van Vechten "exceeded all bounds of silliness in their gross flatteries." He failed to understand the reasons scholars were fascinated with his father's friendship with Melville. As he wrote a researcher in December 1931, their acquaintance "was comparatively slight. It seems to me to contain hardly substance enough for a volume. Melville's genius culminated with *Moby-Dick*; his mind afterward became progressively unbalanced." In the end, only one scholarly project related to his father earned Julian's approval: Ralph Rusk's edition of Emerson's letters. "I shall be glad to see my father's letters" to Emerson in print, he wrote Rusk, because "the two men were good friends," although "their telescopes were not directed to the same point overhead."[18]

He was no less confused by the strange new postwar world. The old targets—Howells, Zola, Wilson, Theodore Roosevelt, Rockefeller—were all dead or dying. So he discovered some new ones—Mussolini and fascism, "the pseudoscience of Freud," "the poison of Bolshevism," and prohibition. So long as the temperance movement had no chance of succeeding, Julian had been a proponent. Carrie Nation was "the female John Brown of this age," he proclaimed in 1901, because hers was a crusade "to free men from the slavery of alcohol." In 1926, however, he bragged lustily when he was able to drink "the Real Stuff!" even when bought from bootleggers.[19]

He was especially chagrined by the inroads made by modernism on the genteel tradition in the arts. He still championed the romantic-allegorical style of his father and decried the writings of Ernest Hemingway, James Joyce, Gertrude Stein, and D. H. Lawrence, whose *Sons and Lovers* he dismissed as "dismal and hopeless." He yearned for the days when a minor poet like Edwin Markham could compose a poem like "The Man with the Muckrake" that challenged the social status quo but, as he wrote Lincoln Steffens, one of the original muckrakers, "our contemporary chirpers and twitterers lack the guts for such achievements." "I for several years tried to stem the tide of modern literature (or call it what you will)," he proclaimed in the *Star-News*, and he contemptuously dismissed such innovations as vers libre: "Ninety-nine hundredth[s] of our best poetry is rhymed; almost none of contemporary unrhymed verse is poetry." Long after the deaths of James Whistler and Lawrence Alma-Tadema, he expressed disdain for cubism and other forms of expressionism. After he bought a radio, he was even disturbed by the ubiquity of "anything like jazz or blatant speaking or vulgar nonsense—of which the radio abounds."[20]

Julian's misgivings about trash culture broadcast on the radio did not prevent him, however, from speaking on the local San Francisco station KPO whenever he was invited. He was a regular guest on a program sponsored by the Sperry Flour Company called "Sperry Smiles," chatting about such luminaries of his boyhood as Louisa Alcott and Oliver Wendell Holmes. He was also interviewed on radio at the close of the Los Angeles Olympics in July 1932 "on the theme of Athletics seventy or more years ago."[21]

He was often invited to speak, in fact, as a sort of doomsaying voice from the past. "Outwardly we seem to have become more humane," he told another interviewer, "but we have not progressed in the spirit since the witch-burning days of Salem. The intolerance of Americans seems to be endless." He was especially outspoken about Americans' intolerance of sexual freedoms. To be sure, "We do not brand unmarried mothers with big 'A's,'" but "we have our own forms of intolerances, the gallows, the K.K.K., evolution trials, prohibition laws and free speech restrictions. . . . The branding-iron of the 17th century and the intolerances of the 20th— they're of the same spirit." At the same time he offered qualified approval of the sexual revolution of the 1920s, believing that the history of Western civilization for the past "two thousand years has been a war against sex."[22] From his perspective, Hester Prynne was a heroic figure because she was both a free lover and a good mother.

*   *   *

Except for his children, Julian outlived everyone he had known before the turn of the century. In 1901 Mother Alphonsa opened a second hospital for the incurably ill in Hawthorne, New York, to her brother's unqualified admiration. "You and your work are never out of my mind: it is a vision of Jacob's Ladder, by which angels descend to earth, and mortals climb toward Heaven," he assured her. "Your little Home, seen from Heaven, is a bright spot in a dark world, and the brightness will spread forever."[23] She became a candidate for sainthood in the Roman Catholic Church seventy-seven years after her death in 1926.

Will Morton continued to invest money in Freeman's dry holes to his inevitable regret. Morton insisted in April 1917 that Freeman's latest mine "is a really big thing," though by September he admitted, "I heartily wish I had my money back." After Will's death in 1920, Bessie was forced to earn her living as a governess, because Freeman "took Will's every penny." Morton was a victim of the "financial harpies," Julian wrote in a final tribute to his friend. "He was never cured of his faith in their honesty, and he died poor."[24]

In 1920, while living with Imogen and her family in West Redding, Connecticut, Minne suffered a paralyzing stroke. On June 5, 1925, she died from a second stroke "without pain, unconscious," as Julian remarked in his journal. A month later, on July 6, Julian and Edith were married at the town hall in La Jolla. It was a "fine sunny day. All well at last." After nearly two decades together, they no longer maintained the ruse that she was his nurse, niece, or aide. After Minne's death, Julian thrice returned to New York and

Julian and Edith Hawthorne, ca. 1930. (Courtesy of the Bancroft Library, University of California, Berkeley [BANC PIC 1987.078 2:2].)

New England to visit his children and grandchildren—during summer and fall of 1928, summer of 1929, and spring of 1932. However, he continued to spread the polite fiction that he and Minne had always been happily married. As he wrote Frederick Macmillan in 1933, "My wife, whom you knew, died years ago, leaving me with seven children—those you knew and two others."[25] He obliquely referred here to Mayflower and Joan for the only time on record after writing his will in 1908.

Despite his marriage to Edith, Julian remained something of a Lothario. Even as an octogenarian, he flirted with women half his age or younger, such as Emily Glass, a friend of the Wilshires. As he wrote her when he was seventy-six and she twenty-five, "I fell in love [with you] at first sight years ago," long before her husband Ray "discovered her ocean cave." (He seemed to regard her as a Siren.) Emily had hosted his most recent birthday party, and he wrote to thank her: "May I never be too old to have a birthday, and you to make magic of it!" He sent her letters surreptitiously. ("Edith hasn't, and she will not, see this letter, or know I'm writing, and needless to say Ray mustn't.") He began one letter to his "precious girl" by declaring that she had "a kiss coming to you," and he closed it with a similar sweet nothing: "You may now disentangle yourself from my yearning arms, and consider how much I shall always be yours."[26]

*   *   *

During his final years in California, as during his New England boyhood, Julian craved sea and mountain air. Just as Lenox had been too stifling for his father in 1851, Pasadena was too far inland to suit him. He and Edith sublet their bungalow there in June 1924 and moved to a small house in Sausalito with a "good view of bay and mountain." "I am much better since arriving," Julian wrote a week later. They spent October in La Jolla, and the next summer they camped beside Lake Tahoe in the Sierra Nevada. Then they moved to the Berkeley Hills within sight of San Francisco Bay for a few months, although Julian, increasingly a curmudgeon, detested the campus atmosphere: "scratch a Berkeley-ite and you find a Vacuum, but of that poisonous sort that spreads a miasma of contagious barrenness," he ranted to Henry Seidel Canby of Yale. Then with a touch of poignancy: "I am an old man and I know the world."[27] In 1926–27 Julian and Edith lived successively in Newport Beach, Sausalito, and La Jolla before finally settling in an apartment on Eighth Street in San Francisco less than a block from Golden Gate Park in December 1927, where they lived for the rest of their lives.[28]

After dining with Julian in San Francisco in the fall of 1929, Hamlin Garland launched a campaign to have him elected to the National Institute of

Arts and Letters. He sounded out William Lyon Phelps, professor of English at Yale, on the subject: Julian was "old and poor," though "a fine, dignified gentleman." To elect him to the institute "would be a fine gesture. After all he is the distinguished son of a very great man, and I have never believed that he meant to defraud." Such an honor "now when he is nearing the end" would "afford him deep satisfaction." Phelps was unconvinced. "I agree with you that he is a gentleman and certainly not a bad man," he replied, "but would it not drag [his conviction and imprisonment] into publicity if we made such a nomination?" (Julian privately dubbed Phelps "the Prince of Philistines.") Garland also sounded out other institute members, including William Allen White, to no avail, and dropped the plan.[29]

Nevertheless, in March 1930 Garland invited Julian to speak in Los Angeles. "If I were 24, instead of 60 years beyond that: or were, like you, in the flush of manhood," Julian replied, "it would be simpler: but life is now in the last pages of its final chapter." He asked for a hundred-dollar honorarium plus expenses and offered to "address two or three audiences instead of one" if necessary to earn the money. Garland arranged for Julian to talk on June 7 before the Hollywood Woman's Club on "Personal Reminiscences of the Concord Group" and to lecture on July 15–17 at the University of Southern California on "Nathaniel Hawthorne at Concord," "The Making of the 'Scarlet Letter,'" "Louisa Alcott and Family," and "Ralph Waldo Emerson."[30]

He was honored on his eighty-fifth birthday with a banquet hosted by the *Pasadena Star-News* at the Huntington Hotel on June 22, 1931. The managing editor of the paper, Charles H. Prisk, reminisced before the 125 guests about his negotiations with Hawthorne in 1923 for the weekly articles the author was to contribute to the *Star-News*. Upton Sinclair, "promising not to make a Socialist speech," described Julian as a "charming, lovable writer." The literary editor of the newspaper, Harold D. Carew, then read letters and telegrams from such luminaries as Garland, White, George Bernard Shaw, Sinclair Lewis, P. G. Wodehouse, H. L. Mencken, Ellen Glasgow, Robinson Jeffers, and Lincoln Steffens. Garland praised Julian's work as an autobiographer. White commended his journalism. Shaw expressed surprise that he was still alive: "I had mourned him for years! Are you sure he is not an impostor?" Julian knew Lewis from summers at Newport Beach, "then a rather primitive and secluded place" near Los Angeles, and the Nobel laureate "wished that I possessed that grace and charm which enabled him to come so close to the great of literary and political England." Lewis would later name a minor character Julian in his novel *It Can't Happen Here* (1935). At the close of the five-hour banquet, in his final public appearance, Julian reminisced about life at the Wayside with his parents and sisters and thanked his friends. Should any of them "live to be 85," he hoped "you will enjoy it as much as I have," and "I like to hope that you will have friends as kind to you as you have been to me." Edith was relieved when he finished: "The way Julian digressed in his speech from what he intended to say made me hot and cold, for the tone of his talk was getting so grewsome, so graveyard, that I wondered how he was going to get out of it."[31]

*   *   *

Julian attributed his longevity to diet and exercise. "At forty, I was very fit, weighed 175, and my general health was perfect. At seventy I was still running three to four miles before breakfast." He continued to walk five to seven miles a day until the age of eighty-six.[32] But he never recovered from a bout of flu in the summer of 1933. He was sick for several weeks and the illness affected his heart. When Garland saw him in late August, he remarked in his diary on Julian's frail appearance, saying he had "failed in mental strength and vigor since I saw him last. He has shrunk in size and has in the face the shadow of approaching death."[33] Julian spent three days in the hospital that winter for medical tests. Hildegarde moved to Berkeley in 1933 to be near her father in his sere and yellow leaf. Early in 1934 he suffered a setback, and on the night of March 21 "he took a decided turn for the worse," as Edith reported to friends. Only an injection of morphine enabled him to rally from a heart attack. Afterward, his eyesight began to fail, and he suffered a second heart attack in June.[34]

Julian Hawthorne died in the early morning hours of July 14, 1934. Edith described his final hours in a confidential letter to Helen Haines four days later. From his bed, he "held out his arms" and "pleaded with me" to join him, "and he held up the blanket for me." His illness had "left him without sex-force" for months and in his final hours "he felt proud to beckon me."

I told him when he got strong we would be lovers again. To keep a grip on myself, I went into another room, but after a while I found him still waiting for me—I lowered the lights hoping he would sleep. For an hour and a half this phase of pleading lasted,—then suddenly his strength was spent—he tried to sit up to get up and I had to exert all my strength to help him. And so that was the last cry of the physical man. I knew if I did not get sleep that night I might break so got a nurse. . . . She came at ten p.m.—I had just finished explaining to her Julian's habits, and that she had to guard against his falling above all, when he began to be really sick and in great pain inside.

During the next three hours—everything happened—Julian gradually became a living human flame. His mind keen, his chivalry on tap thanking us both for every act—asking the nurse to turn away when he had to throw up saying "You are a good girl but you must go away." Fortunately she caught his quality at once—seemed to understand him—"My! but that man loves you" she said—as she saw his eyes following me everywhere. But nature began to break down fast—and everything poured from him from every opening. . . . Every sheet every towel and small cloth in the place was rushed into service—and dashed into the kitchen tubs—as we ran back to his side—

Julian died during a general strike in San Francisco at the nadir of the Great Depression, so the physician Edith summoned had trouble reaching their apartment.

The doctor was finally located—he phoned he could not get there until 12.30 being on a case. By twelve Julian was wild—by twelve thirty he was in agony—yet always thinking of us. "Wonderful woman" he said to me again and again. . . . Then Julian sitting up in bed against the head board—without pillows behind him—spoke firmly. "I want to put my body in a kneeling position—in the attitude of prayer, to thank God for the care I have been getting!" He slipped from the bed to his knees—and as I put a pillow under them on the floor, he bowed his head over the mattress, and thus in prayer, was gone—his head dropped down on the bed, and I knew it was over. His pain was gone.[35]

The funeral was private, as he had requested, with only four attendees, including Edith, Hildegarde, and the minister. At his direction his body was cremated—he was not buried in the family plot in Concord, perhaps to spare Edith the expense, perhaps to spare his other relatives the ignominy—and his ashes were scattered along Newport Beach. When he died, Edith later wrote, "one of earth's rare men passed on" and "to be deprived of such companionship is to me inestimable."[36]

EPILOGUE

At Julian's death Edith lost her only source of income. He had no life insurance. She eked out a living by selling some Hawthorniana, including a draft of *Dr. Grimshawe's Secret* in Sophia's hand and a batch of Elizabeth Hawthorne's letters, to the Rare Book Department at Scribner's for $250. She spoke occasionally on KFRC radio in San Francisco on topics gleaned from his papers. When he died, moreover, the *Star-News* had a backlog of thirty-eight of his columns, and Edith silently wrote seventeen more from his notes "in self-defense."[1] They appeared posthumously and without interruption for eleven months, and the *Star-News* then serialized his *Memoirs*, edited by Edith, from June until December 1935.

Julian continually puttered over these reminiscences in his final years—he finished no fewer than four distinct versions, each with a different title: "Literary Lights of Old Concord," "Giants of Old Concord," "Things in General," and "Thinking Things Over." He realized that literary scholars would "find small value" in them, but he figured archeologists "will grin over the mouldering pages."[2] It was hardly an intimate autobiography; rather, it was a chronicle of his public persona. He nowhere mentions in it either of his wives, any of his children, or his imprisonment. Though publishers were interested, none of them was interested enough to accept it. According to Edith, they "pronounced the material very valuable, but said they were not in shape for publication." So after he died she "took hold of these manuscripts, and after more than two years work on them, again submitted them to Macmillan," which accepted an abridged version of "Thinking Things Over."[3] Julian's valedictory volume was published in April 1938, nearly four years after his death, to favorable reviews. The *Los Angeles Times* proclaimed it "a really valuable contribution to our knowledge of New England and its literary pioneers," and the *Christian Science Monitor* called it "a genuine contribution to the history of American letters." Odell

Shepard, professor of English at Trinity College, supposed in the *Nation* that "there can have been few more successful sons of great and famous men" than Julian. In September 1938, ironically, after blacklisting several of his novels during his life, the Roman Catholic Archdiocese of New York listed Julian's *Memoirs* among books it approved.[4]

Edith died in January 1949 in the same San Francisco apartment she had shared with Julian. In the *Pasadena Star-News*, Helen Haines memorialized her, saying Julian "was her lifework: he was at once her child, her lover, her husband, and her father."[5] He was the only child of Nathaniel and Sophia blessed with adult offspring; all their heirs descend through him, and his children who survived infancy all led long lives. Hildegarde became, like her father and grandfather, a professional author and died at eighty-one; Jack, who nearly died of yellow fever in 1898, enjoyed a successful newspaper career and died at eighty-seven; and after a distinguished career as a sportswriter, Fred died at seventy-two. Henry died at eighty-five; Gwendolen at ninety-four; Beatrix at eighty-eight; and Imogen at seventy-three. Mayflower and Joan lived to the ages of seventy-five and ninety without the recognition they might have received as descendants of the Hawthornes. The present generation of "legitimate" heirs knew nothing about Julian's shadow family until July 2004, when two of Mayflower's descendants attended the bicentennial celebration of Nathaniel Hawthorne's birth in Salem.

NOTES

ABBREVIATIONS

72/236z	Hawthorne Family Papers, Bancroft Library, University of California, Berkeley
87/23c	JH Papers, Bancroft Library, University of California, Berkeley
89/201c	Bancroft Library, University of California, Berkeley
AC	*Atlanta Constitution*
AJ	*Appleton's Journal*
AL	*American Literature*
AM	*Atlantic Monthly*
BA	*Boston American*
Bassan	Maurice Bassan, *Hawthorne's Son* (Columbus: Ohio State University Press, 1970)
BE	*Brooklyn Eagle*
BG	*Boston Globe*
"Biography"	"Biography, New Style," *University Magazine*, 29 Sep 1880, 53–57
BJ	*Boston Journal*
Bridge	Horatio Bridge, *Personal Recollections of Nathaniel Hawthorne* (New York: Harper and Brothers, 1893)
BPL	Boston Public Library
BT	*Boston Transcript*
C&C	JH, *Confessions and Criticisms* (Boston: Ticknor, 1886)
CE	*Centenary Edition of the Works of Nathaniel Hawthorne*
CIO	*Chicago Inter-Ocean*
Columbia	Butler Library, Columbia University
Cosmo	*Cosmopolitan*
CT	*Chicago Tribune*
CW	*Collier's Weekly*
DI	*Dearborn [Michigan] Independent*

DP	*Denver Post*
EPP	Elizabeth Palmer Peabody
GW	*Good Words*
H&HC	JH, *Hawthorne and His Circle* (New York: Harper and Brothers, 1903)
HL	*Human Life*
Houghton	Houghton Library, Harvard University
Hull	Raymona E. Hull, *Nathaniel Hawthorne: The English Experience* (Pittsburgh: University of Pittsburgh Press, 1980)
IA	*Illustrated American*
JH	Julian Hawthorne
LAE	*Los Angeles Examiner*
LAT	*Los Angeles Times*
LC	Library of Congress
LHJ	*Ladies' Home Journal*
LW	*Literary World*
M	JH, *Memoirs* (New York: Macmillan, 1938)
Maynard	Theodore Maynard, *A Fire Was Lighted* (Milwaukee: Bruce, 1948)
Memories	Rose Hawthorne Lathrop, *Memories of Hawthorne* (Boston: Houghton Mifflin, 1897)
NAR	*North American Review*
NH&W	JH, *Nathaniel Hawthorne and His Wife* (Boston: Osgood, 1884)
NHR	*Nathaniel Hawthorne Review*
NYA	*New York American*
NYCA	*New York Commercial Advertiser*
NYH	*New York Herald*
NYJ	*New York Journal*
NYPL	The Henry W. and Albert A. Berg Collection of English and American Literature, New York Public Library, Astor, Lenox and Tilden Foundations
NYS	*New York Sun*
NYTimes	*New York Times*
NYTrib	*New York Tribune*
NYW	*New York World*
PI	*Philadelphia Inquirer*
PNA	*Philadelphia North American*
PO	*Portland Oregonian*
PSN	*Pasadena Star-News*
Ronda	*Letters of Elizabeth Palmer Peabody*, ed. Bruce Ronda (Middletown, CT: Wesleyan University Press, 1984)
Rosary Hill	Rosary Hill Home, Hawthorne, New York
SB	JH, *The Subterranean Brotherhood* (New York: McBride, Nast, 1914)

SEP	*Saturday Evening Post*
SFE	*San Francisco Examiner*
SH	Sophia Hawthorne
Shapes	JH, *Shapes That Pass* (New York: Houghton Mifflin, 1928)
SR	*Springfield [Illinois] Republican*
SS	JH, *Saxon Studies* (Boston: Osgood, 1876)
Tharp	Louise Tharp, *The Peabody Sisters of Salem (*Boston: Little, Brown, 1950)
UVa	Alderman Library, University of Virginia
Valenti	Patricia Dunlavy Valenti, *To Myself a Stranger* (Baton Rouge: Louisiana State University Press, 1991)
WP	*Washington Post*

INTRODUCTION

1. *M*, 3.

2. *M*, 298.

3. *LAE*, 8 Jan 1905, 28.

4. Maud Howe Elliot, *Three Generations* (Boston: Little, Brown, 1923), 29.

5. John Nichol, *American Literature* (Edinburgh: Black, 1882), 388; *Critic*, 12 Apr 1884, 169; 6 Jun 1885, 1.

6. A virtually complete list of JH's publications has appeared in two parts in *Resources for American Literary Study* 33 (2010): 93–132; and 35 (2010): 139–246. A few vagrant pieces are lost because they appeared in periodicals so ephemeral they do not survive.

7. *M*, 52.

8. Edith Hawthorne to Robert B. Carter, 16 Feb 1936 (87/23c box 1).

9. 72/236z carton 2.

10. Sean McCann, "The Novel of Crime, Mystery, and Suspense," in *The Cambridge History of the American Novel*, ed. Leonard Cassuto et al. (Cambridge: Cambridge University Press, 2011), 806.

11. Jean Strouse, "Semiprivate Lives," in *Studies in Biography*, ed. Daniel Aaron (Cambridge: Harvard University Press, 1978), 129.

12. It is also marred by dozens of factual errors and gaps in the record; e.g., Bassan asserts that JH submitted a series of several articles about Dresden to the *London Times* in 1872 (98) when these pieces in fact appeared in the *New York Times*; that he "spent the winter of 1881–82 in Italy" (142), though he was in Ireland; that Albert Freeman "never spent a day in jail" (215), though he was jailed in the Tombs for ten days in March 1913; that Sam Chamberlain was one of his Harvard classmates (221), though Chamberlain attended NYU; that his story "Two Old Boys" appeared "only in serial form in the *World*" (249), though it appeared in neither the *New York World* nor the *London World* but revised under a different title and in a different venue many years later.

PROLOGUE

1. Eugene V. Debs, *Walls and Bars* (Chicago: Socialist Party, 1927), 35; *NYS*, 15 Oct 1913, 1.

2. *NYS*, 16 Oct 1913, 7; *SB*, 76; *Atlanta Journal*, 15 Oct 1913, 1.

3. *NYA*, 16 Oct 1913, 1; *NYS*, 16 Oct 1913, 7.

4. C. W. Stuart to JH, 4 Nov 1913 (72/236z box 6).

5. *NYTrib*, 17 Oct 1913, 18; *NYTimes*, 17 Oct 1913, 20.

6. *Atlanta Journal*, 15 Oct 1913, 3.

7. *AC*, 17 Oct 1913, 8.

8. *AC*, 16 Oct 1913, 1, 16.

9. *NYS*, 11 Jan 1914, 11; 22 Feb 1914, editorial section, 12.

10. *NYS*, 7 Jan 1914, 2.

11. *NYTrib*, 17 Oct 1913, 18.

12. *AC*, 16 Oct 1913, 16.

13. *NYS*, 11 Jan 1914, 11.

14. *Duluth* [Minnesota] *News-Tribune*, 18 Oct 1913, 3.

15. JH to editor of the *NYW*, 15 Oct 1913 (Columbia).

16. *SB*, vii, 20, 95, 112, 210.

17. *Idaho Statesman*, 13 Jan 1914, 6.

18. *NYS*, 19 Feb 1914, 3.

19. *SB*, vi.

20. David Mike Hamilton, *The Tools of My Trade* (Seattle: University of Washington Press, 1986), 40, 150; *PO*, 27 Dec 1914, 9; *Journal of the American Institute of Criminal Law and Criminology* 6 (May 1915): 154–56.

21. *NYS*, 11 Jan 1914, 11; *NYTimes*, 13 Jan 1914, 8.

22. *NYS*, 22 Feb 1914, editorial section, 12.

23. *NYS*, 11 Jan 1914, 11.

24. *WP*, 7 Jan 1914, 2; *Kansas City Star*, 9 Jan 1914, 10; *NYS*, 6 Jan 1914, 1; 7 Jan 1914, 2.

25. *NYTimes*, 23 Jan 1914, 1.

26. *NYTimes*, 23 Mar 1914, 8.

27. *NYTimes*, 29 Mar 1915, 4.

28. *Journal of the American Institute of Criminal Law and Criminology* 6 (May 1915): 138.

29. Debs, *Walls and Bars*, 71, 56, 236.

CHAPTER 1: 1846–64

1. *CE* 16: 173–74, 201.

2. *Century* 93 (Dec 1927): 157.

3. Edwin Haviland Miller, *Salem Is My Dwelling Place* (Iowa City: University of Iowa Press, 1991), 127; 87/23c box 1.

4. Brenda Wineapple, *Hawthorne: A Life* (New York: Knopf, 2003), 15.

5. Philip Young, *Hawthorne's Secret* (Boston: Godine, 1984), 125–26.

6. *CE* 11: 68.

7. *NH&W* 1: 314; *HL* 7 (Sep 1908): 24.

8. *NH&W* 1: 310, 331; *CE* 16: 193; 8: 400, 415, 434; *Memories*, 243.

9. *NH&W* 1: 379, 324; Miller, *Salem*, 259; *Nathaniel Hawthorne: A Biography* (New Haven: Yale University Press, 1948), 91; *CE* 18: 487; 8: 424–25; T. Walter Herbert, *PMLA* 103 (May 1988): 285.

10. *NHR* 15 (Fall 1989): 6–9; *BA*, 16 May 1915, 3G-4G.

11. *H&HC*, 7, 9; *CE* 16: 338; 11: 7; 8: 410, 412, 415; *PSN*, 28 Feb 1931, 5; *NH&W* 1: 407–408.

12. *Bookman* 75 (Sep 1932): 505; *NH&W* 1: 363; *DI*, 3 Sep 1927, 12–13, 25–26.

13. *H&HC*, 32; *Booklover's Weekly,* 30 Dec 1901, 229.

14. *NH&W* 1: 410; Miller, *Salem*, 348; *CE* 8: 484–85; *HL* 7 (Sep 1908): 5–6.

15. *AL* 9 (March 1937): 334–35; *CE* 8: 448, 465, 466, 468; Herman Melville, *Correspondence* (Evanston: Northwestern University Press, 1993), 221–22.

16. *CE* 16: 454; *DI*, 22 Oct 1927, 16; *PSN*, 8 May 1925, 30; *NH&W* 1: 430–31; *H&HC*, 46–50.

17. Wineapple, *Hawthorne*, 251; *H&HC*, 61.

18. *H&HC*, 57; *LAE*, 19 Aug 1905, 10; *PSN*, 12 Dec 1923, 16.

19. *DI*, 26 Jun 1926, 16; *New York Critic*, 24 Nov 1888, 252; *Memories*, 194, 211–12.

20. *Memories*, 210; JH to Nathaniel Peabody, 12 Jan 1855 (NYPL); *H&HC*, 1–2, 23.

21. *Worcester Spy*, 9 Nov 1893, 4; James R. Mellow, *Nathaniel Hawthorne in His Times* (Boston: Houghton Mifflin, 1980), 381; *Lippincott's* 43 (Feb 1889): 254.

22. *CE* 23: 352; *PSN*, 15 Jul 1925, 3.

23. *Shapes*, 7; Hull 9; *H&HC*, 79, 86.

24. *Memories*, 223; *NH&W* 2: 23; *H&HC*, 120.

25. *H&HC*, 87; *DP*, 13 May 1900, 9; *CE* 17: 327; *NH&W* 2: 22.

26. *PSN*, 30 Oct 1925, 12; *Shapes*, 56–58; *H&HC*, 127; 72/236z carton 2; *NH&W* 1: 26.

27. *Bookman* 61 (Jul 1925): 567–71; 75 (Sep 1932): 505; *BA*, 10 Oct 1915, 2, 5; *DI*, 9 Jan 1926, 7; JH, "The Salem of Hawthorne," *Century* 28 (May 1884): 6.

28. *Shapes*, 39–40; *CE* 17: 289–90, 456; *PSN*, 3 Jan 1924, 7; 12 Nov 1927, 10; 7 Dec 1929, 5; 12 March 1932, 5; 4 Nov 1933, 5; 17 Feb 1934, 6; Valenti 13; *H&HC*, 227.

29. *Shapes*, 30; *Memories*, 330; *CE* 17: 351, 482; "Biography."

30. *M*, 15; *DI*, 29 Oct 1927, 5; *NH&W* 2: 133; *CE* 17: 460.

31. Hull 25; *Critic*, 19 Jul 1890, 36; *H&HC*, 2–95; *DP*, 13 May 1900, 9.

32. *PSN*, 28 March 1924, 29; 17 Sep 1927, 18; *DI*, 3 Sep 1927, 25; *H&HC*, 135; *Shapes*, 55; *NH&W* 2: 134.

33. Bassan 33; *NH&W* 2: 44, 49; *Memories*, 273; *H&HC*, 156; *CE* 21: 88, 196, 206.

34. Wineapple, *Hawthorne*, 281.

35. *CE* 17: 456–59; 21: 723; Hull 70, 71.

36. Hull 94; *DI*, 3 Sep 1927, 12; *CE* 5: 139–66; *H&HW* 2: 9; diary entry for 27 Jun 1857 (Pierpont Morgan); *Memories*, 315.

37. *H&HC*, 229–30; *NH&W* 2: 266; Valenti 14; Hull 154; ZA Pearson (Beinecke Rare Book and Manuscript Library, Yale University).

38. *H&HC*, 248; *CE* 14: 13, 25–26; *Shapes*, 17; *DP*, 10 Jun 1900, 16; *PSN*, 8 Sep 1924, 18.

39. *CE* 14: 25–27, 33; *PSN*, 8 Sep 1924, 18; *H&HC*, 260; *DP*, 20 May 1900, 14; *NH&W* 2: 176, 181.

40. *CE* 14: 125, 177; Rebecca Harding Davis, *Bits of Gossip* (Boston: Houghton Mifflin, 1904), 232; *H&HC*, 294; *NYA*, 24 Apr 1907, 10; JH, *A Fool of Nature* (New York: Scribner's, 1896), 167; *All-Story Weekly*, 1 May 1920, 445.

41. *NH&W* 2: 172; *HL* 7 (Sep 1908): 5–6; *H&HC*, 293, 320; *AM* 142 (Sep 1928): 373; *CE* 14: 138.

42. *H&HC*, 335; Mellow, *Nathaniel Hawthorne*, 501; *CE* 14: 258, 270; SH, *Notes on England and Italy* (New York: Putnam's, 1869), 339; *NH&W* 2: 190–91.

43. *Examiner*, 17 May 1879, 646; *DP*, 27 May 1900, 19; *H&HC*, 341; Hull 158; *CE* 14: 300–301; *PSN*, 4 Jun 1933, 10; 28 Jul 1934, 6; Caroline Dall, *Daughter of Boston*, ed. Helen R. Deese (Boston: Beacon, 2005), 45.

44. *DP*, 3 Jun 1900, 16; *PSN*, 22 Dec 1924, 19; 16 Jun 1934, 6.

45. *NH&W* 2: 198; *H&HC*, 343.

46. *CE* 14: 441, 613; 4: 145; *H&HC*, 43; *DP*, 20 May 1900, 14; *NH&W* 2: 202.

47. *H&HC*, 358; *M*, 160; *NH&W* 2: 206, 210; *PSN*, 15 Jul 1925, 3; *CE* 14: 508.

48. *CE* 4: 168–71, 382–89; 14: 505; Maynard 92.

49. *CE* 14: 557, 598; "Biography"; *Booklover's Weekly*, 30 Dec 1901, 226.

50. *H&HC*, 366; *CT*, 3 Jun 1879, 3.

51. *H&HC*, 368; *NH&W* 2: 230; 72/236z carton 2.

52. 72/236z carton 2; *CE* 18: 284.

53. *H&HC*, 371; *PSN*, 16 Mar 1929, 30; 25 Feb 1933, 5; *M*, 81; *Critic* 45 (Jul 1904): 67.

54. Hull 179; *PSN*, 28 Dec 1923, 28; 24 Jan 1924, 10; *NH&W* 2: 264, 267, 330; *BA*, 30 May 1915, 9L.

55. *CE* 18: 317–18, 353.

56. *DP*, 29 Apr 1900, 19; *PSN*, 28 Dec 1923, 28; 24 Sep 1932, 20.

57. *PSN*, 24 Jan 1924, 10; 20 Jan 1926, 7; *Worcester Spy*, 18 Apr 1904, 5; Maynard 140; *DI*, 24 Jul 1926, 14–15, 26; *DP*, 29 Apr 1900, 19.

58. *PSN*, 3 Jan 1924, 7; *DI*, 10 Sep 1927, 14–15, 21–22; 87/23c box 1; *CE* 18: 440.

59. Frank B. Sanborn, *Hawthorne and His Friends* (Cedar Rapids, IA: Torch, 1908), 13–16; *CE* 3: 47; *New England Quarterly* 20 (Jun 1947): 226.

60. *M*, 61; *Selected Letters of Louisa May Alcott*, ed. Joel Myerson and Daniel Shealy (Athens: University of Georgia Press, 1995), 57, 167; *Louisa May Alcott*, ed. Ednah D. Cheney (Boston: Roberts Brothers, 1889), 31; *The Letters of Ellen Emerson*, ed. Edith E. W. Gregg (Kent, OH: Kent State University Press, 1992), 1:

227, 260, 338, 410; *Critic* 45 (Jul 1904): 67; *DP*, 8 Apr 1900, 19; *NYA*, 28 Jul 1905, 6; *LHJ* 39 (Oct 1922): 120; *LW*, 1 Sep 1871, 62.

61. JH to SH, 21–23 Aug 1862 (NYPL); *Journals of Louisa May Alcott*, ed. Joel Myerson and Daniel Shealy (Boston: Little, Brown, 1989), 110; Cheney, *Letters*, 141; *M*, 61, 63, 68; *San Francisco Bulletin*, 11 Jun 1879, 4; *NYTimes Sunday Magazine*, 27 Nov 1932, 17; *PSN*, 29 Jul 1933, 10; 87/23c box 1; *LHJ* 39 (Oct 1922): 25, 120.

62. *Critic* 45 (Jul 1904): 67–71; *PSN*, 15 Oct 1927, 36; *CE* 18: 358, 597.

63. Hull 204; JH to Una Hawthorne, 20–21 Aug 1862 (NYPL); *NH&W* 2: 315–18; *PSN*, 11 Jun 1927, 20; *CE* 18: 478, 481–82.

64. *CE* 18: 379–81; 87/23c box 1; *Bookman* 75 (Sep 1932): 506; *DP*, 25 March 1900, 16; Albert J. Von Frank, *Emerson Chronology* (New York: Hall, 1984), 371; Frank Stearns, *The Life and Genius of Nathaniel Hawthorne* (Philadelphia: Lippincott, 1906), 405.

65. *DP*, 22 Apr 1900, 8; *PSN*, 12 Dec 1923, 16.

66. *More Books* 19 (1944): 267; JH to SH, 8 Nov 1864 (NYPL); *PSN*, 18 May 1929, 32; 27 Dec 1930, 5; Tharp 292; *M*, 18; M. A. DeWolfe Howe, *Memories of a Hostess* (Boston: Atlantic Monthly Press, 1922), 15.

67. Tharp 305; *CE* 18: 540, 545; *New Letters of James Russell Lowell* (New York: Harper, 1932), 103–104; *PSN*, 14 Sep 1925, 7; *DP*, 6 May 1900; *DI*, 2 Oct 1926, 13.

68. JH to EPP, 14 Jun 1863 (NYPL); *NH&W* 2: 330; *CE* 18: 545, 583; JH to SH, "Monday, Cambridge" [fall 1863] (St. Lawrence); *PSN*, 7 Oct 1925, 22.

69. *CE* 18: 595; Myerson and Shealy, *Selected Letters of Alcott*, 92.

70. *PSN*, 7 Oct 1925, 22.

71. *CE* 18: 601, 603; *PSN*, 8 Sep 1924, 18.

72. *San Francisco Call and Post*, 19 Jul 1924, 13, 18; *M*, 178–79.

73. "Biography"; 72/236z box 6; Bridge 191–92; *CE* 18: 610; Stearns, *Life and Genius*, 409; *PSN*, 27 Aug 1927, 28.

74. "Biography."

75. *HL* 7 (Sep 1908): 5–6; *NH&W* 2: 335.

CHAPTER 2: 1864–74

1. *AL* 27 (Jan 1956): 563; *NH&W* 2: 347.

2. Stearns, *Life and Genius*, 418.

3. Bridge 179; *AL* 27 (Jan 1956): 563; qtd. in Bassan 36.

4. JH to James T. Fields, 22 May 1864 (Ms.C.1.11 [10] BPL). Courtesy of the Trustees of the Boston Public Library/Rare Books.

5. *DI*, 8 May 1926, 23; *NH&W* 2: 347; *BT*, 24 May 1864, 4; Maynard 134.

6. *M*, 19, 158; *Bookman* 75 (Sep 1932), 505–6; *AL* 27 (Jan 1956): 563; Maynard 138; *DI*, 15 Oct 1927, 5.

7. *PSN*, 13 May 1925, 5; 15 Jul 1925, 3; *M*, 189–90; 87/23c box 1.

8. Mellow, *Nathaniel Hawthorne*, 572; JH to Franklin Pierce, 1 and 11 Sep 1864 (Franklin Pierce Papers, #1929-1, New Hampshire Historical Society).

9. *M*, 180, 195; "Biography"; 87/23c box 1; *BA*, 23 May 1915, 4E-5E; *PSN*, 5 Feb 1926, 5.

10. *CIO*, 19 Dec 1886, 22; *SR*, 16 Nov 1874, 3; Charles Honce, *A Julian Hawthorne Collection* (New York: privately printed, 1939), 17; *IA*, 4 Apr 1896, 438–39.

11. *DI*, 3 Sep 1927, 13, 26; *DP*, 10 Jun 1900, 16; *PSN*, 28 Mar 1924, 29; 2 Jun 1924, 11; 8 Jan 1927, 20; 23 Feb 1935, 5; 87/23c box 1; *Shapes*, 184.

12. *PSN*, 23 Jul 1927, 28; Claire Louise Kellogg, *Memoirs of an American Prima Donna* (New York: Putnam's, 1913), 49.

13. *NYA*, 3 Aug 1905, 6; JH to Pierce, 30 Sep 1864 (Franklin Pierce Papers, #1929-1, New Hampshire Historical Society).

14. *NYA*, 6 Oct 1905, 10; JH to Pierce, 13 Oct 1864 (Franklin Pierce Papers, #1929-1, New Hampshire Historical Society); Bassan 41.

15. *PNA*, 30 March 1929, 5; *BG*, 30 Dec 1883, 16; 6 Jan 1884, 13; 13 Jan, 13; 20 Jan, 13; 27 Jan, 13; JH, *Fool of Nature*, 24–25.

16. *NYA*, 12 Jul 1905, 10; *CIO*, 2 Nov 1890, 25; 9 Nov 1890, 25.

17. JH to Pierce, 26 Apr 1865 (Franklin Pierce Papers, #1929-1, New Hampshire Historical Society); Pierce to Horatio Bridge, 27 Nov 1865 (Franklin Pierce Papers, #1929-1, New Hampshire Historical Society); *More Books* 21 (1946): 43–46.

18. *More Books* 21 (1946): 255, 259, 263; *Booklover's Weekly*, 28 Oct 1901, 25–31; Susan Coultrap-McQuin, *Doing Literary Business* (Chapel Hill: University of North Carolina Press, 1990), 125; JH to J. R. Osgood, 20 Apr 1871 (MS Thr 470 [40], Houghton); JH to Rose and Una Hawthorne, 5 May 1871 (NYPL); *PSN*, 28 Jun 1924, 30.

19. *SR*, 16 Nov 1874, 3; *CIO*, 19 Dec 1886, 22.

20. JH to SH, 8 Nov 1864 (NYPL); JH to Minne Amelung, 13 Sep 1870 (private collection).

21. Ephraim Gurney to SH, 9 Feb 1866 (NYPL).

22. *DI*, 2 Oct 1926, 13; "Biography"; Tharp 305–6.

23. R. C. Beatty, *James Russell Lowell* (Nashville: Vanderbilt University Press, 1942), 198; Bridge 199; Maynard 152.

24. *More Books* 21 (1946): 47–48; Judith Roman, *Annie Adams Fields* (Bloomington: Indiana University Press, 1990), 50; Rita Gollin, *Annie Adams Fields* (Amherst: University of Massachusetts Press, 2002), 103.

25. Maynard 151.

26. "Biography"; Bassan 43; *More Books* 21 (1946): 48; Maynard 152.

27. *M*, 186; *DI*, 11 Sep 1926, 23; *PSN*, 10 Mar 1924, 12; *Shapes*, 36; Bassan 90; *DI*, 4 Dec 1926, 12–13.

28. "Biography"; *H&HC*, 191; 87/23c box 1.

29. *M*, 249; *NHR* 6 (1976): 115; *PSN*, 7 Aug 1926, 20.

30. *Another's Crime* (New York: Cassell, 1888), 71; JH, Dresden journal for 1868–69 (NYPL); *PSN*, 8 Jul 1925, 5; 7 Aug 1926, 20.

31. JH, Dresden journal entries for 3 Jan and 7 Jan 1869 (NYPL); JH to EPP, 13 Mar 1869 (Rosary Hill); 87/23c box 1.

32. JH to EPP, 13 Mar 1869 (Rosary Hill); 87/23c box 1; JH, *The Professor's Sister* (Chicago: Belford, 1890), 12.

33. JH to EPP, 13 Mar 1869 (Rosary Hill); Bassan 49; JH, Dresden journal for 20 Mar 1869 (NYPL); "Biography"; *NYA*, 27 Sep 1905, 10.

34. JH, Dresden journal for 10 and 15 Apr 1869 (NYPL).

35. JH, Dresden journal for 25 Apr and 11 Jun 1869 (NYPL); JH, *Ellice Quentin and Other Stories* (London: Chatto and Windus, 1880), 1.

36. JH, Dresden journal for 22 Jul 1869 (NYPL).

37. JH, Dresden journal for 13 Sep 1869 (NYPL); *Putnam's* 4 (Aug 1869): 165; *Nation*, 29 Jul 1869, 96.

38. JH to Minne Amelung, 30 May, 22 Jul, 4 Sep, 22 Oct, 12 Dec, 22 Dec 1869 (private collection); JH, Dresden journal for 21 Nov 1869 (NYPL).

39. *Lippincott's* 46 (Jul 1890): 136; JH to Minne Amelung, 10 Apr 1870 (private collection); JH, Dresden journal for 11 Nov 1869 (NYPL); *NH&W* 2: 358.

40. *NHR* 6 (1976): 101; Bassan 45; Valenti 42–43, 49.

41. JH to Minne Amelung, 10 Apr 70, 5 Mar 1870 (private collection).

42. *Elizabeth Manning Hawthorne: A Life in Letters*, ed. Cecile Ann de Rocher (Tuscaloosa: University of Alabama Press, 2006), 135; JH to Minne Amelung, 5 Mar 1870 (private collection).

43. *NH&W* 2: 353; "Biography"; *PSN*, 28 Jul 1926, 5.

44. Valenti 44; 87/23c box 1; *NH&W* 2: 367; Maynard 183.

45. *Elizabeth Manning Hawthorne*, ed. De Rocher, 138; JH to Una Hawthorne, 22 Jul 1873 (NYPL).

46. *NYA*, 3 Oct 1905, 10; 25 Nov 1905, 10; *NYCA*, 23 Jul 1873, 2; *M*, 181; *IA*, 4 Apr 1896, 438–39; *PSN*, 24 Nov 1925, 5; 15 Jun 1929, 40.

47. 87/23c box 1; JH to Osgood, 9 Sep, 19 Sep, 19 Dec, 23 Nov 1871 (MS Thr 470 [40], Houghton).

48. *PSN*, 3 Sep 1926, 5; 87/23c box 1.

49. 72/236z boxes 4 and 5; *PSN*, 3 Sep 1926, 5; JH to Una and Rose Hawthorne, 22 Jun 1871 (NYPL); *PSN*, 29 Apr 1926, 18; *BE*, 24 Feb 1872, 2.

50. *PSN*, 29 Apr 1926, 18; *C&C*, 10, 17; JH to Osgood, 10 Apr 1872 (MS Thr 470 [40], Houghton); *San Francisco Bulletin*, 2 Jul 1872, 1.

51. Frank Luther Mott, *American Journalism: A History 1690–1960* (New York: Macmillan, 1962), 411; Charles Johanningsmeier, *Fiction and the American Literary Marketplace* (Cambridge: Cambridge University Press, 1997), 2, 15; Daniel H. Borus, *Writing Realism: Howells, James, and Norris in the Mass Market* (Chapel Hill: University of North Carolina Press, 1989), 40, 119; John Tebbel, *A History of Book Publishing in the United States* (New York: Bowker, 1972), 154.

52. William Charvat, *The Profession of Authorship in America, 1800–1870* (1968; rpt. New York: Columbia University Press, 1992), 293; Johanningsmeier, *Fiction*, 165–66.

53. *Bret Harte's California*, ed. Gary Scharnhorst (Albuquerque: University of New Mexico Press, 1990), 140; Richard Grant White, "Why We Have No Saturday

Reviews," *Galaxy*, 15 Nov 1866, 544; Frank Luther Mott, *A History of American Magazines* (Cambridge: Belknap, 1967), 3: 14; Gary Scharnhorst, *Horatio Alger Jr.* (Boston: Twayne, 1980), 28; Herman Melville, *Correspondence* (Evanston, IL: Northwestern University Press, 1993), 191.

54. *San Francisco Bulletin*, 11 Jun 1879, 4; *AM*, 142 (Sep 1928): 375.

55. 87/23c vol. 1; 72/236z box 6; *NYTimes*, 29 Jul 1872, 2.

56. JH to EPP, 29 Jun 1873 (NYPL); *SR*, 16 Nov 1874, 3; *PSN*, 7 Oct 1925, 22.

57. *NYTrib*, 31 Jul 1873, 4–5; George Knox, "Dissonance Abroad: JH's *Saxon Studies*," *Essex Institute Historical Studies*, 96 (1960): 137; JH to Una Hawthorne, 9 Mar 1873 (NYPL); *PSN*, 5 Jul 1926, 18; 21 May 1927, 20; *AJ*, 4 Jan 1873, 49–52; *Independent*, 4 Dec 1873, 1531.

58. *C&C*, 10; JH to EPP, 29 Jun 1873 (NYPL); JH to Una Hawthorne, 25 Feb 1873 (NYPL); *SR*, 16 Nov 1874, 3; JH to Robert Carter, 24 Feb 1873 (Peabody Essex); Carter to JH, 14 Nov 1872 (72/236 box 4).

59. JH to Osgood, 24 Apr 1872 (MS Thr 470 [40], Houghton); 72/236z box 4; Carter to JH, 27 Jun 1873 and n.d. (72/236 box 4); *Henry James Letters*, ed. Leon Edel (Cambridge: Belknap, 1975), 2: 243.

60. JH, *Bressant* (New York: Appleton, 1873), 1: 257; 2: 149, 209; Valenti 48.

61. 87/23c vol. 1; *Correspondence of William James*, ed. Ignas K. Skrupskelis and Elizabeth M. Berkeley (Charlottesville: University Press of Virginia, 1997), 4: 448–49; *Athenaeum*, 17 May 1873, 626; JH to Una Hawthorne, 26 May 1873 (Rosary Hill); 87/23c, pp. 10–60; *London Graphic*, 5 Jul 1873, 12; JH to EPP, 29 Jun 1873 (NYPL); *Spectator*, 21 Jun 1873, 794–95; 72/236z box 5.

62. *BG*, 12 Jun 1873, 1; *NYTimes*, 28 Jun 1873, 9; 87/23c, pp. 10–60; *NYTrib*, 8 Jul 1873, 6; *Christian Union*, 6 Aug 1873, 107; JH to Henry Ward Beecher, 29 Aug 1873 (Cornell); *DP*, 23 Sep 1900, 13; *Spectator*, 20 Sep 1873, 1183; 26 Aug 1876, 1077; *M*, 280; *Bookmart* 5 (Dec 1887): 270–75.

63. *DP*, 14 Oct 1900, 15.

64. 72/236z box 4; *AJ* 5 (Jul 1878), 32; *SS* 211.

65. Hull 232, 106; JH to Una Hawthorne, 24 Jan 1873, 22 Mar 1873 (NYPL).

66. JH to Una Hawthorne, circa 19 Jan 1873 (Rosary Hill); JH to Una Hawthorne, 17 Feb 1873 (NYPL); *C&C*, 11–12; 87/23c box 2.

67. *Bookmart* 4 (Apr 1887): 433–38; W. D. Howells, *Literary Friends and Acquaintance* (1911; rpt. Bloomington: Indiana University Press, 1968), 251.

68. *Bookman* 73 (Apr 1931): 170–71; JH, *Idolatry* (Boston: Osgood, 1874), 145; Carter to JH, 3 Mar 1874 (72/236 box 4).

69. *DP*, 23 Sep 1900, 13; *PSN*, 23 Jan 1926, 5; *Henry James Letters* (Cambridge: Belknap, 1975), 2: 264.

70. 72/236z carton 2; *SR*, 16 Nov 1874, 3; JH to Una Hawthorne, 24 Jun 1873 (NYPL).

71. JH to Una Hawthorne, 30 Jul 1874 (NYPL).

72. *Shapes*, 70.

CHAPTER 3: 1874–81

1. *Shapes*, 70.

2. *CW*, 17 Jun 1897, 22–23; JH to William Peckham, 4 Oct 1874 (UVa); *Book-Lover* 5 (May 1904): 529–35.

3. *Critic*, 19 Jul 1890, 36; *PSN*, 20 Jun 1925, 22; Bassan 97.

4. *PSN*, 1 Oct 1925, 14; 6 Jun 1931, 5.

5. Bassan 104; *Shapes*, 198; *PSN*, 14 Sep 1929, 5.

6. 87/23c box 1.

7. Journal entries for 1 Jan, 31 Jan, 10 Feb, and 25 Feb 1875 (72/236z carton2); JH to Strahan, n.d. (Pierpont Morgan).

8. *AM* 34 (Dec 1874): 748; *London Times*, 5 Jan 1875, 3; *Scribner's* 9 (Jan 1875): 385; *Galaxy* 18 (Dec 1874): 856; *Saturday Review*, 24 Oct 1874, 540; *Athenaeum*, 17 Oct 1874, 511; *Spectator*, 17 Oct 1874, 1300; *Philadelphia Inquirer*, 16 Nov 1874, 3; *London Academy*, 28 Nov 1874, 580.

9. *NYTrib*, 23 Sep 1874, 6; *NYTimes*, 6 Oct 1874, 3; *NYA*, 5 Sep 1905; *CW*, 11 Feb 1897, 10–11.

10. *Shapes*, 78; *DP*, 5 Aug 1900, 19; *NYW*, 22 Aug 1886, 11; *AM* 97 (Jun 1906): 817–24; *Book-Lover* 5 (May 1904): 529–35.

11. 72/236z box 5; *PNA*, 16 Sep 1900, 14; 23 Oct 1900, 8; *PSN*, 14 Sep 1925, 7; 29 Apr 1926, 18; 2 Jun 1928, 28; *NYA*, 13 Dec 1906, 18; *LAE*, 23 Sep 1905, 16; *H&HC*, 125.

12. *PSN*, 7 Sep 1929, 5; *DP*, 14 Oct 1900, 15.

13. JH to Francis Bennoch, 21 Feb 1875 (Georgetown); Virginia Harlow, *Thomas Sergeant Perry: A Biography* (Durham: Duke University Press, 1950), 294–95; JH to Carter, 10 Jan 1876 (Beinecke Rare Book and Manuscript Library, Yale University); 87/23c box 1; *PSN*, 30 Sep 1926, 31; JH to Peckham, 9 Dec 1875 (UVa).

14. *SS* 116, 24; *PSN*, 30 Sep 1926, 31; 22 Oct 1932, 24; *Dresdener Nachrichten*, 1 Feb 1876.

15. *PSN*, 22 Oct 1932, 24; *Spectator*, 5 Dec 1874, 1535; *Nation*, 30 Mar 1876, 214–15; *NYH*, 6 Jan 1876, 5; *Athenaeum*, 1 Jul 1876, 14; *PNA*, 28 Jan 1876, 1; *AJ*, 8 Jan 1876, 59.

16. JH to Una Hawthorne, 25 Feb 1873 (NYPL); 72/236z scrapbook 1.

17. 72/236z box 5; JH to Bennoch, 16 Nov 1875 (Georgetown); 72/236z carton 2.

18. JH to Bennoch, 21 Feb 1875 (Georgetown); 72/236z carton 2.

19. JH to Mary Louise Booth, 11 March 1875 (Harry Ransom Center, University of Texas); *NYH*, 18 Apr 1875, 8; *NHR* 6 (1976): 107; JH to Carter, 10 Jan 1876 (Beinecke Rare Book and Manuscript Library, Yale University).

20. JH to Osgood, 5 Apr 1876, 22 May 1876 (MS Thr 470 [40], Houghton).

21. *NYTrib*, 8 Jul 1876, 2.

22. Valenti 56; Ronda 381; Maynard 183.

23. JH to Carter, 10 Jan 1876 (Beinecke Rare Book and Manuscript Library, Yale University); 72/236z carton 2.

24. JH to Bennoch, 5 Apr 1876, 17 Oct 1876 (Georgetown); 72/236z carton 2.

25. 72/236z carton 2.

26. *DP*, 6 May 1900, 16; 72/236z carton 2.

27. 72/236z carton 2; JH to Bennoch, 6 Nov 1877 (Georgetown).

28. *NH&W* 2: 373; 72/236z carton 2; *PSN*, 14 Feb 1931, 5.

29. *NH&W* 2: 374; *M*, 222.

30. 87/23c box 2; JH to Richard Bentley, 17 Nov 1878 (87/23c box 2); *M*, 52; *Athenaeum*, 1 Mar 1879, 276; Carl Weber, *The Rise and Fall of James Ripley Osgood* (Waterville, ME: Colby College Press, 1959), 171.

31. JH to Bennoch, 17 Oct 1876 (Georgetown); 72/236z carton 2.

32. "Kildhurm's Oak" (1880) contains a character named Hilda, *Noble Blood* (1885) a Beatrice, "Professor Weisheit's Experiment" (1886) a Priscilla, "Her Soul and Body" (1893) a Wakefield, and both *The Golden Fleece* (1892) and "A Cosmic Courtship" (1917) a Miriam. Several of JH's stories feature "elixirs of immortality": *Fortune's Fool* (1883); "Carlo Carrambo" (1885); "The Book of the Flood" (1886); *A Messenger from the Unknown* (1892); "A Daughter of Love" (1898); "Absolute Evil" (1918); and "The Jewels of Nobleman Jack" (1921).

33. *C&C*, 13; 72/236z carton 2.

34. 72/236z carton 2.

35. *AJ* 3 (Aug 1877): 191; *Examiner*, 28 Jul 1877, 950; *Portland Press*, 9 Jun 1877, 1; Mayo Hazeltine, *Chats about Books* (New York: Scribner, 1883), 89–90; *London World*, 2 Oct 1878, 19; *NAR* 125 (Sep 1877): 315; *Nation*, 21 Jun 1877, 369; *Saturday Review*, 6 Jun 1877, 741; *NYTimes*, 10 Jun 1877, 10.

36. JH to Bennoch, 6 Nov, 17 Nov, 24 Nov 1877, 6 Jan, 21 Jan 1878 (Georgetown); Minne Hawthorne to Bennoch, 13 Oct 1878 (Georgetown); 72/236z carton 2.

37. Bassan 125; 72/236z carton 2; *NYA*, 1 Jul 1905, 16.

38. JH to Bennoch, 20 Sep 1879 (Georgetown); 72/236z carton 2.

39. JH to Bennoch, 25 Jan 1878, 16 Aug 1878, 18 Apr 1879, 24 Sep 1879 (Georgetown).

40. JH to Bennoch, 24 Sep 1879 (Georgetown); 72/236z carton 2; Ronda 400; Strange and Brother to Bennoch, 16 Jan 1879 (Georgetown).

41. JH to Bennoch, 21 Jan 1878 (Georgetown).

42. *Letters of Bret Harte*, ed. Geoffrey Bret Harte (Boston: Houghton Mifflin, 1926), 252; Brenda Murphy, *American Realism and American Drama* (Athens: Ohio University Press, 1992), 61; JH to Bennoch, 22 Jul 1878 (Georgetown); *Shapes*, 107.

43. *Booklover's* 1 (May 1903): 477–91; *PSN*, 28 Nov 1924, 23; 72/236z carton 2.

44. 72/236z carton 2; JH to Bennoch, 16 Aug, 24–25 Aug 1878 (Georgetown); 72/236z carton 2; *PSN*, 2 Oct 1926, 35; *NYA*, 20 Jun 1905, 10.

45. J. M. Morriss to Bennoch, 25 Nov 1878 (Georgetown); JH to Bennoch, 7 Sep 1878, 26 Nov 1878, 8 Dec 1878 (Georgetown); 72/236z carton 2.

46. JH to Bennoch, 16 Dec 1878 (Georgetown); 72/236z carton 2.

47. *BE*, 1 Nov 1885, 10; JH to Bennoch, 13 May 1879 (Georgetown); 72/236z

carton 2; Basil Champneys, *Memoirs and Correspondence of Coventry Patmore* (London: Bell, 1900), 1: 259–60; *PSN*, 4 Sep 1924, 10; *Examiner*, 9 Aug 1879, 1028–29.

48. 72/236z carton 2; *NYA*, 2 Mar 1907, 14; *C&C*, 13, 15; *Nation*, 22 May 1884, 450.

49. *Dublin University Magazine* ns 1 (May 1878): 573–80; JH, *Constance and Calbot's Rival* (New York: Appleton, 1889), 149; *PSN*, 5 Mar 1927, 20; 22 Sep 1928, 36; 30 Sep 1933, 4.

50. 72/236z carton 2; JH to Alexander Strahan, 11 Feb 1878 (Georgetown); qtd. in Michael Anesko, *"Friction with the Market": Henry James and the Profession of Authorship* (New York: Oxford University Press, 1986), 76; JH to Bennoch, 12 Feb 1880 (Georgetown); 72/236z box 4.

51. 72/236z carton 2; JH to Bennoch, 8 Dec 1878, 20 Dec 1878 (Georgetown).

52. *NYTrib*, 4 Jun 1878, 2; *Nation*, 23 May 1878, 338–39; *Book-Lover* 5 (Jun 1904): 661–67; *Shapes*, 247.

53. *PNA*, 3 Dec 1900, 8; *Lippincott's* 2 (Sep 1890): 413; Vincent O'Sullivan, *Aspects of Wilde* (New York: Holt, 1936), 133; *Harper's Bazar*, 19 Feb 1881, 114–15; 19 Mar 1881, 177; 30 Apr 1881, 273; 14 May 1881, 306–307; *PSN*, 17 Jul 1924, 8; Minne Hawthorne to Lilian Aldrich, 17 Jan 1882 (MS Thr 470 [40], Houghton); *Complete Letters of Oscar Wilde*, ed. Merlin Holland and Rupert Hart-Davis (New York: Holt, 2000), 134, 138.

54. *AL* 50 (Nov 1978): 462.

55. *PSN*, 3 Apr 1924, 32; *LHJ* 39 (Oct 1922): 124.

56. *Modern Fiction Studies* 36 (Summer 1990): 211–17; *Henry James Letters* 2: 216–17, 263; *Nation*, 3 Apr 1879, 228–29. In December 1897 James bought Lamb House in Rye, only ten miles from Hastings.

57. JH to Bennoch, 30 Dec 1878 (Georgetown); *PSN*, 12 Oct 1929, 5; *DP*, 11 Nov 1900, 4; JH to Richard Bentley, 26 Jul 1879 (87/23c box 2); *NYTrib*, 15 Mar 1880, 4; *LW*, 28 Feb 1880, 72; *Examiner*, 27 Dec 1879, 1678–79.

58. 72/236z carton 2.

59. Ibid.; JH to Bennoch, 13 May 1879 (Georgetown); *Shapes*, 198.

60. JH to Bennoch, 18, 21, 22 Jun 1879, 20, 24 Sep 1879 (Georgetown).

61. JH to Bennoch, 29 Oct 1879, 8 Nov 1879 (Georgetown).

62. *London Times*, 3 Jan 1880, 4; JH to Bennoch, 6 Dec 1879 (Georgetown); 72/236z carton 2.

63. JH to Bennoch, 25 Apr 1880 (Georgetown); 72/236z carton 2.

64. 72/236z carton 2; JH to Bennoch, 15 Jul 1879, 12 and 14 Feb 1880, 28 Mar 1880 (Georgetown); *Christian Union*, 28 Jul 1880, 71; *Ronda* 400.

65. *WP Book World*, 13 Dec 1987, 9; JH to Strahan, 5 March 1879 (Georgetown); 72/236z carton 2; JH to Sampson, Low, 15 Mar 1880 (Georgetown); Strahan to JH, 19 Mar 1880 (Georgetown).

66. 72/236z carton 2; *NYTrib*, 12 Mar 1883, 5; *C&C*, 15, 26.

67. 72/236z carton 2.

68. JH to Rose and George Lathrop, 15 Mar 1881 (Rosary Hill); Ronda 412–13; Bassan 119.

69. *Booklover's* 1 (May 1903): 477–91; *NYA*, 19 Aug 1905, 6; *WP*, 15 Jun 1885, 1; *PSN*, 15 Jan 1927, 20; *NYTimes*, 14 Mar 1882, 8.

CHAPTER 4: 1881–86

1. W. D. Howells, *My Mark Twain* (New York: Harper and Brothers), 61; *DI*, 24 Jul 1926, 14–15, 26; 87/23c box 1; *Letters of Ellen Emerson* 2: 458, 484; *Harper's* 65 (Jul 1882): 278–81.

2. *BE*, 12 Jan 1885, 2; 72/236z carton 2; "Syndicate Matter," *America*, 7 Jul 1888, 12; JH, *Dust* (New York: Fords, Howard, 1882), 88; *Our Continent*, 23 Aug 1882, 219; 13 Sep 1882, 316; Bassan 144–45; *AC*, 7 Sep 1891, 4; *AM* 51 (May 1883): 706; *Saturday Review*, 24 Mar 1883, 381–82; *Nation*, 10 May 1883, 405.

3. JH to Chatto and Windus, 15 Nov 1881 (UVa); JH to Ben Ticknor, 15 Apr 1882, 1 May 1882 (LC); Houghton Mifflin contract file (Houghton).

4. *PSN*, 5 Oct 1929, 8; JH to Osgood, 30 Jun 1882 (Pierpont Morgan).

5. Edward H. Davidson, *Hawthorne's Last Phase* (New Haven: Yale University Press, 1949), 158–59; JH to George Hellman, n.d. [HM 7729] (Huntington); JH to Ben Ticknor, 25 Apr 1882, 20 Aug 1882 (LC).

6. *Boston Traveller*, 14 Aug 1882, 2; George Parsons Lathrop, *A Study of Hawthorne* (Boston: Osgood, 1876), 278; JH to Osgood, 15 Aug 1882 (MS Thr 470 [40], Houghton); *NYS*, 27 Aug 1882, 2; Valenti 68; JH to Ticknor, 20 Aug 1882, 25 Nov 1882 (LC); JH, Preface to *Dr. Grimshawe's Secret* (Boston: Osgood, 1883), ix.

7. *Athenaeum*, 23 Dec 1882, 848; *NH&W* 2: 302; JH to Ben Ticknor, 20 Aug 1882, 28 Aug 1882 (LC); Edward H. Davidson, *Hawthorne's Dr. Grimshawe's Secret* (Cambridge: Harvard University Press, 1954), vi; Davidson, *Hawthorne's Last Phase*, vii–viii, 161–65; JH to George Hellman, n.d. [HM 7729] (Huntington).

8. *Independent*, 1 Feb 1883, 10; *Pall Mall Gazette*, 1 Jan 1883, 4–5; *Saturday Review*, 6 Jan 1883, 25–26; *Nation*, 18 Jan 1883, 66.

9. 72/236z carton 2; JH to Ticknor, 8 Jul 1883; 31 Jan 1884 (LC); *WP*, 15 Jun 1885, 1.

10. JH to Osgood, 22 Sep 1882 (MS Thr 470 [40], Houghton); *Letters of Ellen Emerson* 2: 484; 72/236z carton 2.

11. JH to Ticknor, 16 Nov 1884 (MS Thr 470 [40], Houghton); JH to Bridge, 27 Dec 1882 (Bowdoin College); qtd. in Marc Pachter, *Telling Lives* (Washington, DC: New Republic, 1979), 18; JH to Osgood, 30 Sep 1883 (MS Thr 470 [40], Houghton).

12. JH to Ticknor, 8 Jul 1883; 6 Aug 1883 (LC); JH to Rose Hawthorne Lathrop, 12 Dec 1883 (Rosary Hill); *H&HC*, 33; *NH&W* 2: 135; 87/23c box 1; Harrison Hayford, *Melville and Hawthorne* (PhD diss., Yale University 1945), 334.

13. *Unitarian Review* 23 (May 1885): 423; Ronda 424–25.

14. 72/236z carton 2; JH to "Mr. Peatrie," 4 Dec 1885 (Peabody Essex); *PSN*, 24 Jan 1931, 5; *Epoch*, 11 Feb 1887, 10–12; *America*, 21 Jul 1888, 12; *Bookmart* 6 (Sep 1888): 218–19.

15. *NH&W* 1: 260–61; *American Literary History* 7 (Summer 1995): 210–33.

16. *BT*, 2 Jan 1885, 4; 9 Jan 1885, 6; 16 Jan 1885, 4; *LW*, 10 Jan 1885, 14; Ronda 424–26, 436.

17. *NH&W* 2: 304, 311; Aldrich to Higginson, 24 Nov 1884, 13 Dec 1884 (Huntington); *BT*, 5 Feb 1885, 4; *DP*, 7 Jan 1900, 10; *Bookmart* 5 (Feb 1888): 355–57.

18. *American Literary History* 7 (Summer 1995): 219; *Athenaeum*, 20 Dec 1884, 799–800; *Saturday Review*,13 Dec 1884, 759–60; London *Academy*, 29 Nov 1884, 350–52; *Boston Beacon*, 22 Nov 1884, 3; *Independent*, 1 Jan 1885, 10; *NYTrib*, 16 Nov 1884, 4; Charles F. Richardson, *American Literature* (New York: Putnam, 1888), 2: 447.

19. *Worcester Spy*, 22 Feb 1883, 1; *PI*, 26 Feb 1883, 8; *NYTimes*, 20 Mar 1883, 8; *Critic*, 26 Mar 1887, 169; 72/236z carton 2; *NYTrib*, 21 Mar 1883, 5; *Lippincott's* 6 (Jul 1883): 89.

20. *NYTrib*, 5 Apr 1883, 5; *Shapes*, 314.

21. *NYTrib*, 12 Mar 1883, 5; 5 Apr 1883, 5; 1 Apr 1883, 1.

22. *NYTrib*, 12 Mar 1883, 5; 5 Apr 1883, 5; 72/236z carton 2.

23. *C&C*, 15, 28; JH, *Dust,* 196, 468; Bassan 171–72.

24. *Spectator*, 3 May 1884, 587–88; *Century* 27 (Dec 1883): 313; *Critic*, 10 Nov 1883, 451; *Nation*, 15 Nov 1883, 421.

25. 72/236z carton 2; *LW*, 19 May 1883, 165; *Life*, 28 Feb 1884, 122; *LW*, 9 Feb 1884, 35.

26. *LHJ* 39 (Oct 1922): 25; *BJ*, 1 Aug 1883, 3.

27. *Harper's* 89 (Aug 1894): 442; *PI*, 20 Jul 1896, 7; *Princeton Review* 13 (Jan 1884): 14; *Letters of Ellen Emerson* 2: 531; *Manhattan* 4 (Aug 1884): 199–207; *The Genius and Character of Emerson*, ed. F. B. Sanborn (Boston: Osgood, 1884), 68–91.

28. JH to Rose Hawthorne Lathrop, 16 Oct 1883 (Rosary Hill); JH to Osgood, 8 Sep 1883 (MS Thr 470 [40], Houghton); JH to Mary Mapes Dodge, 9 and 19 Sep 1883 (Princeton).

29. JH to Rose Hawthorne Lathrop, 16 Oct 1883 (Rosary Hill); *CIO*, 19 Oct 1890, 26.

30. JH to Rose Hawthorne Lathrop, 12 Dec 1883 (Rosary Hill); JH to Osgood, 8 Sep 1883 (MS Thr 470 [40], Houghton); JH to Ticknor, 15 and 24 Jun 1884 (LC); *Pacific Rural Press*, 16 Dec 1882, 481; JH to Laurence Hutton, 25 Feb 1884 (Princeton).

31. 72/236z carton 2; JH to Osgood, 26 May 1883 (MS Thr 470 [40], Houghton); Valenti 72.

32. JH to Osgood, 14 May 1884 (MS Thr 470 [40], Houghton); JH to Ticknor, 15 May 1884 (LC); *SR*, 30 Jul 1884; JH to Barrett Smith, 23 Nov 1884 (UVa); *BE*, 12 Jan 1885, 2; Hildegarde Hawthorne, *Makeshift Farm* (New York: Appleton, 1925), 3, 158.

33. JH to Rose Hawthorne Lathrop, 1, 13, and 28 Sep 1884 (Rosary Hill); *BE*, 12 Nov 1884, 2; *NYTrib*, 29 Nov 1884, 6; 72/236z scrapbook 3; Valenti 73; JH to T. B. Aldrich, 9 Oct 1884 (MS Thr 470 [40], Houghton); *SR*, 17 Feb 1886, 6; 72/236z box 4.

34. *NYTimes*, 12 Nov 1884, 5; *BE*, 12 Jan 1885, 2; *Independent*, 27 Nov 1884, 7; *Pilgrim* 3 (Nov 1901), 8; *PSN*, 29 Aug 1931, 9; 72/236z box 6; *Boston Advertiser*, 23 Oct 1885, 1; *DKE Quarterly* 3 (Jan 1885): 101–107; 4 (Apr 1886): 185–91.

35. *Christian Union*, 18 Jun 1885, 6; *SR*, 2 Jan 1886, 4; JH to Minne Hawthorne, 7 and 10 Jun 1885 (NYPL).

36. JH, *Love—or a Name* (Boston: Ticknor, 1885), 227; *WP*, 1 Nov 1885, 6; *LW*, 3 Oct 1885, 342; *Nation*, 19 Nov 1885, 428.

37. Lowell to JH, 28 Nov 1885 (Huntington); JH to Paul Hamilton Hayne, 24 Dec 1885 (Duke).

38. *Autobiography of Mark Twain*, ed. Harriet E. Smith et al. (Berkeley: University of California Press, 2010), 384, 601; *Life*, 30 Apr 1885, 248; *PSN*, 2 Dec 1925, 5.

39. JH to Charlton Lewis, 21 Dec 1885 (Beinecke Rare Book and Manuscript Library, Yale University); *San Jose Mercury News*, 28 Aug 1886, 32; *NYH*, 14 May 1886, 3; JH to Augustin Daly, 6 Jan 1886 (Y.c.4105 [1], Augustin Daly Collection, Folger Shakespeare Library); *Critic*, 19 Jun 1886, 307; *PSN*, 1 Oct 1925, 14; 12 Mar 1927, 20.

40. Maynard 196; *NYW*, 8 Aug 1886, 11; *CW*, 24 Sep 1896, 7, 10; *PNA*, 16 Mar 1901, 8; 2 Aug 1901, 8; *NAR* 147 (Jul 1888): 117; *Phantasms of the Living* (London: Society for Psychical Research, 1886), 76; *Independent*, 1 Oct 1885, 1278–79; 8 Oct, 1310–11.

41. *PSN*, 2 Dec 1925, 5; JH to Mark Twain, 11 Dec 1885 (Bancroft Library, University of California, Berkeley).

42. Mark Twain to JH, 18 Dec 1885 (Bancroft Library, University of California, Berkeley); JH to Mark Twain, 23 Dec 1885 (Bancroft Library, University of California, Berkeley); *NYTimes*, 16 Jan 1886, 8; *St. Louis Missouri Republican*, 5 Sep 1888, 11; 17 Jan 1895.

43. *AM* (Apr 1886): 471–85; *PSN*, 11 Mar 1933, 8; JH to Ben Ticknor, 25 May 1886 (LC).

44. JH to Ticknor, 28 Mar 1886 (LC); *PSN*, 24 Dec 1924, 7; *San Francisco Bulletin*, 11 Sep 1886, 1.

45. *BE*, 20 Mar 1887, 11; 3 Jun 86; *NYTimes*, 11 Jul 1885, 5; *CT*, 11 Jul 1885, 2; *BE*, 23 Jul 1886, 4; *Washington Critic*, 24 Jul 1886, 1; *SR*, 4 Jul 1886, 4; *BE*, 1 Jun 1887, 5.

46. *PSN*, 10 Jun 1926, 5; 21 Feb 1931, 5; *SR*, 18 Nov 1886, 2; *Critic*, 2 Oct 1886, 166; *Booklover's Weekly*, 28 Oct 1901, 25–31; *NYW*, 29 Oct 1886, 3.

47. *NYW*, 24 Oct 1886, 9.

48. *Boston Advertiser*, 26 Oct 1886, 1; *Letters of James Russell Lowell*, ed. Charles Eliot Norton (New York: Harper and Brothers, 1893), 2: 319; Horace C. Scudder, *James Russell Lowell: A Biography* (Boston: Houghton Mifflin, 1901), 336–38; *Boston Herald*, 27 Oct 1886, 2; *NYW*, 1 Nov 1886, 5; 11 Nov 1886, 5.

49. *CIO*, 19 Dec 1886, 22; *Chicago Daily News*, 1 Nov 1886, 2; *SR*, 27 Oct 1886, 4; *NYCA*, 9 Jul 1889, 1; W. D. Howells, *Selected Letters 1882–1891* (Boston: Twayne, 1980), 167, 175; *Essex Institute Historical Collections* 95 (Oct 1959), 348–54; Henry James, *The Reverberator* (London: Rupert Hart-Davis, 1949), 136.

CHAPTER 5: 1887–96

1. *LAE*, 8 Jan 1905, 28.

2. Qtd. in *Worcester Spy*, 29 Apr 1889, 4.

3. JH to Ticknor, 25 Dec 1886 (LC); JH to "Mr. Clark," n.d. [Nov 1889?] (Peabody Essex); Borus, *Writing Realism*, 43.

4. *AC*, 7 Sep 1891, 4.

5. *Critic*, 23 Jul 1887, 186; *PSN*, 11 Dec 1924, 22.

6. *NYH*, 30 Nov 1890, 14.

7. Jacob Riis, *The Making of an American* (New York: Macmillan, 1904), 341.

8. *Kansas City Star*, 20 Aug 1887, 2; *San Francisco Bulletin* supplement, 16 Jul 1887, 1; 10 Sep 1887, 4; *LW*, 17 Sep 1887, 298; 14 Apr 1888, 123.

9. *Current Literature* 2 (Apr 1889): 360.

10. *America*, 28 March 1889, 12–13; 17 Oct 1886, 10; *PNA*, 16 Feb 1900, 9; *Spectator*, 7 Aug 1880, 1015.

11. *American Magazine* 7 (Mar 1888): 617–18. Julian had invoked the same phrase ("dismal fraud") to describe Margaret Fuller in 1884 during the controversy over his biography of his father.

12. *NYTimes*, 5 Jan 1887, 5.

13. *NYW*, 29 Aug 1886, 11.

14. Edwin Cady, *The Road to Realism* (Syracuse, NY: Syracuse University Press, 1956), 241; *London Spectator*, 13 Nov 1880, 1451–52.

15. *Bookmart* 4 (Apr 1887): 433–38; *C&C*, 59; *America*, 25 Oct 1888, 11–12; JH to Minne Hawthorne, 14 Feb 1891 (NYPL); *PNA*, 9 Feb 1900, 6; 14 Jun 1901, 8.

16. *Bookmart* 5 (Aug 1887): 102–103; *NYW*, 5 Sep 1886, 11; *America*, 7 Apr 1888, 7; JH to E. C. Stedman, 2 Sep 1886 (Columbia).

17. *PSN*, 5 Aug 1926, 5.

18. JH to Stoddart, 12 Jun 1889 (Ms.Am.1491 [59] BPL). Courtesy of the Trustees of the Boston Public Library/Rare Books.

19. *CIO*, 13 Mar 1892, 17.

20. *PNA*, 28 Jan 1901, 13; *PSN*, 28 Oct 1925, 8.

21. *PSN*, 19 Sep 1931, 5; 16 Jul 1927, 28. Mark Twain to Lorenz Reich, 2 December 1882 (Mark Twain Papers, Bancroft Library, University of California, Berkeley).

22. *NYCA*, 16 Aug 1889, 3; *PSN*, 29 Jan 1927, 10; *St. Louis Republic*, 11 Aug 1889, 12.

23. *DP*, 13 May 1900, 9; *PSN*, 14 Apr 1934, 6.

24. *NYH*, 30 Nov 1890, 14; *PNA*, 16 Nov 1899, 16; *Jenness-Miller Magazine* 5 (Apr 1891): 306–309.

25. *Pall Mall Gazette*, 17 Aug 1889, 1–2; *NYCA*, 23 Aug 1889, 3; 27 Aug 1889, 3; 30 Aug 1889, 3; 3 Sep 1889, 7; 13 Sep 1889, 3; *NYTimes*, 25 Aug 1889, 5; *PO*, 18 Jan 1890, 10.

26. *NYCA*, 22 Aug 1889, 3; 26 Aug 1889, 3; 13 Sep 1889, 3; 17 Sep 1889, 4; 19 Sep 1889, 3; *NYTimes*, 25 Jul 1889, 5.

27. *BE*, 24 Aug 1890, 14; *NYW*, 1 Feb 1891, 15.

28. *NYW*, 1 Feb 1891, 15; *Outing* 15 (March 1890): 60; *PSN*, 6 Nov 1925, 28.

29. *NYTimes*, 18 Nov 1925, 40.

30. JH to Stedman, 15 Jan 1892 (Beinecke Rare Book and Manuscript Library, Yale University); 72/236z box 5; *PSN*, 14 Jun 1930, 5.

31. JH and Leonard Lemmon, *American Literature: An Elementary Textbook for Use in High Schools and Academies* (Boston: Heath, 1891), 26, 48, 211, 162.

32. *NYTimes Book Review*, 17 Oct 1896, 1; *The Letters of Theodore Roosevelt and Brander Matthews*, ed. Lawrence J. Oliver (Knoxville: University of Tennessee Press, 1995), 37; Borus, *Writing Realism*, 43.

33. 72/236z carton 2.

34. *Lippincott's* 2 (Oct 1890): 536.

35. *PO*, 29 Mar 1893, 10; *NYTimes*, 30 Mar 1893, 2.

36. *NYW*, 1 Feb 1891, 15; *Belford's* 8 (Oct 1891): 194–98; *CT*, 2 Mar 1890, 26; JH to "Miss Hume," 12 Apr 1891 (NYU); *C&C*, 16; *America*, 30 Jun 1888, 12; 20 Sep 1888, 12; 17 Jan 1889, 12; Charles Honce, *A Julian Hawthorne Collection* (New York: privately printed, 1939), 23; Valenti 123; JH to ?, 15 Jun 1892 (Rosenberg Library, Galveston, Texas).

37. JH to Minne Hawthorne, 11 Oct 1891 (NYPL); *America*, 16 May 1889, 214–15; JH to ?, 15 Jun 1892 (Rosenberg Library, Galveston, Texas; *BJ*, 30 Jul 1892, 5; *San Francisco Call*, 1 Nov 1896, 23; *CT*, 1 Nov 1896, 42.

38. *Engineering Magazine* 3 (Sep 1892): 759–64.

39. JH to Rose Hawthorne Lathrop, 28 Jul 1892 (Rosary Hill).

40. *Publishers' Weekly*, 29 Oct 1892, 693; JH to "My dear Boy," 4 Nov 1892 (Peabody Essex); Maynard 227–28; *LAT*, 15 Oct 1893, 12.

41. *CT*, 17 Feb 1893, 8;

42. *Once a Week*, 25 Nov 1893, 10.

43. JH, *Humors of the Fair* (Chicago: Weeks, 1893), 5, 65, 72, 143, 200–201.

44. *Shapes*, 105–106; *PSN*, 12 May 1926, 5.

45. *Kingston Gleaner*, 11 Dec 1893, 2; journal for 1 and 13 Jan 1894 (private collection); Hildegarde Hawthorne, *Island Farm* (New York: D. Appleton, 1926), 17, 19; *NYA*, 16 Jan 1907, 3; *Wilkes-Barre Times*, 21 Mar 1895, 6; *Once a Week*, 10 March 1894, 6.

46. *NYA*, 27 Oct 1905, 10; *PNA*, 13 Dec 1900, 8; *Dallas Morning News*, 10 Feb 1895, 16; JH to "Mrs. Lincoln," 9 Sep 1895 (Beinecke Rare Book and Manuscript Library, Yale University); *CIO*, 24 Dec 1894, 4; JH to Ticknor, 10 Apr 1889 (LC); journal for 1 Jan 1894 (private collection).

47. Hildegarde Hawthorne, *Island Farm*, 19; *CW*, 26 Nov 1896, 11–12; 5 Nov 1898, 4–6.

48. *Wilkes-Barre Times*, 21 Mar 1895, 6; journal for 4 Mar 1895 (private collection); *Island Farm*, 144, 153.

49. JH to Julius Chambers, 28 Jul 1895 (NYU); JH to Lorenz Reich, 1 May 95 (Pierpont Morgan).

50. JH to Reich, 1 May 95 (Pierpont Morgan).

51. Journal for 28 Jan, 9, 12 Mar, and 12 Apr 1895 (private collection); *Worcester Spy*, 17 Apr 1895, 7; *CIO*, 24 Dec 1894, 4.

52. Journal for 28 Jan, 6 Feb, and 26 Jul 1895 (private collection); JH, *Love Is a Spirit* (New York: Harper, 1896), 82, 51.

53. JH to Rose Hawthorne Lathrop, 27 Mar 1891; 20 May 1891 (Rosary Hill); journal for 20 Feb 1895 (private collection); Valenti 126–27.

54. Journal for 11 March, 1–8 Apr 1895 (private collection).

55. Journal for 22–23 Feb and 18 Apr 1895 (private collection); JH to Reich, 1 May 1895 (Pierpont Morgan).

56. *NYH*, 1 Dec 1895, VI, 1; *PSN*, 20 Dec 1930, 36; journal for 26 May, 6 Jun, 15 Jun 1895 (private collection); *Book Buyer* 13 (May 1896): 214.

57. *PSN*, 20 Dec 1930, 36; *NYH*, 14 Jul 1895, 2.

58. JH to Reich, 10 and 19 Jun 1895 (Pierpont Morgan); *PSN*, 8 May 1926, 38.

59. 87/23c scrapbook 3.

60. Ibid.; *NYH*, 1 Dec 1895, 6: 1; Edward Bok, "Literary Leaves," *NYCA*, 21 Dec 1895, 13.

61. 72/236z box 4; *Bookman* 3 (Jun 1896): 365; *NYTimes*, 5 Apr 1896, 31; *Dial*, 16 Aug 1896: 95; *CT*, 1 Jul 1902, 1.

62. Journal for 30 Nov 1895, 28 Dec 1895 (private collection).

63. *NYTrib*, 25 Jan 1896, 6; *NYTimes*, 10 May 1896, 8; JH to Stoddart, 23 Mar 1896 (Boston College); *Knoxville Journal*, 9 Apr 1896, 1; JH to Annie Godwin de Castro, 3 Jun 1896 (Harry Ransom Center, University of Texas); *PI*, 20 Jul 1896, 7; *Worcester Spy*, 18 Oct 1896, 3; *Current Literature* 19 (May 1896): 378; *NYH*, 28 Apr 1896, 3.

64. *NYJ*, 1 Aug 1896, 1–2.

65. *DP*, 9 Jul 1900, 10; *NYA*, 7 Jul 1906, 2; JH, Introduction to "Nineteenth Century Literature," in *The Nineteenth Century* (Washington, DC: American Book and Bible House, 1900), 388–91; *Duluth* [Minnesota] *News-Tribune*, 5 Jul 1906, 4.

66. *NYJ*, 11 Dec 1896, 1.

67. *NYJ*, 28 Nov 1896, 4; 11 Dec 1896, 1.

68. *PI*, 20 Jul 1896, 7; *DP*, 10 Sep 1899, 7; *NYJ*, 11 Aug 1896, 1, 5;13 Aug 1896, 5; 30 Oct 1896, 1, 4; *PSN*, 4 Aug 1925, 7; 14 Jul 1926, 5.

69. *Omaha World Herald*, 1 Nov 1896, 6; *PSN*, 4 Aug 1925, 7; *NYJ*, 28 Oct 1896, 1–2; 30 Oct 1896, 1, 4; 2 Nov 1896, 1–2; 3 Nov 1896, 1–2.

70. *NYJ*, 2 Nov 1896, 1–2; *Omaha World-Herald*, 16 Jul 1900, 7; *BG*, 6 Nov 1896, 1; *NYJ*, 7 Nov 1898, 6; *CW*, 16 Sep 1897, 21; 27 Jan 1898, 16–17.

CHAPTER 6: 1897–1907

1. 72/236z box 4.

2. *PSN*, 25 Jul 1931, 5.

3. *PNA*, 23 Jan 1900, 6; *AM* 142 (Sep 1928): 377.

4. *BG*, 30 May 1897, 3.

5. *M*, 291.

6. Ibid.; *Cosmo* 23 (Jul 1897): 238; 23 (Aug 1897): 370; 23 (Sep 1897): 515; 24 (Nov 1897): 12–15; 9 Mar 1902; JH to John Brisbane Walker, 24 May 1897 (BYU).

7. *PSN*, 13 Sep 1930, 5; *BG*, 30 May 1897, 3; *CW*, 5 Nov 1898, 4–6; *Cosmo* 23 (Aug 1897): 370, 372, 374; 23 (Sep 1897): 517.

8. *New Voice*, 28 Jan 1899, 2, 14; *PSN*, 9 Jun 1934, 6; JH to Minne Hawthorne, 7 Jun 1885 (NYPL); *Town Topics*, 11 Dec 1902, 53–58; *BE*, 22 May 1897, 6.

9. JH to Walker, 24 May 1897 (BYU); qtd. in *Indiana State Journal*, 14 Jul 1897, 8; *Dallas Morning News*, 5 Nov 1897, 4.

10. *NYJ*, 2 Sep 97, 16; *Dallas Morning News*, 5 Nov 1897, 4; Robert Loerzel, *Alchemy of Bones* (Urbana: University of Illinois Press, 2003), 107.

11. *NYJ*, 4 Sep 4; 5 Sep 2; 1 Oct 12; 2 Oct 1897, 4.

12. *NYJ*, 9 Nov 2; 12 Nov 1–2; 30 Nov 1897, 1–2.

13. Kenneth Whyte, *The Uncrowned King* (Berkeley: Counterpoint, 2009), 170–71.

14. *NYJ*, 15 Oct 1897, 1; *CW*, 2 Dec 1897, 18–19.

15. *NYJ*, 12 Feb 1898, 2; JH to U.S. consul in Havana, 9 Feb 1898 (private collection).

16. *NYJ*, 13 Feb 1898, 34–35; Ben Proctor, *William Randolph Hearst: The Early Years, 1863–1910* (New York: Oxford University Press, 1998), 118; Marcus M. Wilkerson, *Public Opinion and the Spanish-American War* (New York: Russell and Russell, 1932), 55; *Congressional Record,* 55th Congress, 2 Sess., XXXI, pt. 2, 1875.

17. *NYJ*, 19 Feb 1898; *CW*, 5 Mar 1898; *Washington Evening Times*, 26 Feb 1902, 2.

18. W. A. Swanberg, *Citizen Hearst* (New York: Scribner, 1961), 382; Gregory M. Pfitzer, *Popular History and the Literary Marketplace* (Amherst: University of Massachusetts Press, 2008), 322; Mott, *American Journalism,* 532.

19. *New York Evening Journal*, 19 Feb 1898, 3; *Los Angeles Herald*, 20 Feb 1898, 1; *Omaha World-Herald*, 20 Feb 1898, 1.

20. *NYJ*, 12 Feb 1898, 2; *Washington Evening Times*, 26 Feb 1902, 4; *San Francisco Call*, 7 Mar 1898, 6; Proctor, *William Randolph Hearst*, 117.

21. *NYA*, 28 Aug 1898, 37–38; JH, *History of the United States* (New York: Collier, 1898), 1108.

22. JH to Minne Hawthorne, 11 Oct 1891 (NYPL); Charles King to Minne Hawthorne, 17 Feb 1892 (NYU); JH to Rose Hawthorne Lathrop, 28 Jul 1892 (Rosary Hill); *PNA*, 6 May 1901, 14.

23. *NYJ*, 28 Aug 1898, 37–38; 29 Aug 1898, 6; 28 Nov 1898, 4; JH, *History of the United States,* 1109, 1100.

24. Stephen Crane, *New York World*, 14 Jul 1898; *DP*, 4 Feb 1900, 7; *PSN*, 17 Mar 1934, 8; *PNA*, 29 Dec 1899, 10; *LAE*, 27 May 1905, 8.

25. *NYJ*, 7 Nov 1898, 6; *Worcester Spy*, 22 Feb 1883, 1; Swanberg, *Citizen Hearst,* 167; *NYA*, 21 Feb 1906, 4; *PNA*, 8 Feb 1901, 16; *NYJ*, 3 Sep 1898, 6.

26. *NYJ*, 7 Oct 1898, 2; 8 Oct 1898, 3; 11 Oct 1898, 5; JH, *History of the United States,* 1126–27.

27. 72/236z carton 2. Bassan, the only other scholar known to have examined this memo book, suggests "it records primarily business transactions" (257).

28. The "second anniversary" of the consummation of their affair.

29. *American Mercury* 6 (Sep 1925): 72–73; *Washington Herald*, 15 Nov 1908, 5.

30. *NYTrib*, 16 Jul 1905, 18; 72/236 vol. 3; *Harper's Monthly* 91 (Sep 1895): 489.

31. *NYTimes*, 18 Jul 1905, 7; *NYTrib*, 17 Apr 1903, 10; 20 Dec 1903, 5; JH's last will and testament (private collection); *New Orleans Picayune*, 7 Dec 1915, 5.

32. JH to E. Leslie Gilliams, 16 Oct 1897 (Beinecke Rare Book and Manuscript Library, Yale University); journal for 15 Mar 1899 (72/236z carton 2); JH to Henry H. Clements, 21 Feb 1902 (Amherst).

33. *AL* 28 (March 1958): 75; JH to George S. Hellman, 4 Jun 1904, 29 Jun 1906, 1 Dec 1907 (Huntington); JH to Houghton and Mifflin, 31 Mar 1904 (MS Thr 470 [40], Houghton); JH to Harper and Brothers, 28 Aug 1905 (Columbia).

34. *PSN*, 12 May 1926, 5; JH, *Story of Oregon* (New York: American Historical Pub. Co., 1892), 1: vii; JH, *History of the United States*, ix, 41, 91, 399, 638, 887, 906, 913, 920.

35. Pfitzer, *Popular History*, 317.

36. JH, *Spanish America* (New York: Collier, 1899), 51, 126, 128, 294.

37. JH to James C. Young, 31 Jul 1901 (Notre Dame); *CIO*, 22 Mar 1896, 26; *NYTimes*, 8 Apr 1900, 6.

38. Gene Fowler, *Timber Line* (New York: Covici, Friede, 1933), 105–108; 72/236z carton 1; *DP*, 25 Aug 1899, 1; 6 Sep 1899, 3; 8 Sep 1899, 6.

39. *DP*, 17 Sep 1899, 5; 24 Sep 1899, 28; 8 Oct 1899, 8; 15 Oct 1899, 8; *PSN*, 27 Mar 1926, 5.

40. *PNA*, 6 Jul 1900, 24; *DP*, 4 Jul 1900; rpt. *Omaha World-Herald*, 16 Jul 1900, 7; *PSN*, 26 May 1934, 10.

41. *PNA*, 4 Sep 1900, 1, 6; 5 Sep 1900, 1–2; 6 Sep 1900, 1, 7; 10 Sep 1900, 3, 12; 13 Sep 1900, 3, 9.

42. *Challenge*, 27 Feb 1901, 1–2; *Wilshire's* 3 (Apr 1902): 14–20.

43. *PNA*, 14 Sep 1900, 1–2; 18 Sep 1900, 3; 19 Sep 1900, 1–2; 20 Sep 1900, 11–12; *New Orleans Picayune*, 22 Sep 1900, 10.

44. *PNA*, 19 Oct 1900, 2; 26 Oct 1900, 8.

45. *NYJ*, 16 Sep 1898, 8; 17 Jul 1900, 8.

46. *Smart Set* 1 (Mar 1900): 63–78; *PSN*, 17 Jul 1924, 8; *PNA*, 3 Dec 1900, 8.

47. *Studies in American Naturalism* 5 (Winter 2010): 189–95; *CW*, 5 Feb 1898, 16–17; 72/236, scrapbook 2.

48. *NYTrib*, 2 Feb 1886, 2; *PNA*, 31 Jan 1901, 16; 8 Feb 1901, 16; 27 May 1901, 1, 5; *PSN*, 17 Jan 1925, 30, 10 Feb 1926, 20.

49. *Once a Week*, 21 Oct 1893, 6; *Birmingham Age-Herald*, 18 Apr 1900, 2; *NYJ*, 27 Apr 1900.

50. 72/236 vol. 2; *PNA*, 23 Apr 1901, 8; 26 Apr 1901, 8; 11 May 1901, 8; *AC*, 22 Apr 1901, 7; *CW*, 12 Nov 1896, 7; *NYJ*, 28 May 1899, 27.

51. *Bookmart* 6 (Nov 1888): 341–43; *NYJ*, 7 Nov 1898, 6; *Forum* 27 (Jun 1899): 441–44.

52. JH, *History of the United States*, 1133–34; JH, unpublished editorial, "Anarchy and the Terror" (MS Am 1758 [534], Houghton); *PNA*, 14 Sep 1901, 4; 30 Oct 1901, 8.

53. *NAR* 176 (March 1903): 391–400; JH to Joseph Stoddart, 16 Aug 1904 (Houghton).

54. *H&HC*, 18, 52; JH to Annie Fields, 22 Jun 1904 (Ms.C.1.11 [1] BPL), Courtesy of the Trustees of the Boston Public Library/Rare Books.

55. *NYS*, 7 Feb 1904, 9; *H&HC*, 224; *CE* 20: 447; 21: 505; *NYS*, 7 Feb 1904, 9; *New York Evening World*, 6 Feb 1904, 10; *PSN*, 16 Apr 1927, 32.

56. *WP*, 21 May 1904, 18; *NAR* 77 (Dec 1903): 872; JH to W. D. Howells, 8 Nov 1903 (Houghton); JH to L. W. Payne, 31 Jan 1932 (Harry Ransom Center, University of Texas).

57. *LAE*, 9 Jan 1905, 1, 9.

58. *LAE*, 10 Jan 1905, 1, 4; *The Letters of Jack London*, ed. Earle Labor, Robert C. Leitz, III, and I. Milo Shepard (Stanford: Stanford University Press, 1988), 1: 373, 478.

59. *LAE*, 12 Jan 1905, 3.

60. *LAE*, 16 Feb 1905, 11–12; 5 Mar 1905, 61; 26 Mar 1905, 2: 34; 9 Apr 1905, 33–34.

61. *LAE*, 27 Mar 1905, 3; Richard Salmon, *Henry James and the Culture of Publicity* (New York: Cambridge University Press, 1997, 188.

62. *NYA*, 11 Jun 1899, 43; 4 Nov 1899, 1; 12 May 1900, 8; *PSN*, 22 Aug 1931, 5; 31 Aug 1900, 16; 19 Jun 1905, 6; 17 May 1907, 10; *Kansas City Star*, 23 May 1905, 3.

63. *NYA*, 15 Apr 1904, 8; 9 Feb 1906, 4; 15 Feb 1906, 7; 14 Mar 1906, 4; 29 Mar 1906, 10; 10 Apr 1906, 6; 1 May 1906, 5; 9 May 1906, 5.

64. *NYA*, 16 May 1906, 3; 24 May 1906, 9; Jacob M. Appel, *Western New England Law Review* 26 (2004): 204.

65. *PSN*, 5 May 1926, 14; *NYA*, 11 Feb 1907, 2; *BJ*, 17 Jan 1907, 6.

66. *PSN*, 21 Jul 1924, 15; *NYA*, 23 Jan 1907, 2, 4; 24 Jan 1907, 3; 1 Feb 1907, 3; 6 Feb 1907, 4; 11 Feb 1907, 2.

67. Michael Macdonald Mooney, *Evelyn Nesbit and Stanford White* (New York: Morrow, 1976), 256; E. L. Doctorow, *Ragtime* (New York: Random House, 1975), 70; *NYA*, 8 Feb 1907, 3, 7; *Kansas City Star*, 30 Mar 1907, 2; *HL* 5 (Apr 1907): 3–4, 24.

68. *CW*, 1 Oct 1896, 7; 26 Mar 1898, 17; *Pearson's* 4 (Oct 1907): 409–16.

69. *CW*, 25 Nov 1897, 5; *NYA*, 15 Nov 1903, 51; 28 Nov 1905, 11; 2 Dec 1905, 10.

70. JH to Mayo Hazeltine, 28 Mar 1908 (87/23c box 2); *PSN*, 20 Jul 1926, 11.

71. *NYTimes*, 6 Dec 1905, 1; *NYTrib*, 10 Nov 1906, 6.

CHAPTER 7: 1908–14

1. JH to Seymour Eaton, 7 Dec 1907 (Beinecke Rare Book and Manuscript Library, Yale University).

2. *NYTimes Book Review*, 14 Mar 1908, 137.

3. 87/23c box 2; Mott, *American Journalism*, 603.

4. *NYS*, 10 Jan 1913, 7; *U.S. v. Hawthorne* (U.S. Second Court of Appeals case file 5109).

5. *NYTimes*, 27 Nov 1912, 7; *Dallas Morning News*, 20 Feb 1913, 20.

6. JH to Edith Garrigues, 10 Jul 1908 (72/236z box 6).

7. 72/236z box 6.

8. *NYS*, 7 Feb 1913, 11; *NYTimes*, 6 Jan 1912, 17.

9. *NYTimes*, 10 Jan 1913, 20; *U.S. v. Hawthorne* (U.S. Second Court of Appeals case file 5109).

10. *NYTimes*, 15 Mar 1913, 1; *U.S. v. Hawthorne* (U.S. Second Court of Appeals case file 5109).

11. *Colorado Springs Gazette-Telegraph*, 13 Mar 1913, 2; U.S. v. Hawthorne (U.S. Second Court of Appeals case file 5109).

12. *PO*, 11 Feb 1913, 1.

13. *NYTimes*, 27 Nov 1912, 7.

14. 72/236 box 5.

15. JH to Mark Twain, 8 Aug 1908 (Bancroft Library, University of California, Berkeley).

16. *NYTimes*, 24 Apr 1910, 3.

17. 72/236z box 4; JH to Edith Garrigues, 6 Aug 1908 (72/236z box 6).

18. *NYTimes*, 13 Oct 1909, 1; 15 Jan 1910, 15; 72/236z scrapbook 3; *NYTrib*, 16 Feb 1909, 8; *WP*, 20 Oct 1909, 5.

19. 72/236z carton 1.

20. *The Lyric Year*, ed. Ferdinand Earle (New York: Kennerley, 1912), 111–19.

21. *BJ*, 13 Dec 1912, 3; *NYTimes*, 24 Oct 1911, 22.

22. *NYTimes*, 13 Dec 1912, 9; *BJ*, 13 Dec 1912, 3.

23. Mother Alphonsa to JH, 9 May 1911 (72/236z box 5).

24. W. J. Morton to JH, 18 Sep 1908 (72/236z box 5).

25. *NYTimes*, 11 Dec 1912, 8; *U.S. v. Hawthorne* (U.S. Second Court of Appeals case file 5109).

26. *NYTimes*, 7 Dec 1912, 9.

27. *Mines and Minerals* 29 (Mar 1909): 367; *NYTimes*, 7 Dec 1912, 9.

28. *NYTimes*, 27 Nov 1912, 7; 7 Dec 1912, 9.

29. Dan Plazak, *A Hole in the Ground with a Liar at the Top* (Salt Lake City: University of Utah Press, 2006), 313–14; *U.S. v. Hawthorne* (U.S. Second Court of Appeals case file 5109).

30. *Montgomery Advertiser*, 19 Nov 1912, 1; JH to Seymour Eaton, 17 Nov 1911 (72/236z box 4).

31. *PO*, 30 Oct 1911, 5; *WP*, 6 Jan 1912, 1.

32. *NYTimes*, 26 Nov 1912, 24; 27 Nov 1912, 7; 8 Jan 1913, 3; *U.S. v. Hawthorne* (U.S. Second Court of Appeals case file 5109).

33. Plazak, *Hole in the Ground*, 311; *NYTimes*, 11 Dec 1912, 8.

34. *NYTimes*, 6 Jan 1912, 17.

35. *NYS*, 8 Jan 1913, 16; *NYTimes*, 8 Jan 1913, 3.

36. *NYTimes*, 10 Jan 1913, 20.

37. *NYTimes*, 16 Jan 1913, 1; *SB*, 287.

38. *SB*, 10; *Colorado Springs Gazette-Telegraph*, 13 Mar 1913, 2.

39. *NYS*, 15 Mar 1913, 1–2.

40. *SB*, 41; *NYS*, 15 Mar 1913, 1–2; *NYTimes*, 15 Mar 1913, 1; *U.S. v. Hawthorne* (U.S. Second Court of Appeals case file 5109).

41. *SB*, 17; *NYTimes*, 15 Mar 1913, 1.

42. *AC*, 16 Mar 1913, 5.

43. *NYTimes*, 22 Mar 1913, 14; 17 Oct 1913, 20; JH prison records (National Archives–Atlanta Region).

44. 72/236z box 6; *NYS*, 6 Mar 1914, 2; *BJ*, 26 Mar 1914, 2; *WP*, 27 Mar 1914, 5; Plazak, *Hole in the Ground*, 315.

45. *NYTimes*, 17 Dec 1913, 7.

46. *SB*, 36; 72/236z box 4.

47. Taft Papers; *PI*, 5 Apr 1913, 2; 72/236z box 5; *NYS*, 10 Jan 1915, IV: 10.

48. *NYTrib*, 17 Oct 1913, 18; *WP*, 6 Aug 1913, 2.

49. *SB*, 227; *GW*, 1 Nov 1913, 2; 1 Jun 1913, 3; 72/236 scrapbook 2; *WP*, 9 Jun 1913, 6.

50. *GW*, 1 Jun 1913, 1, 2; 1 Jul 1913, 1, 3; 1 Aug 1913, 1, 2, 6; 1 Sep 1913, 2; 1 Oct 1913, 2, 5; 1 Nov 1913, 2; Michel Foucault, *Discipline and Punish* (1975; rpt. New York: Vintage, 1979), 174.

51. *GW*, 1 May 1913, 3; *NYA*, 2 Jul 1913, 16; 72/236z box 4; JH prison records (National Archives–Atlanta Region).

52. JH prison records (National Archives–Atlanta Region); *WP*, 8 Jun 1913, 4.

53. *GW*, 1 May 1913, 3; *SB*, 304; *LAT*, 24 Apr 1913, 18; *NYS*, 22 Feb 1914, editorial section, 12; JH to Zona Gale, 10 Jan 1928 (Wisconsin Historical Society); *Chicago Defender*, 27 Jan 1923, 17.

54. *SB*, 79, 223–24, 249.

55. *AC*, 15 Oct 1915, 1.

CHAPTER 8: 1915–34

1. 72/236z box 6.

2. *PSN*, 30 Sep 1925, 5.

3. *NYA*, 14 Jun 1905, 6; *BA*, 28 Feb 1915, 3: 1–2; 6 Mar 1915, 4; 4 Apr 1915, 2: 6; *Macon Telegraph*, 1 Mar 1915, 5; *PSN*, 28 May 1927, 24.

4. *BA*, 18 Apr 1915, 5–6; *LHJ* 39 (Oct 1922), 25.

5. *BA*, 20 Jun 1915, 2: 1, 8; 87/23c vol. 1.

6. *BA*, 4 Jul 1915, 2: 1, 8. Louis Harap alleges in *The Image of the Jew in American Literature* (Philadelphia: Jewish Publication Society of America, 1974), 308, that Julian was "one of the worst practitioners [of anti-Semitism] in American fiction." While he was hardly immune to the race prejudices common at the time, he was by no means a virulent anti-Semite, as his interview with Brandeis suggests. In fact, he once declared in print that "the Jews are one of the most effective and successful concrete forces in contemporary civilization" (*NYA*, 6 Jul 1907, 14).

7. *PSN*, 8 Oct 1927, 28.

8. 72/236z box 4.

9. *PSN*, 8 Jun 1935, 6; JH to Benjamin Hamilton, 12 Apr 1920 (72/236z box 4).

10. JH to Houghton Mifflin, 14 Feb 1920 (MS Thr 470 [40], Houghton); JH to Seward Collins, 21 Mar 1933 (Beinecke Rare Book and Manuscript Library, Yale University).

11. 72/236z box 5.

12. *Smart Set* 51 (Mar 1917): 75–80.

13. *San Francisco Chronicle*, 16 Jun 1929, 4F.

14. *NYTimes Book Review*, 28 Oct 1928, 65.

15. *PSN*, 22 Feb 1930, 5; 22 Apr 1933, 5.

16. *PSN*, 29 Apr 1933, 15.

17. *Saturday Review of Literature*, 16 Apr 1927, 728; *San Francisco Chronicle*, 23 Jun 1929, 4D; Randall Stewart, Preface to *American Notebooks* (New Haven: Yale University Press, 1932), vi–viii; *NYTimes*, 6 Dec 1932, 4.

18. JH to Raymond Weaver, 5 Dec 1919 (Columbia); *PSN*, 7 Mar 1924, 32; 87/23c box 1; 89/201c box 4; JH to Ralph L. Rusk, 6 May 1932 (72/236z box 4). JH asked W. T. H. Howe of the American Book Company in Cincinnati in the early 1930s whether he had been "the purchaser of that correspondence between my mother and Melville, relating to his Moby Dick." These letters are unknown to scholarship. Howe bought at least a single Melville letter to Sophia for $3100 (72/236z box 4).

19. *PSN*, 3 Oct 1931, 5; *Shapes*, 332; *PNA*, 5 Feb 1901, 8; JH to Helen E. Haines, 27 Jun 1926 (Helen Elizabeth Haines Papers, Bancroft Library).

20. *PSN*, 19 Sep 1924, 12; 2 Apr 1932, 5; 28 May 1932, 20; 29 Jun 1933, 10; JH to Lincoln Steffens, 17 Apr 1932 (Columbia); 87/23c box 2.

21. 72/236z box 5; 87/23c box 2.

22. 72/236z box 6; 87/23c box 1.

23. JH to Mother Alphonsa, 11 Dec 1923 (Rosary Hill).

24. Plazak, *Hole in the Ground*, 315; 72/236z box 5; *PSN*, 7 Oct 1925, 22.

25. Journal for 5 Jun and 6 Jul 1925 (72/236z carton 2); JH to Houghton Mifflin, 22 Jul 1928 (MS Thr 470 [40], Houghton); *PSN*, 6 Jul 1929, 5; JH to Frederick Macmillan, 9 Feb 1933 (89/201c box 4).

26. JH to Emily Glass, 28 Jun 1922; 12 Oct 1924; 3 Nov 1924 (UCLA).

27. Journal for 15 Apr 1924 (72/236z carton 2); *PSN*, 27 Mar 1926, 5; JH to Henry Seidel Canby, late 1925 (Beinecke Rare Book and Manuscript Library, Yale University).

28. *Selected Letters of Hamlin Garland*, ed. Keith Newlin and Joseph B. Mc-Cullough (Lincoln: University of Nebraska Press, 1998), 352; JH to Canby, late 1925 (Beinecke Rare Book and Manuscript Library, Yale University).

29. JH to Hamlin Garland, 29 Mar 1930 (University of Southern California); *LAT*, 8 Jun 1930, B6; 20 Jun 1930, A10.

30. *PSN*, 19 Jul 1930, 28; 23 Jun 1931, 9, 13; *LAT*, 21 Jul 1931, 13; 72/236z box 6; Edith Garrigues Hawthorne to Haines, 1 Jul 1931 (Helen Elizabeth Haines Papers, Bancroft Library).

31. *DI*, 4 Dec 1926, 12; *San Francisco Call-Bulletin*, 14 Jul 1934, 2

32. *Hamlin Garland's Diaries*, ed. Donald Pizer (San Marino: Huntington Library, 1968), 144.

33. 87/23c box 2; *PSN*, 14 Jul 1934, 1.

34. 87/23c box 2.

35. *LAT*, 5 Aug 1934, E5; Edith Garrigues Hawthorne to Seward Collins, 9 Oct 1935 (Beinecke Rare Book and Manuscript Library, Yale University).

36. 87/23c box 2.

EPILOGUE

1. *M*, 3.

2. Edith Garrigues Hawthorne to L. W. Payne, 22 Mar 1938 (Harry Ransom Center, University of Texas).

3. *LAT*, 17 Apr 1938, C6; *Christian Science Monitor*, 22 Apr 1938, 22; *Nation*, 23 Apr 1938, 479; *NYTimes*, 25 Sep 1938, 34.

4. *PSN*, 16 Jan 1949.

INDEX

GARY SCHARNHORST is Distinguished Professor Emeritus of English at the University of New Mexico and the author of *Kate Field: The Many Lives of a Nineteenth-Century American Journalist*.

The University of Illinois Press
is a founding member of the
Association of American University Presses.

Composed in 10/13 Sabon
by Lisa Connery
at the University of Illinois Press
Designed by Dennis Roberts
Manufactured by Sheridan Books, Inc.

University of Illinois Press
1325 South Oak Street
Champaign, IL 61820-6903
www.press.uillinois.edu